The Frontman:
Bono (In the Name of Power)

Harry Browne

VERSO
London • New York

First published by Verso 2013
© Harry Browne 2013

Lyrics to 'Flights of Earls', composed by Liam Reilly, used by permission of
Bardis Music Co. Ltd

1 3 5 7 9 10 8 6 4 2

Verso
UK: 6 Meard Street, London W1F 0EG
US: 20 Jay Street, Suite 1010, Brooklyn, NY 11201
www.versobooks.com

Verso is the imprint of New Left Books

ISBN-13: 978-1-78168-082-7

British Library Cataloguing in Publication Data
A catalogue record for this book is available from the British Library

Library of Congress Cataloging-in-Publication Data
A catalog record for this book is available from the Library of Congress

Typeset in Minion Pro by MJ & N Gavan, Truro, Cornwall
Printed in the US by Maple Vail

HARRY BROWNE is a lecturer in the School of Creative Arts and Media at Dublin Institute of Technology. His journalism has appeared in *CounterPunch*, the *Dublin Review* and many Irish newspapers. Born in Italy and raised in the United States, he has lived in Ireland since the mid-1980s. His previous book is *Hammered by the Irish: How the Pitstop Ploughshares Disabled a US War-Plane – With Ireland's Blessing.*

COUNTERBLASTS

COUNTERBLASTS is a series of short, polemical titles that aims to revive a tradition inaugurated by Puritan and Leveller pamphleteers in the seventeenth century, when, in the words of one of their number, Gerard Winstanley, the old world was 'running up like parchment in the fire'. From 1640 to 1663, a leading bookseller and publisher, George Thomason, recorded that his collection alone contained over twenty thousand pamphlets. Such polemics reappeared both before and during the French, Russian, Chinese and Cuban revolutions of the last century.

In a period where politicians, media barons and their ideological hirelings rarely challenge the basis of existing society, it is time to revive the tradition. Verso's Counterblasts will challenge the apologists of Empire and Capital.

CONTENTS

INTRODUCTION: 'THIS IS NOT A REBEL SONG'

Celebrity philanthropy comes in many guises, but perhaps no single figure better encapsulates its delusions, pretensions and misdirections than does the lead singer of rock band U2, Paul Hewson, aka Bono.

That's because Bono is more than a mere giver of charity – indeed, his fame in this realm has nothing to do with the spending of his own considerable fortune on the needs of the poor. He is, instead, an 'advocate', and as such has become a symbol of the essentially benign character of the West's rich elite, ever ready to help the world's poor – just waiting for a little encouragement, and a few good ideas, to eliminate hunger and poverty forever. This makes him an ideal frontman for a system of imperial exploitation and war whose depredations and depravity remain as savage as ever.

Bono's own description of what he does for a living is 'travelling salesman', latest in a line:

> A lot of our family are traveling salesmen. And of course that is what I have become! I am very much a traveling salesman. And that, if you really want to know, is how I see myself. I sell songs from door to door, from town to town. I sell melodies and words. And for me, in my political work, I sell ideas. In the commercial world that I'm entering into, I'm also selling ideas. So I see myself in a long line of family sales people.[1]

He has certainly been a more-than-competent seller of his musical work, and of himself. In his own version of the metaphor, politically he travels the world selling ideas about how to help the world's poor – selling them mainly to the powerful people and institutions that can turn those ideas into reality. This is at best a partial account, however: in reality the idea that he is most seriously engaged in selling is the one about how those powerful people and institutions are genuinely committed to making the world a more just and equitable place. And he's selling that to us.

Bono is nothing if not cosmopolitan. As an Americanised Irishman who has conspicuously joined forces with the British government in the past and is linked in the public eye with the fate of Africa, Bono is among the most thoroughly transatlantic of elite figures. (Former Irish attorney-general Peter Sutherland, chairman of Goldman Sachs International, ex-chairman of BP, and before that the first head of the World Trade Organization, is perhaps his nearest globe-bestriding equivalent – an adviser to banks and governments who has been called 'the father of globalisation'[2] – and we shall see that Bono's similarities to such a thoroughly establishment character go beyond their moneyed Dublin accents.) In the United States, the belief that Bono brings some vaguely understood 'European' value-set to the global discussion may be part of the reason that he is viewed widely there as a largely benign and politically left-liberal figure. At one of George W. Bush's warmest public appearances with the singer ('Bono, I appreciate your heart'), the then-president couldn't resist an anecdote that relied for its humour on the perception that Bono was his political opposite: 'Dick Cheney walked in the Oval Office, he said: "Jesse Helms wants us to listen to Bono's ideas." ' This brought the house down, with Bono himself smiling and clapping.[3] This political perception, however, is based upon a misunderstanding of both his own 'values' and those of institutional Europe: neither Bono nor the EU is nearly as committed to social justice and collectivist values as US pundits are wont to insist. Meanwhile, his tendency to verbal and emotional Americanisms is part of the reason he is viewed with greater suspicion in Europe – or at least, strikingly, in Britain and Ireland, where Bono is largely a figure of ridicule and the object of often-nasty abuse. The British comic magazine *Viz* called him 'the little twat with the big heart', while writer Jane Bussmann suggested in the *Guardian* that Bono purveys 'self-serving bollocks', with Africa serving a 'masturbatory function' for him.[4] Then there is the oft-heard, surely apocryphal story of a Glasgow U2 gig when Bono silenced the audience and began a slow handclap, then whispered weightily: 'Every time I clap my hands, a child in Africa dies.' A voice cried out from the audience: 'Well, fucking stop doin' it then.'[5]

Ridicule of this sort is widespread in Ireland but rare in the Irish media, where U2's friends are many and their influence and patronage large. Indeed, consideration of Bono in his home country is complicated by the peculiarly Irish concept of 'begrudgery', an alleged national tendency to tear down those who are successful. This tendency, insofar as it exists, is born of a healthy, possibly postcolonial suspicion that the world is less meritocratic than it makes out, or that success has often come at a moral cost. Sadly, begrudgery is more often bemoaned than typified: 'fuck the begrudgers' is Ireland's ancient and venerable and ubiquitous version of 'haters gonna hate'.

Petty begrudgery certainly exists; most Dubliners have probably either said or heard the following: 'I saw Bono in town today, but I pretended not to recognise him – I wouldn't give him the satisfaction.' In reality, however, Ireland was all too short of begrudgers during the 1990s and 2000s boom years known as the Celtic Tiger, when financiers, bond-holders, politicians, journalists, property developers and even rock stars were inflating a mad bubble that, when it burst, decimated economic life in the country. This book, in any case, has nothing to do with envy and doesn't question the basis for Bono's success – the music industry is probably slightly more meritocratic than most – but rather how he has chosen to use it politically.

The widely varying views of Bono across and within countries pose a dilemma for the writer, especially one writing for an international audience. How seriously can you treat a figure who is so often ridiculed, in such a range of venues, for so many reasons? There's also the fact that Bono, as a public figure, can be hard to pin down because he works in so many registers even by the standards of our frictionless, boundaryless celebrity culture: one day, it seems, you read that he is meeting the leaders of the G8, the next that he is pursuing his ex-stylist through the courts to recover a hat; this morning he's selling you an iPod, this evening it's his version of the Irish peace process. Ultimately, I have endeavoured to take him as seriously as he appears to take himself, which is to say 'very' but with regular efforts at deprecation and light relief. The reason I take seriousness as a starting point has a only a little to do with the respect that any person is due – too much of the ridicule of Bono is dumb and misguided anyway – but more to do with the fact that he appears to be taken seriously (his organisations funded, him personally invited on to prestigious platforms) by the world's most powerful people. To understand why they do that means rising above mere terms of abuse, most of the time anyway.

I adopt this relatively high tone with some regret – as you move down the social scale the dislike of Bono gets stronger: if Tony Blair is at one, loving extreme, then the graffiti-scrawlers of inner-city Dublin are at the other, and I would hate to think of the latter feeling entirely neglected. But in a world where the *New York Times* mostly treats Bono like a guru, whereas many *Guardian* writers treat him like a fool; where countless continental Europeans regard him as a great artist, while America's *South Park* satirists depict him as literally a piece of shit; where the BBC does a slightly probing TV documentary called *Bono's Millions* in 2008, then devotes a whole day of promotional radio programming to the release of U2's new album in 2009; where a friend I meet in the pub wonders why I would want to criticise Bono, then one I meet on the street reckons my task is too easy to be a proper challenge – in such a world there is no perfect way to approach this book. I hope the way I've chosen makes it more likely that some of Bono's many fans and admirers will be prepared to engage with my arguments.

I am myself neither a big fan nor a dedicated detractor of U2's music. *The Frontman* considers Bono largely as a political operator, rather than as a cultural producer. Bono himself many years ago said he saw the roles as separate, and music as a largely useless vehicle for political change. So this will not be the book that decides if *Achtung Baby* is really better than *War*. But, even within those limits, it would be remiss for this book not to consider, for example, what 'Sunday Bloody Sunday' tells us about Bono's posturing on Irish politics, or whether U2's turn from an American toward a European visual and musical aesthetic in the early 1990s had any political analogue. Insofar as the business, the politics and the music are intertwined, it is important to reflect that, as well as to try to unravel them.

This is, obviously, not conventional biography; nor is it an effort at psychological profiling of its subject. Although I indulge in occasional speculation about his thoughts and motives, it will not, sadly, be possible to get right behind the wrap-around shades and discern what interplay of idealism and cynicism gives rise to a figure like Bono. I am loath to judge another man's motivation, but nor would it be appropriate simply to assume, despite what many of his acquaintances have told me, that in his political and humanitarian roles 'he means well'. The point of *The Frontman* is to focus not on what motivates Bono but on his rhetoric, his actions, and their consequences. For nearly three decades as a public figure, and especially in this century, Bono has been, more often than not, amplifying elite discourses, advocating ineffective solutions, patronising the poor, and kissing the arses of the rich and powerful. He has been generating and reproducing ways of seeing the developing world, especially Africa, that are no more than a slick mix of traditional missionary and commercial colonialism, in which the poor world exists as a task for the rich world to complete. In big and small ways, he has turned his attention to a planet of savage injustice, inequality and exploitation, and it is not unreasonable to argue that he has, in some ways, helped make it worse.

Has he also helped make it better? There is no doubt that some of his campaigning and the work of the organisations he supports have improved the lives, health and well-being of many people in Africa. It would be silly to insist otherwise. And it would be presumptuous in the extreme to suggest that this or any other book can omnisciently weigh up the faults and accomplishments and deliver a definitive, objective verdict. I have endeavoured to give credit to Bono where I believe it's due, but I don't pretend to be a neutral arbiter. I could build and wallpaper an outhouse with the literally hundreds of books and articles that explicate How Bono Makes It Better: they are readily available online and in your local library. This one sets out to make the opposite case.

Bono himself is not shy about taking a lot of credit. He recently called his campaigning 'a movement that changed the world'.[6] In the midst of the George W. Bush years, he said: 'People openly laughed in my face when I suggested that this administration would distribute antiretroviral drugs to Africa. They said, "You are out of your tiny mind." There's 200,000 Africans now who owe their lives to America'.[7] The construction of those sentences makes it impossible to resist the invitation to substitute the word 'America' with the word 'me'.

The idea that Bono makes it worse is, one might reasonably object, simply a political opinion – one based on what I think is clear-sighted, well informed analysis, but an opinion nonetheless. Other writers have looked at the same career, the same facts, and drawn opposite conclusions. Readers are invited to judge for themselves. However, the depoliticising language of humanitarianism, the image of Bono as outside, above and beyond politics, has often rendered the expression of mere political difference about him difficult to express. So whether or not you ultimately agree that Bono 'makes it worse', the point of this book is to place him and, by extension, celebrity humanitarianism firmly in the realm of politics, and therefore of political difference. To do that means to underline a few indisputable facts: that he stands for a particular set of discourses, values and material forces within a wider debate about global poverty, development and justice; that though these discourses, values and forces are often vaguely and misleadingly expressed, these can broadly be characterised as conservative, Western-centric and pro-capitalist; that they are seen as fundamentally non-threatening by the elites that have wreaked havoc on the world; and that they are capable of being vigorously contested and criticised both in principle and in terms of their effectiveness. In other words, after reading this book, you might well still believe that Bono is right, but perhaps no longer believe that his rightness is self-evident, beyond argument.

Whether or not Bono is right, I hope it will be difficult for anyone who has read this book to maintain that he is 'left'. Indeed, since 2005 he and his organisations have been frequently derisive of approaches that they see as leftish. 'It … would be really wrong beating a sort of left-wing drum, taking the usual bleeding-heart-liberal line' is a typical Bono statement about where he locates his campaigning politics.[8] Of course he would also say, in the unlikely event that he were asked, that he is not right-wing either. It is precisely the notion that the technocratic 'problem-solving' approaches that he advocates are somehow apolitical that needs to be contested.

The rise of Bono as a political operator since the late 1990s is tied to larger and disquieting developments in transnational governance, by which the biggest states, corporations, foundations and multilateral institutions have undermined democratic accountability and sovereignty throughout the world, often in the name of humanitarianism. Bono is a relatively small (though nonetheless significant) player in this project, and to consider it fully is beyond the bounds of this volume. By the end of the book, as Bono's close ties to the Bill and Melinda Gates Foundation and its agenda for African development are considered, readers may be encouraged to learn more.

Before you get to that point, *The Frontman* is divided into three thematic strands that are drawn in part from the chronology and geography of Bono's own story. Chapter 1, 'Ireland', looks, among other things, at the myths and realities of Bono's origins in Dublin; the way he and U2 related to the Irish Troubles; their emergence as symbols of Irish confidence and regeneration, and then as major players in domestic business and property investment, before and after the collapse of the Irish economy. Chapter 2, 'Africa', examines how Africa has been constructed in Bono's work and how he came to steal the show at Live Aid in 1985, eventually overtaking its progenitor Bob Geldof as the main 'African' advocate in Western politics and show business, pushing neoliberal solutions to the continent's problems. Chapter 3, 'The World', looks at Bono's multinational business interests and his role in events such as G8 summits, cosying up to the likes of Jesse Helms and Paul O'Neill, whitewashing war criminals of the Iraq invasion such as Tony Blair and Paul Wolfowitz, and acting as a sidekick to shock-doctrine economist Jeffrey Sachs. Some important but non-political aspects of his career are absent entirely; some of the most important political events and issues are dealt with in two or even three of the chapters, examined each time from a slightly different perspective.

The great genius and the great danger of Bono is that – not unlike that 'community organiser' Barack Obama – he does a plausible imitation of an activist. His discourse rings with familiar cries for justice, and some of us who should know better hear our yearnings in his voice: he is, after all, an accomplished singer. British journalist George Monbiot wrote after the 2005 G8 summit, in which Bono played such a clever and shameful role:

> The G8 leaders and the business interests their summit promotes can absorb our demands for aid, debt relief, even slightly fairer terms of trade, and lose nothing. They can wear our colours, speak our language, claim to support our aims, and discover in our agitation not new constraints, but new opportunities for manufacturing consent. Justice, this consensus says, can be achieved without confronting power.[9]

Bono comes in the name of that power, assuring us that if we make our peace with it – 'campaigning', sure, but only within its terms – it will make everything all right. That power, true to its pretensions as an equal-opportunity employer, is happy to employ a talkative Irish rock star in designer sunglasses and leather trousers to deliver the message, if that's what it takes.

It's nothing personal, Bono, but I'm afraid one of the first steps for people seeking real justice is that we stop buying the message you're selling.

1 IRELAND

'WHAT A THRILL FOR FOUR IRISH BOYS FROM THE NORTHSIDE OF DUBLIN ...': ORIGINS

Bono is rich: he wears designer clothes, flies around in private jets, drives any one of five luxury cars, loves the finest of food and wine – his net worth has been estimated at more than a half-billion dollars.

Bono is famous: he fronts the most consistently popular band of the last three decades, has millions of fans, sings several of our era's best-known songs – he wears sunglasses that draw attention to him rather than deflect it.

Bono is powerful: his counsel is sought, heard and heeded at the very highest levels of national and international governance – he is, as the Ramones might say, friends with the president, friends with the pope.

But Bono wants you to know he hasn't forgotten where he comes from. As thousands gathered on Washington's Mall in January 2009, and millions watched on TV, he told the man who would be inaugurated as US president two days later: 'What a thrill for four Irish boys from the northside of Dublin to honour you, sir.'

When Bono, preening for Barack Obama and the wider world outside the Lincoln Memorial, chose these words of pseudo-self-deprecation to capture the all-round awesomeness of U2's presence, he was indulging in a mashup of signifiers, typical of those who carefully craft their own images. At its most basic level, the 'What a thrill for ...' was just an adaptation of American Dream boilerplate, which was flowing especially thick in those Obama-worshipping days: 'We were just four Irish boys', was what he meant, 'and now look at us.' 'Irish', though, doesn't necessarily signify a foreign nationality for many people in the US, so much as a certain kind of Americans, or even just a bout of bad temper. However, Bono did throw in a few extra words of geographic specificity – 'from the northside of

Dublin' – and in context one got the impression it was the realm of the working class, the baddest part of town. And it probably doesn't hurt that 'north' and 'Irish' may also conjure up memories of old TV news footage of bombs and barbed wire. Suddenly, Bono, Adam, Larry and The Edge are cast in the mind's eye as street urchins who dodged the crossfire of the Irish Troubles and lived to sing about it. Hey, didn't they call two of their first three albums *Boy* and *War*?

This discussion of origin-mythmaking is not simply meant to suggest that Bono and his band are somehow inauthentic (though it is true that the concept of 'authenticity' and its discontents have stalked U2's career). Nor is it meant to provoke the arguably racist questioning of 'how Irish are they really?' beloved of some hostile commentators, who point out that 'Paul David Hewson' bears no trace of Gaelic origins – but the same can be said about the names of millions of people who are unquestionably of Irish origin.

It is meant to disentangle the facts of Bono's life from his rhetoric. In Dublin, the often-capitalised Northside and Southside are states of mind as much as states of geography, and are class signifiers to such an extent that, for example, the working-class Liberties south of the river Liffey are often described as 'not really Southside'; similarly, the seaside urban villages of Clontarf, where Bono and the boys met at Mount Temple Comprehensive School, and Malahide, where Adam and The Edge lived as kids, are posh enough to be rhetorically exempted from the Northside that abuts them.

To be fair, we have no idea whether the word 'northside' carried a capital N in Bono's mind's eye when he drawled it outside the Lincoln Memorial. However, there's no doubt that's the way it was heard in Ireland: the *Irish Times*, quintessential Southside newspaper, devoted a column after the Obama affair to the trashing of Bono's claim to real Northside-icity. (It is one of the small ironies of Dublin's division that it is generally Southsiders who are most protective of the Northside and Real-Dub – 'real Dublin' – brands, treating them like Appellations Contrôlées, the guarantees of regional authenticity on bottles of French wine, denouncing any suspiciously middle-class figures, of whatever geographic origin, who attempt to wear the labels as badges of street-credibility.) Bono, it seems, with his unDubby mid-Atlantic accent and his mansion overlooking the most-definitely-Southside Killiney Bay, is forever to be condemned for alluding significantly to the fact that he grew up, genuinely, on the northside of Dublin city.

That *Irish Times* columnist remarked: 'It's not as if most of Bono's friends are either dead or in jail. Last time I looked, they were making soundtracks and bowls.'[1] This rather strangely and cleverly inverted put-down perhaps says more than it intends to about how the *Irish Times* sees the essence of Northsidedness – 'dead or in jail', like something out of a rapper's boast about his unlikely rise from the streets. But it also helps us to get a handle on how misleading, or at least inadequate, Bono was being when he summarised U2 as 'four Irish boys from the northside of Dublin', a description that in the circumstances certainly signified (to listeners and viewers of whatever sensitivity) origins distant and isolated from centres and moments of cultural power like the one he was enjoying on Washington's Mall, whether or not it signified full-blown poverty and deprivation.

The reality is that Bono grew up in a middle-class (that term is more upmarket in Ireland and Britain than in the US) and slightly counter-cultural enclave of the poor and working-class north Dublin area called 'Ballymun' (another signifying Appellation Contrôlée that he is occasionally abused for employing). 'Violence ... is the thing I remember most from my teenage years', he has said, but without giving any more detail than a suggestion that, when he and his pals strayed into working-class territory, it was, you know, kind of scary.[2] Ballymun's notorious, now-demolished tower blocks may have been evoked in Bono's 'Running to Stand Still', but he grew up a safe distance away on Cedarwood Road, full of comfy semi-detached homes with nice gardens, lawns and driveways.

In the early 1990s Bono tried to convince an American journalist, Bill Flanagan, that as a child he used to hustle tourists in (Protestant) St Patrick's Cathedral:

> 'I would charge them for tours of the cathedral', [Bono] says. 'I made good money.'
>
> 'Oh', I say, 'you were an *urchin*.'
>
> 'I was!' Bono says brightly, at which [Bono's wife] Ali bursts out laughing. She knows her husband never urched.[3]

Bono was no child of the streets; nor were the city and country he inhabited the complete backwaters that they look like in so much retrospection. Born in 1960, Bono was raised in a Republic of Ireland that was economically and culturally emerging from the isolation of the first four decades after independence. Emigration had slowed very dramatically, and with a new economic strategy of seeking foreign investment, the country was even attracting families from Britain like those of Bono's future bandmates: Edge's dad was an engineer, Clayton's a pilot – higher earners than Bono's father, with his white-collar job in the postal service. The sometimes-maddening tendency of the Irish economy to be out of sync with its neighbours was occasionally a good thing: for example, while Britain went slouching toward the Winter of Discontent in the late 1970s, Ireland, including the boys of U2, enjoyed a mini-boom.

New political winds were blowing through the era too: a leading politician could credibly claim that 'the Seventies will be socialist'; there was a vigorous women's liberation movement that got a good airing in broadcast and printed media; and there was of course a civil rights movement and 'armed struggle' across the border in British-controlled Northern Ireland. By the time Bono was starting secondary school at the new, liberal, Protestant-run, multi-denominational, co-educational Mount Temple, one of Britain's favourite blues guitarists was Cork-based Rory Gallagher, and within another year or two Thin Lizzy – with a black Dubliner, Phil Lynnott, as frontman – were blasting up the rock charts on both sides of the Atlantic. And that's to say nothing of the centrality of Irish music and musicians in the ongoing international 'revival' of traditional and folk music. Ireland wasn't rich, but it was a reasonably cool place to be from, and in, with nothing much cooler and more connected than to be a teenage rock 'n' roller at Mount Temple, with its largely well-off student body. When 1977 came along, some of the punk bands made it to Dublin on tour.

You might call them cosmopolitan provincials, or provincial cosmopolitans; either way, middle-class young people in Dublin in the 1970s were capable of being clued-in about the wider world, and even feeling that they could exert some influence over it. Pirate radio and a TV aerial that could pick up the BBC meant that you needn't miss a thing. In 1977 Niall Stokes launched an ambitious and specifically Irish title, *Hot Press*, an irreverently liberal music magazine, which quickly turned into a must-read for local fans and bands alike, especially in Dublin.

Ah, but there was, of course, the power of the Catholic church to spoil all that, and for many people it was a terrible scourge on their lives. Its role shouldn't, however, be exaggerated, as it often is in the memories and polemics of those who get over-excited about Ireland's eventual liberation from its yoke. While it was true that the Catholic hierarchy cast a long shadow, including over national legislation on matters such as divorce and birth control – U2 would eventually play their first benefit gig in 1978 for the Contraception Action Campaign[4] – it didn't especially darken places like Mount Temple.

Bono has made much of his parents' religiously mixed marriage: 'My mother was a Protestant, my father was a Catholic; no big deal anywhere else in the world but here' – benighted Ireland, the only place in the world where denominational differences matter. Except that Bono has never shown that his parents' mixed marriage was anything like a 'big deal' in the circles he inhabited. Indeed, it is striking that in an Ireland where the Catholic church's *Ne temere* doctrine of 1908, ruling that children in mixed marriages must be raised Catholic, had been declared by the Supreme Court in 1950 to be enforceable in law, Bobby and Iris Hewson felt free to make their own arrangements: they agreed to raise their children alternately, the first Protestant, the second (Paul, later to become Bono) Catholic – or, by another telling, boys Catholic and girls Protestant – and then didn't stick to that arrangement in practice, with Bobby leaving their two boys in their mother's (Protestant) spiritual care. Young Paul went to mainstream Protestant primary schools.[5]

The Hewsons' mixed marriage, and whatever agonies they may have suffered because of it, is of course a private matter; it may well have been harder than we'll ever know. No one would dream of questioning the real trauma and loss that accompanied Iris Hewson's death when young Paul was fourteen. But it is difficult not to suspect that Bono locates himself as a childhood victim of sectarian pressures at least partly to associate his origins with the conflict in Northern Ireland, understood in much of the rest of the world to be a sectarian Protestant-versus-Catholic war. Bono's repeated insistence that he had a little piece of the war in his very own childhood home – he had, he said in a Washington speech in 2006, 'a father who was Protestant and a mother who was Catholic in a country where the line between the two was, quite literally, often a battle line'[6] – is part of the backdrop to his decades of posturing on that conflict. (Strangely enough, in that speech he reversed his parents' actual religious affiliations.) In reality the Troubles took place almost in their entirety sixty-plus miles up the road in Northern Ireland; and when the conflict made rare, bloody intrusions into the Republic, it didn't discriminate between Protestant, Catholic and 'mixed' victims.

The four boys in U2, meanwhile, were not very different from most of the people who would become their fans across Europe and North America: comfortably off, liberally raised, and drawn inexorably to the international language of rock 'n' roll. Somewhat more unusually for teenagers at that time and in those circumstances, Bono and his mates were attracted by another global language: that of Christianity.

DANDELION MARKET: U2 EMERGES

In many ways, their enthusiasm for Jesus was more outré and cutting-edge than their musical aesthetic. Under their first two names of Feedback and The Hype, the band that would become U2 played covers of songs by middle-of-the-road chart acts such as Peter Frampton, the Eagles and the Moody Blues well into 1977 – many months after the Sex Pistols had released 'Anarchy in the UK' and the older fellas in Dublin band the Boomtown Rats had headed off to join the punk scene in London. When young Bono wrote his first song, 'What's Going On?', he apparently didn't realise that Marvin Gaye had got to the title first. Only after the Clash came to town in October 1977 did the band begin to punk up their sound and their look, and finally their name.[7]

Paul Hewson grabbed his own stage-name not from any Christian commitment to doing good but from a prominent hearing-aid shop in central Dublin that advertised 'Bono Vox' (good voice) devices. (The name is pronounced, as one of his detractors notes, to rhyme with 'con-oh' rather than 'oh-no'.[8]) His youthful religious explorations began at an early age, when he befriended neighbour Derek Rowan (later to become 'Guggi', a successful painter), who belonged to an evangelical Protestant sect that had been founded in Dublin in the 1820s, the Plymouth Brethren.[9] The intensification of his religious curiosity, at home and in school, has been attributed to the loss of his mother when he was fourteen; when Larry Mullen's mother died a few years later, the two teenagers delved together into Bible study. Religious observance was high in Ireland, among both Protestants and Catholics; religious identity was important to a substantial portion of the population; but religious enthusiasm was and is seen as a distinctly odd phenomenon in the Republic. Back in the 1980s many Irish observers would wrinkle their noses in suspicion and tell you that U2 were 'some kind of born-agains' – the phrase suggesting an Americanised Protestant evangelicalism. Or, on the other hand, they would raise eyebrows and explain that U2 'had gone charismatic' – a term which, unlike 'born-again', pointed to the possibility of a basically Catholic orientation, but one far removed from the quietly muttered rituals that dominated most Irish-Catholic practice.

Ireland is a country where you can still be half-seriously asked if you're 'a Catholic atheist or a Protestant atheist', but most Irish people seem to have lost interest long ago in whether Bono and two of his bandmates (bassist Adam Clayton stayed out of the Bible scene) were or are Protestant Christians or Catholic Christians – though the interest in scripture points to the former. The prayer group they joined in 1978, and eventually left more than three years later when they came under pressure from fellow members to abandon rock 'n' roll and its trappings, was called Shalom; but, despite the name, Shalom's members were not Jewish Christians, and, just to add to the confusion, the organisation has been described as both 'evangelical' and 'charismatic', with 'Pentecostal' thrown in for good measure.[10] Bono's wedding in 1982 was conducted in the conventionally Protestant Church of Ireland – part of the Anglican communion – to which his wife

Ali Stewart belonged, but with some of his friends' Plymouth Brethren colouring thrown in.[11]

Whatever words you use to describe the band's early Christianity, it doesn't appear to have made much of a mark on the Dublin music scene. In February 1979 Bono told *Hot Press* writer Bill Graham about the religious commitments of his circle of friends in the earnest, creative, post-hippy imagined community they called Lypton Village, 'One thing you should know about the Village: we're all Christians.' Graham, however, chose to leave that revelation out of his published interview with the band he was already growing to love, in order to protect their reputation.[12] Oddly enough, U2 were apparently stalked for a few weeks in 1979 by a group of young toughs from Bono's neighbourhood styling themselves the 'Black Catholics', who denounced U2 as 'Protestant bastards'. But this seemingly had more to do with class than religion – 'Protestant' translated in this case as 'posh and stuck-up'; and after a couple of tussles the harassment was ended by Bono marching down Cedarwood Road to confront the daddy of one of his persecutors.[13] The Christians of U2 weren't, in any case, persecuted for their religious beliefs; nor did they make much of proselytising them.

But even as U2 were embracing God they came face to face with Mammon, in the form of Paul McGuinness. Bono has described U2 as 'a gang of four, but a corporation of five',[14] with the fifth and equal partner being the hard-headed capitalist who has managed the band from nearly their start. McGuinness, a decade older than the band, was and is a traditional Irish Catholic, which is to say a man without a shred of obvious, let alone ostentatious, Christianity. (He famously shot down the band when they were hesitating over a set of gigs, under pressure from Shalom comrades: 'If God had something to say about this tour he should have raised his hand a little earlier.'[15]) From the time he took on management of the band after passionate encouragement from Graham of *Hot Press*, McGuinness served the purpose of deflecting and absorbing criticism: he could be a tough, obsessive bastard so they didn't have to. He aroused far more resentment among other musicians than anything involving U2's religion ever did. One false rumour doing the rounds in 1979 suggested that McGuinness made a phone call pretending to be a London A&R man in order to get U2 a gig opening for the popular English New Waver Joe Jackson, insisting that local rivals Rocky De Valera & the Gravediggers had to be dumped so he could see U2. (That change was never in fact made.) When *Heat* magazine printed the untrue rumour, McGuinness initiated a lawsuit that soon shut the magazine down.[16] McGuinness was a man who was tough enough to attract conspiracy theories, and dealt firmly with adversity.

Commercial success didn't immediately follow upon McGuinness's manoeuvres, but his ambition and U2's discipline meant that they left no stone unturned. Ireland was, unbeknown to itself, coming to the end of its era of the showbands, typically eight-piece sharp-suited groups who toured the highways and byways playing cover songs for dancing. These bands were still, in 1979, making more money than the small collection of post-punk groups like U2 that constituted an incestuous Dublin scene. The Boomtown Rats were big, but their profits seemed to underline the truism that London was where the action was. McGuinness eventually took his 'Baby Band'[17] to play in London, but built them up even to London journalists and industry scouts as Dublin's quintessential live act. He got them signed to a small, non-exclusive deal with the CBS subsidiary in Ireland, and built their live following remorselessly, putting on a famous series of Saturday-afternoon shows in the half-derelict Dandelion Market next to St Stephen's Green to cater for U2's under-eighteen following, who couldn't go to pub and club gigs. The shows at the 'Dando' would become the stuff of legend: few Dubliners of a certain age will admit to having not seen them there, though a few will tell you they were rotten. The climax of McGuinness's efforts came when – as something of a last throw of the dice – he booked them to tour Ireland and to play the National Stadium on Dublin's South Circular Road. 'National Stadium' is a grand name for a boxing venue that seated a couple of thousand people, but McGuinness put them there knowing full well that they couldn't possibly fill it: top international acts sometimes failed to do so. Sure enough, there were hundreds of empty seats when U2 took the stage on 26 February 1980, but the declaration of importance and ambition of that winter was enough to seal a good deal at last with Bill Stewart – a British army intelligence officer turned ad-man turned music scout – on behalf of an international label, Island Records, which had made its fortune with Bob Marley but, according to Graham, was a bit at a loss when it came to the current state of rock.[18]

That was okay, because U2 didn't sound like they had much of a clue either. Listen to the first U2 singles and you may find it hard to believe that this is a 'great' band working in the aftermath of, say, the Clash's *London Calling* – released a few months before U2 signed with Island. Musical range, lyrical wit, political sensibility: U2 had none of the above. They were, it's true, still young, five or six years younger than the youngest members of the Clash, but youth alone doesn't fully explain just how callow they sound. It's easy to conclude that this is an Eagles cover-band that picked up some pace from punk and some posturing from David Bowie but simply hadn't listened to enough good, passionate music to understand how it might work technically and emotionally. Their devotion, meanwhile, to what authors Sean Campbell and Gerry Smyth have identified as the main animating discourse of Irish 'beat' music in its formative decades, 'creative self-expression' – the idea that one performed music in order to explore and reveal allegedly deep emotional truths – is all too earnestly apparent in these tracks.[19] Bono was writing almost all of the lyrics, but from the start the four members of U2 shared the song-writing credits, and eventually the royalties, equally.

While many English bands in this period went chasing after black sounds, mainly reggae and ska, U2 were a whiter shade of pale. A series of 'London spies' – talent-spotters from the big city – had previously found the band 'gauche and formless',[20] and it's easy to hear why. Yes, there is something interesting and different about Edge's guitar-playing – and once he had added an echo-unit to his paraphernalia that playing would remain the band's major sonic contribution to the rock canon over the coming decade or three. But to understand why this mediocre band was preparing to take on the world requires some understanding of what Bono contributed, other than banal lyrics and what was then still a fairly ordinary voice.

One thing was his stagecraft. He and his friend Gavin Friday (of arty band Virgin Prunes) had studied theatre techniques with a teacher, Conal Kearney, who had himself studied with the internationally famous mime artist Marcel Marceau; Irish actor and playwright Mannix Flynn, who would later go on to national fame with his robust explorations of his traumatic youth, also helped out. Bono was a 'boy from the northside' with a sophisticated, trained sense derived from leading practitioners of how to use his body and eyes to seduce an audience.[21] Then there was his charm, a sort of face-to-face stagecraft. Bono was, by all accounts, friendly and un-aloof, his motor-mouth not suggestive of excessive calculation, despite Bill Graham's conclusion that Bono and U2 'were always rather skilled at discovering people to discover them'.[22] *Hot Press* fell into U2's orbit, and has remained there permanently. Bono just happened to be especially good at making friends with, say, Ireland's best music writer, Graham, and Ireland's favourite rock DJ, Dave Fanning. Writing in 1985, Fanning, who would remain a favoured insider for decades, freely admitted that U2's initial charm had little to do with music: it was 'Bono's histrionics which gave U2 an air of more substance than was suggested by the evidence of their overall performance', he wrote. More than their records, their 'late night rock show interviews' on his own pirate-radio show meant that 'insomniacs all over Dublin could quite clearly see U2's unique passion, commitment and dedication to the idea of the potential of the song as something heartfelt and special, and the uplifting power of live performance'.[23] In other words, Bono talked a great gig.

When the time came, he wove similar personal magic in London, New York and beyond. Bono 'had the ability to persuade the interviewer that U2 were his own private discovery and that the journalist had been cast by the fates to play his own absolutely personalized role in U2's crusade against the forces of darkness', wrote Graham.[24]

Where the journalists and DJs went, other listeners followed. It's a pop-critical cliché to say that vague lyrics like Bono's invite you to project your own circumstances into the emotions they evoke. But in the case of U2, the invitation came embossed and with a charming, effusive personal greeting from the lyricist himself. How could anyone resist?

WAR: NEGOTIATING IRISH POLITICS

Bono and U2 were, however, stuck with their Irishness, and in the early 1980s, with violence raging in Northern Ireland and the republican hunger-strikes escalating both tension and international interest, it was not always easy to be vague about one's views and commitments. While their near-contemporaries, Derry's the Undertones, could skirt artfully around the Troubles of which they were indubitably children, the bombastic and moralising U2 found the crisis that they had, and had not, lived through to be a more difficult and almost unavoidable subject.

In truth, they were probably unambivalent about the Northern crisis, insofar as any people living on the island could be. In keeping with the by now established consensus of most of their class in the Republic, they probably believed the Provisional IRA to be thugs and murderers whose campaign of violence must somehow be stopped, though the worst excesses of British and, especially, loyalist-paramilitary violence evoked some distaste too. For the most part, at least in U2's well-off and liberal circles, fundamental critiques of the Northern state established by the partition of the island in 1921 had faded, and those who attempted to raise them again were often derided as 'sneaking regarders' of republican violence, apologists for the IRA. This suite of views would pose little problem for U2's entrée into culturally enlightened society in Britain, where only a few brave Irish immigrant groups and leftists were prepared to stand up, even amid occasional IRA bombs, for the right of Northern Irish nationalists to resist discrimination and state violence, and to insist that Britain withdraw its troops from Northern Ireland. But it would pose more of a problem in the US, where open adherence to 'the cause' was more widespread in and beyond Irish communities.

Thus, for example, U2's plans to ride a float in the 1982 New York St Patrick's Day parade were abandoned when they learned that dead IRA hunger-striker Bobby Sands had been named as honorary grand marshal.

The hunger-strikers – seeking political status in Northern prisons against a British government, led by Margaret Thatcher, that insisted on treating them as criminals – evoked great respect in the US and around the world. In Northern Ireland the respect was sufficient to see Sands elected as MP in Fermanagh and South Tyrone just weeks before he starved to death. In U2's Dublin, however, Sands was beyond the pale, and even an association as remote as would have been represented by a then still obscure U2 on a float in that parade was more than they could bear.[25]

'Of necessity, Irish rock has striven to escape into a non-sectarian space, even at the cost of being apolitical', Bill Graham wrote with typical certainty in 1981. While this quest for safe spaces was understandable for those working in the midst of the conflict, the nature of the 'necessity' for a Southern-based band is never explained by the highly influential Graham. But the punishment for transgressing the rules that said music should be escapist, for engaging with the Troubles beyond bland condemnation or rocking through the heartache, is evident in the same article in which Graham makes that strange and prescriptive assertion. It's a *Hot Press* interview with the great trad-rock fusion group Moving Hearts, in which Graham excoriates them for supporting the hunger-strike campaign and badgers them to clarify whether they support the IRA itself.[26]

The unstated assumption is that it was 'apolitical', just common sense, to oppose the IRA. Even if they had been inclined to do so, it would have been unwise in the Ireland of the 1980s and early 1990s for U2 to adopt anything other than this version of an apolitical stance – a studied pseudo-neutrality that was essentially an endorsement of the political status quo (or the status quo if only the thugs would stop all the killing). Certainly, the tightly enforced Dublin consensus went, there was no injustice in the North that was worth shedding blood over, and the reasons many Northern Catholics felt otherwise – from discrimination and segregation in jobs and housing to the historic splitting of the island of Ireland and the ongoing provocation of a British military presence – were largely ignored in favour of a generic deploring of violence. (The hypocrisy of this rhetorical pacifism was exposed every time its proponents refused to condemn various acts of violence by, say, the US or British government.)

The personification of this consensus was Garret FitzGerald, who served as taoiseach (prime minister) for most of the 1980s, heading coalitions between his own Fine Gael party and the Labour Party. Virtually every biography of Bono tells of his admiration for FitzGerald, who combined bristling contempt for Northern republicans (his response to a desperate delegation of hunger-strikers' families was to 'lay all the blame for the hunger strikers on the republican movement and to suggest an

immediate unilateral end to their military campaign'[27]) with a determination to launch a 'crusade' to reduce the Catholic hierarchy's influence over
social legislation in the Republic. This was an alluring combination not
merely for Bono but for a generation of Irish social liberals who saw the
vaguely professorial Fitzgerald as someone who could lead the state away
from the backwardness represented by Catholic nationalism.

But the hapless FitzGerald saw his crusade backfire in 1983 when anti-
abortion activists successfully campaigned to have a 'pro-life' amendment
added to the constitution, and again in 1986 when his attempt to introduce
divorce was defeated. Bono and U2 were nowhere to be seen in either of
these bitter referendum campaigns, though Bono had chanced an election
photo-op with FitzGerald in 1982. In September 1983, just a few days after
the disastrous abortion referendum, FitzGerald appointed the increasingly
famous Bono as a member of a minor face-saving distraction called the
'National Youth Policy Committee', a new and (it turned out) short-lived
initiative, chaired by a high-court judge but without any actual powers,
that allegedly aimed to address the myriad social and cultural problems
faced by young people in those recessionary times.[28] One hagiographic
biography of Bono, written long after the fact, suggests without citing any
evidence that Bono resigned after a few months, in frustration at the committee's bureaucracy,[29] but there is no sign in the *Irish Times* archives of his
doing so publicly, and thus embarrassing his friends in government. (U2
did not put all its eggs in one political basket: the hard-headed McGuinness
was closer to the opposition Fianna Fail party – a fact that kept U2 close
to the levers of power after 1987, when that party settled into government
for twenty-one of the next twenty-four years; McGuinness himself would
serve on the state's Arts Council, an important funding body, for more
than a decade.)

To paint Bono in his proper Dublin middle-class Fine Gael colours
is not to endorse those who were conducting the 'armed struggle' in
Northern Ireland. Most people genuinely abhorred the violence of the
IRA. However, it is obvious in retrospect that the ongoing campaign of
vilification and demonisation of Northern Irish nationalist communities
during this period deepened their marginalisation and made it easier to
ignore the reasons those communities supported the 'Provos' (Provisional
IRA). And thus it prolonged the violent conflict.

It is in this context that one can see what a faintly absurd statement of
the obvious it was for Bono to introduce the 1983 song 'Sunday Bloody
Sunday' in concert after concert with the famous words, 'This is not a rebel
song' – a 'rebel song' being, in Irish parlance, a pub-republican come-all-
ye that denounces the Brits and/or celebrates the resistance to them. And

yet there was a certain revisionist something-like-genius in the way that song – its writing started by The Edge and completed by Bono – appropriated republican ideas, including that of 'Bloody Sunday' itself, to create the impression that U2 were in some way the true rebels for the way they bravely rejected rebellion.

Bloody Sunday can refer to two events in Irish history: a date during the War of Independence in 1920 when the IRA killed British intelligence officers across Dublin, and soldiers retaliated by shooting into a Gaelic-football crowd in Croke Park, killing fourteen spectators; or an afternoon in 1972 when British paratroopers again killed fourteen unarmed civilians, this time after a civil rights march in Derry, in Northern Ireland.[30] Thus the term 'Bloody Sunday' mainly denotes the idea, and reality, of brutal and indiscriminate state violence. The U2 song, however, says nothing about who perpetuated the scenes of carnage that it vaguely describes, and makes no reference to the state. Indeed, in its original form, in lyrics written by The Edge, the song started out with a direct condemnation of the IRA and, implicitly, of those supporting its members' rights in situations such as the hunger-strikes that had taken place so recently when the song was written: 'Don't talk to me about the rights of the IRA.'[31] This line is especially revealing of its writer's ignorance, or at least his readiness to offend Northern nationalists: the innocent dead of Bloody Sunday in Derry were protesting against Britain's internment-without-trial of suspected republicans; so in a sense Bloody Sunday's victims, the apparent object of the song's sympathy, had died for trying to 'talk about the rights of the IRA' – and of course of the many non-IRA members who had been picked up in violent military trawls of nationalist communities.

The group thought better of that 'Don't talk to me …' line, which turned into 'I can't believe the news today'. It's perhaps the most fateful edit of U2's entire career, moving the song just far enough into ambiguity to ensure it would anger no one. The protagonist is someone watching the war on television, and the repetition in the song title conveys the weariness of someone observing a society that has degenerated into savagery. How long are we going to have to keep watching this, the song asks, with 'bloody' a curse that in Ireland and Britain commonly suggests 'boring' as much as it does 'horrible', as in the title of John Schlesinger's 1971 film from which the track borrows its name. There are some portentous ruminations on the observers' mediated distance from the events – 'And it's true we are immune / When fact is fiction and TV reality' – and a Christian coda after the instrumental break; there's also some powerful noise coming from the band; what there *isn't* is an ounce of insight, empathy or courage.

Writing in 1987, Irish journalist Brian Trench cogently observed that the song 'turned part of the current war in the North into an anthem for no particular people with no particular aim'. Years later, Northern Irish academic Bill Rolston, in the course of proposing a typology of how songs dealt with the conflict, persuasively assigned 'Sunday Bloody Sunday' to his third of four categories, songs of accusation, which 'condemn the protagonists' but concentrate their ire on republicans. The song has even been read as first proposing, then rejecting, the 'simple republican solution' embodied in the phrase 'We can be as one tonight', abandoning that in favour of a militantly Protestant cry of 'onward Christian soldiers'.[32] One recalls with some sense of irony that this was one of a set of songs that Bono wrote in response to criticism aimed at his previous song-writing of 'not being specific enough in the lyrics'.[33]

U2 drummer, Larry Mullen Jr, said in 1983 that the song was born partly out of annoyance at the pub-and-pew republicanism of Irish-Americans. 'Americans don't understand it. They call it a religious war, but it has nothing to do with religion. During the hunger strikes, the IRA would say, "God is with me. I went to Mass every Sunday." And the Unionists said virtually the same thing. And then they go out and murder each other.'[34] But you can search high and wide to no avail for an IRA statement to the effect that it was a religious war and that God would take the side of mass-goers.

Larry's contempt for those who viewed the Northern Irish conflict as a religious war was lacerating, albeit confused. One wonders how he felt when Bono said, years, later: 'Remember, I come from Ireland and I've seen the damage of religious warfare.'[35]

Despite the hostility to militant nationalism and the sense in 'Sunday Bloody Sunday' of distance from the events it describes, Bono was always ready to declare that the Troubles took place in Ireland, 'my country'. This sounded less like united-Ireland defiance of the border imposed by Britain's partition of the island than a means of conferring credibility on U2 for their proximity to and involvement in the situation.

And however one interprets 'Sunday Bloody Sunday', what is beyond question is that the song, and that (false) sense that U2 intimately knew whereof they spoke, played an enormous role in turning U2 into international stars. Bono's own version of the story says that on the previous tour, for the *October* album, he had already begun deconstructing the Irish tricolour on stage: he tore the green and orange away to leave only a white flag, which became the constant prop for performances of 'Sunday Bloody Sunday' thereafter.[36] Whether that was the origin of it or not, the image of Bono marching to the martial beat of that song with a white flag in the misty rain at a 1983 festival gig in Colorado was part of the band's breakthrough video on MTV. For those who didn't know much about the Irish Troubles, it seemed that this song and the way Bono performed it were saying something terribly defiant about something or other of great, albeit obscure, political importance. And few people were prepared to point out that, in reality, he was defying no one except a beleaguered, oppressed community of mainly working-class people who were already under physical and ideological assault and were themselves looking for ways to break the cycle of violence.

By 1987, U2 were big enough, and the IRA bomb that killed eleven people at an Enniskillen war memorial was horrible enough, for Bono to make very publicly explicit that the song's ire was directed at the Provos, as well as their Irish-American supporters. In a powerful US performance on the night of that bombing, featured in arty black-and-white in the film *Rattle and Hum*, he took a mid-song break to declare:

> I've had enough of Irish-Americans who haven't been back to their country in twenty or thirty years come up to me and talk about the resistance, the revolution back home, and the glory of the revolution, and the glory of dying for the revolution. Fuck the revolution! ... Where's the glory in bombing a Remembrance Day parade of old-age pensioners, their medals taken out and polished up for the day. Where's the glory in that? To leave them dying or crippled for life or dead under the rubble of the revolution that the majority of the people in my country don't want.[37]

He then, as always, led the crowd in chanting 'No more!' – this time with no question about whom the words were targeting. The target most definitely wasn't the state that had conferred those harmlessly polished medals on those old-age pensioners, perhaps, or perhaps not, for their services to the cause of nonviolence.

The truth was that this seemingly courageous, militant stance for Peace was no more than an impassioned dramatisation of the useless, war-weary but war-prolonging shibboleths of the Irish and British establishments, which cast the conflict as fundamentally the fault of a mad, blood-crazed IRA. In this respect, Bono Vox was no more than a 'good voice' of his adopted class, a young man whose career benefited greatly from the Northern conflict.

In a twenty-first century interview Bono indulged in considerable revisionism about this time: 'I could not but be moved by the courage of Bobby Sands, and we understood how people had taken up arms to defend themselves, even if we didn't think it was the right thing to do. But it was clear that the Republican Movement was becoming a monster in order to defeat one.'[38] Such understanding, including an acknowledgment that Sands was courageous and the British presence in Northern Ireland constituted a 'monster', was, however, unspeakable and unspoken by Bono in the 1980s. Writing in the *New York Times* in 2010 as he visited Derry to see the British apologise for 1972's Bloody Sunday, he was even critical of his younger self when describing his newfound respect for Sinn Fein's Martin McGuinness, by that time deputy first minister of Northern Ireland: 'Figures I had learned to loathe as a self-righteous student of nonviolence in the '70s and '80s behaved with a grace that left me embarrassed over my vitriol.'[39] His studies of nonviolence had nonetheless left him strikingly unconcerned about the violence of the state responsible for the very atrocity that he so blithely name-checked in 'Sunday, Bloody Sunday' – the song for which he was invited to Derry that day.

His revisionism, in any case, should come as no surprise. In the years after the ceasefires of the mid 1990s Bono, U2 and most of the rest of the Irish and British establishments learned to speak a retrospective 'peace-process' language of respect, dialogue and inclusion. But it was not their native tongue.

And whatever the truth of the deconstructing-the-tricolour story, Bono would not always be so sensitive about the dangers of associating 'Sunday Bloody Sunday' with nationalism, even violent nationalism. On stage in Madison Square Garden in October 2001, as the US dropped bombs on Afghan cities, during that song he 'embraced the Stars and Stripes' and otherwise 'reverently' handled the US flag.[40] He didn't tear it apart.

SELF AID: CELEBRITY AT HOME

It was obvious by the mid 1980s, when *Rolling Stone* called U2 the 'Band of the Decade' – not an entirely obvious characterisation in 1985, since their five albums (including a 'live' one) had sold millions of copies but not reached any higher than number twelve in the US charts – Bono and the band had successfully used their Irishness as a calling card in the United States. Back home in Ireland, it was also clear that their American success could in turn be a route to domestic power and influence. But despite their increasing association with a liberal human-rights discourse inter-nationally (see Chapters 2 and 3), U2's interventions in Ireland were of a distinctly cautious and conservative hue. As noted above, they kept their heads down during the huge, and hugely divisive, referendum campaigns in 1983 and 1986, on abortion and divorce respectively, when Irish liberals were demoralisingly trounced.

Six weeks before the divorce referendum, however, U2 did lend their credibility and popularity to a local follow-up to the previous summer's global Live Aid concerts. Especially given that Live Aid's creator was Irishman Bob Geldof, and Bono had proved one of its most telegenic stars (see Chapter 2), 'Self Aid' was a predictable enough response to widespread populist grumbling about the readiness of celebrities, and indeed of ordinary donors, to help poor people in faraway Africa – Ireland had led the world in per capita giving to Live Aid – but not the poor on our own doorstep. The grumbling gained depth and resonance from the devastating recession that had taken hold in the Republic in the early 1980s. By May 1986, when Self Aid took place, there was anaemic growth, but no one would have mistaken Ireland for a thriving country, with Irish unemployment having hovered for years between 15 and 20 per cent, and emigration back at levels not seen since the 1950s, tens of thousands of young people, from a total population for the Republic of only 3.5 million, leaving each year.

But the organisers of Self Aid were determined not to see it become a focus for the country's growing political anger. U2 themselves had already begun to be appropriated by politicians and pundits as a reason for the nation to be cheerful and encouraged; in the words of one historian of the period, they were seen as 'proof that a better Ireland was possible'.[41] Self Aid too, as it approached, began to look more and more like a starstudded, TV-friendly paean to the power of positive thinking. And while there were many big Irish stars involved – the Boomtown Rats doing their last gig, Thin Lizzy returning only a few months after singer Phil Lynott's death, the London-and-Liverpool-Irish Elvis Costello – by now there was no doubt that Bono was the biggest of them all.

There was a groundswell of opinion on much of the Irish Left that Self Aid, with its emphasis on positivity and the 'pull up by our bootstraps' type of capitalism of much of its rhetoric, would do more harm than the little good it would achieve through fundraising for jobs-creation projects. In addition to a charitable trust that raised more than a million pounds, and to which community groups and start-ups could subsequently apply for funds, viewers were encouraged to phone in if they could offer employment themselves: thousands of dubious 'jobs' were thus 'created' by the concert/telethon.[42] This sort of charade, critics argued, was letting the state and economic elites off the hook by suggesting that the economic crisis could be solved by some apolitical form of 'self' activity by the unemployed and employers, who suddenly discovered they could employ people and get their names on TV in the bargain. Bono hadn't been especially noisy in the run-up to the concert, but as its most recognisable face he became the target for left-wing criticism as the day approached. Posters featuring Bono went up around Dublin and other cities, parodying the Self Aid 'Make It Work' slogan by declaring: 'Self Aid Makes It Worse'.

The left-wing posters would have been insulting enough to Bono's vanity – campaigners had chosen a less than attractive mulleted photo, though Bono had finally abandoned that hairstyle – but worse was to come. On the Thursday before the weekend Self Aid gig, listings magazine *In Dublin*, normally reliable in its support of U2, appeared on the stands with Bono on the cover. 'The Great Self Aid Farce', the magazine declared, constituted 'Rock Against the People'.[43] Inside, several pieces denounced the concert and singled out U2 for odium for allowing themselves to be used in this way. The polemics were led by the great Derry Marxist and journalist Eamonn McCann (then still a fan, later to become Bono's most trenchant Irish critic), along with the magazine's editor, John Waters (later to become an increasingly conservative grouch, and who rarely had another bad word to say about Bono).

Anyone who hoped that Bono might take the opportunity of the Self Aid gig to answer his critics by underlining his genuine radicalism – and there were still some in Ireland who wanted to believe in that – was to be sorely disappointed. The most political speech he made for the occasion came in the middle of a vamping little version of Bob Dylan's 'Maggie's Farm': U2 were starting their 'exploring the blues' period, and were checking out how their elders and betters had done it, incorporating a bit of John Lennon's 'Cold Turkey' in the mix. Because many young Irish people were emigrating to Margaret ('Maggie') Thatcher's Britain, Bono reckoned it would be clever to present Dylan's great, funny, devastating broadside about power relations as an earnest plea to be able to stay in Ireland rather than emigrate. In effect, 'I ain't gonna work on Maggie's farm, coz I'm gonna stay and work on Garret's farm.'

The result was the effective emasculation of the cocky anger of Dylan's song, whose protagonist runs through a list of people for whom he will no longer work, making it clearer and clearer that they probably include every conceivable species of boss. Dylan's rejection of any chance to 'sing while you slave' wasn't clear enough, however, to emerge intact in Bono's telling, as he made clear in a rather pathetic spoken interlude over the pumping riff: 'You see I like it just where I am. Tonight that's Dublin city, Ireland. And I prefer to get a job in my own hometown, mister.' The American twang in Bono's accent had rarely stood out quite this strongly. The distinctly unDublin phrasing, including the faux-proletarian 'mister', pointed to the other major influence at play: Bruce Springsteen was still near the height of his popularity, and the previous summer had played a huge outdoor gig at Slane Castle in nearby County Meath; U2 had even done a (reportedly dismal) cover version of his song 'My Hometown' during a Dublin show in June 1985.

It was striking that Bono made his watery political declaration sound such a false and borrowed note. But he had more to say. In an extraordinary bout of self-pity, he turned part of the long and winding final section of 'Bad' into an apparent tribute to himself. Singing over the repeating guitar figure to the tune of Elton John's terrible, maudlin song about Marilyn Monroe, 'Candle in the Wind', Bono achingly intoned: 'You have the grace to hold yourself, while those around you crawl. They crawl out of the woodwork, on to pages of cheap Dublin magazines. I have the grace to hold myself. I refuse to crawl.'[44]

Refuse to crawl he might, but even today the effect of viewing this outburst via YouTube may make the viewer's skin crawl. It was clear that the attack on 'cheap Dublin magazines' was aimed at McCann and Waters, but to whom on earth was he directing his refusal to crawl? Was he really just declaring himself satisfied with his display of courage in belittling his critics? And this grace – then as now among his favourite words – did it come direct from God? U2 biographer Eamon Dunphy, critical by the standards of Dublin journalists but still inclined to cut Bono slack on this incident, wrote that it showed that 'Dublin still got to them' – that their hometown's mode of badmouthing had a knack for getting under their skin – but also that, 'this being Dublin', Bono and McCann had chatted and cleared up any 'misunderstandings' at a party after the gig.[45] What could hardly be misunderstood was that this young man had a disproportionate sense of his own righteousness.

However, Bono's strange and chilling onstage attack may have had some effect. It would be more than two decades, until the time when U2's tax arrangements were revealed, before there was any comparable sustained criticism of Bono in the major Irish media. (Paul McGuinness was also capable of his own brand of chilling: when in 1991 a Dublin paper rounded up a few mildly mocking comments about Bono's lyrics for 'The Fly', the band's burly manager wrote a nasty letter to the bylined journalist, calling him 'a creep', and CCing the chief executive of the newspaper company.[46])

The main exception to Irish press quiescence in the face of Bono's power and glory was the small investigative and satirical magazine *Phoenix*. While *Phoenix* mostly kept a close eye on the band's business interests in Ireland, it wasn't above teasing Bono on other fronts. When, for example, in the year 2000 the magazine reported on the legal negotiations then ongoing between Bono and a local tabloid over paparazzi shots of the singer's sunbathing buttocks, his lawyers threatened *Phoenix* with prosecution under the Offences Against the State Act – generally employed against serious crime and 'subversion' – for revealing '*sub judice*' material, and said they had sought the intervention of the attorney-general over the matter. *Phoenix* responded by reproducing the lawyers' letter under the unusually large headline: 'L'ETAT C'EST MOI! KING BONO INVOKES OFFENCES AGAINST THE STATE ACT' – and by continuing to produce story after story about 'Bono's bum deal'.[47]

It was also *Phoenix* magazine that reported on how Bono's wife Ali described their relationship with journalists. Ali had been contacted by an old acquaintance named Dónal de Róiste, the brother of one of her closest charitable partners. De Róiste was still fighting to clear his name more than thirty years after being unjustly 'retired' from the Irish army under a cloud of suspicion of IRA connections. Ali refused to help, though in the nicest possible Christian way: 'I wish I knew a journalist that one could entrust with this cause … but I'm sorry to say I don't at present … the nature of our position unfortunately means that we stay as removed as possible from the press.' She continued sympathetically: 'I am sorry that you feel so wronged. I, iike you, believe in fair play and justice … which I know you will receive in the next life …'[48]

MOTHER: NURTURING NEW U2'S

Bono was rarely shy about where he felt U2 fit, in this life, into the history of rock 'n' roll, the art form and the business. 'I don't mean to sound arrogant,' he told *Rolling Stone* rather redundantly soon after their first album had appeared, 'but at this stage, I do feel that we are meant to be one of the great groups. There's a certain spark, a certain chemistry, that was special about the Stones, the Who and the Beatles, and I think it's also special about U2.'[49]

So it is not surprising that U2 established a record label, in the mode of the Beatles' Apple Corps, with the stated ambition of nurturing Irish talent, though it is perhaps surprising how quickly they got around to this task: they established Mother in August 1984, before they had even started playing arenas, let alone stadia, in the US (and almost exactly ten years after the death of Bono's mother, Iris). The Beatles left the task till rather later in their development as the world's biggest group – that is to say, when they were indisputably on the top of the world and were in a position to establish a sophisticated corporate apparatus in the heart of London, then probably the world's pop capital – and still made a mess of it.

Perhaps the worst that can be said with certainty about U2's label, Mother, is that it fits quite comfortably within a history of poorly performing record labels founded by artists themselves. That is not the worst that is said about Mother, however. While U2 have benefited from a compliant press in Ireland, the gossip that plays such an important role in this small, talkative society is often far less kind. One persistent and false strand of local discourse – now of course searchable on the internet – has long suggested that Mother was deliberately established, and operated, to kill off the Irish competition, to ensure that, far from a 'next U2' emerging from a thriving scene, Irish acts who threatened U2's hegemony would be signed up to Mother, then mismanaged into obscurity. This false theory is the writing-large of the false story of Paul McGuinness's malevolent impersonating phone call to promote U2 from the band's early days, and frankly it has just as little evidence to support it. It vastly overestimates the power of U2 to affect the behaviour of a whole range of international companies that would have been delighted to make stars of an Irish 'next U2', and it equally underestimates the extent to which plans and intentions can go awry and astray with just a little nudge from incompetence and complacency, and no help at all from conspiracy.

But how did Mother, and the associated distribution company Record Services, even manage to offer a plausible imitation of an enterprise established to kill off promising Irish acts? The answer is somewhat surprising, given how quickly and capably Paul McGuinness and U2 had professionalised the management of their own affairs in the early 1980s. The fact appears to be that, with Mother, U2 deliberately set their sights unusually low, then lacked the commitment and professional capacity to achieve even a modest set of notional targets. A label established in the mid 1980s to help young acts in Ireland ended up with its only really notable success being the Icelandic artist Björk in the early-to-mid 1990s. Indeed, Mother may be the only cause ever associated with Bono to have been allowed to fade quietly into obscurity.

One mark of Mother's lack of ambition was its explicitly stated determination to limit its nurturing function to getting artists' singles out on the label. Once an act was at the stage of releasing an album, the theory and practice went, it could and should move on to another label. This was a little strange given that U2 were already themselves recognised as the latest in the long line of quintessentially album-oriented rock groups, and the 1980s as an album-oriented era like no time before or since in the history of popular music.

Irish music-industry insiders don't need especially complex explanations for Mother's failure. U2 may have been helping to drag the business out of the showband era, dominated as it was by cowboy impresarios and their network of dance-halls around the country, with only a thin veneer of a recording industry slapped on to this live-music infrastructure. But the dragging was slow, and the priorities of those, like McGuinness, who were doing the dragging were understandably ruled mainly by U2's concern for their own increasing global success. Given the structures that had prolifer-ated in the previous era, limping weakly into the economic gloom of 1980s Ireland, industry insiders recall that there simply was not the record-label expertise in Ireland to spread around another dozen young bands in the hopes of leading one or two of them to international stardom. It would have been unrealistic to think that Mother could establish a competent version of Apple Corps in Dublin with the people available in the city to staff it. Limiting Mother to the early stages of an act's development rec-ognised the daunting complexity of mentoring and promoting musicians beyond those stages.

But given U2's growing global riches after 1987, when *The Joshua Tree* reached the top spot on album charts all over the world, Mother could eventually have afforded to import the professional capacity to set a more ambitious agenda, or indeed just to do the early-stages work more com-petently; indeed, according to *Magill* magazine in 1987, Mother was being run out of an office in the London headquarters of Island Records (where U2 had acquired a 10 per cent stake) anyway.[50] Its staff never grew past a handful; its spending was a drip-drip of thousands at a time. What emerges from an overview of its history is what may seem like a surprising description for any enterprise involving Bono: 'half-hearted'. Or perhaps, given that U2 were always generous with rhetorical support, with 'love', to up-and-coming bands, but failed to invest in them adequately, 'half-assed' is the more appropriate term: Mother didn't put the staff in place to deliver the uplifting boost that the Irish music scene was hoping for. The result is that a list of the Irish acts that Mother signed and promoted will lead Irish readers to nod in vague recollection of a series of one-time next-big-things, and most readers outside Ireland to stare blankly: In Tua Nua, Engine Alley, Cactus World News, Hothouse Flowers … When the revamped Mother released an album by Dublin-based novelty punk band the Golden Horde in 1991 – a good three or four years after that band's Ramones-with-pretensions joke had started to wear thin even with their core audience – it was all too clear that, in Ireland, Mother would be no more than an amusing plaything, at most, rather than a serious developer of new talent. By that time, as a knowledgable Irish journalist has recalled, 'Bono, U2's point man on Mother, [had] stepped aside, and [Larry] Mullen took over, resolving difficulties brought about by the singer's reluctance to say no to people.'[51] Mother stopped functioning completely by the mid 1990s, and the company was finally wound up a decade later.

Mother comes in for remarkably little discussion in either official or unofficial histories of U2. In one long interview, with Michka Assayas,

Bono refers vaguely to how the band had invested in loss-making enter-prises after profiting from the sale of Island Records in 1989: 'Losing money was not a nice feeling, and you've got to be careful because nothing begins the love of money more than the loss of money. But on the positive side it made us take more charge and interest in our business. This was, I guess, very early nineties.'[52]

He doesn't mention Mother explicitly in that context, nor does he do so in another long interview in which he discusses the mid-1980s scene that Mother was launched to promote. But, reading between the lines, it's easy to hear him blaming the scene rather than Mother's inadequacy for the failure of a 'next U2' to emerge from Ireland, at least in the form of one of Mother's early acts, Hothouse Flowers:

> We were starting to hang out with The Waterboys and Hothouse Flowers. There was a sense of an indigenous Irish music being blended with American folk music coming through. The Hothouse Flowers were … sexy, they spoke Irish and the singer sang blue-eyed soul … but, you know, Irish music tends to end up down the pub, which really diluted the potency of the new strains. The music got drunk, the clothes got bad and the hair got very, very long.[53]

U2 were of course doing more than 'hang out' with Hothouse Flowers: they were the directors of a company that had briefly taken charge of the band's career – and indeed sent them aloft to a middling international record deal and career that never realised its promise, including a miserable spell opening for the Rolling Stones. Unspoken amid Bono's puritanical disdain for the drunken longhairs is the plaintive question: How could we be expected to make stars of such people?

PEACE OF THE ACTION: NORTHERN INTERVENTION

In the decades after 1986, U2 didn't involve themselves very deeply in the political life of Ireland. Bono's 2002 endorsement of a Yes vote in a referendum on an EU treaty, for example, was not only a relatively rare intervention, but also comprised his typical and easily ignored mix of self-praise and establishment boilerplate: 'I go to meetings with politi-cians in Europe, they always bring it up … I think to vote No is going to make Ireland look very selfish.'[54] U2's cultural contribution is, as we have seen, also open to some question. They played gigs in Ireland, certainly, but scarcely any more than a major rock act with a huge Irish following might be expected to do, and always stadium-sized shows in a couple of big cities, mostly Dublin. In fact, they became something of a symbol of not-being-in-Ireland, the band that provided solace and an apolitical, uncontroversial form of Irish nationality abroad for the generation of emigrants who had fled the country through the 1980s and into the 1990s, Self Aid notwithstanding.

When, in the late 1980s, songwriter Liam Reilly came to write 'Flight of Earls', a sentimental emigrant ballad for that generation – which Reilly saw part-accurately as more educated and mobile than previous emigrants – he naturally mentioned what everyone knew to be the generation's preferred musical badge:

> Because it's not the work that scares us
> We don't mind an honest job
> And we know things will get better once again
> So a thousand times adieu
> We've got Bono and U2
> And all we're missing is the Guinness and the rain

Reilly's allusion was somewhat ironic, given its clear implication that the 1980s emigrants cared more for arena-rock than for folk-pop balladeers like himself. The song nonetheless joined the playlist in countless Irish bars in the US and elsewhere, and was a substantial hit in Ireland in a version by singer Paddy Reilly – reaching number one and still in the charts when U2's 'Desire' overtook it en route to the top. Indeed, for all the awkwardness of its lyrics – yes he did rhyme 'adieu' with 'U2' – 'Flight of Earls' is more likely to get an Irish sing-along going than all but a handful of U2's own songs, and even made something of a comeback among the new emigrants of the post-2008 era.

Bono was not a complete absentee superstar by any means. He lived in Ireland, and as an internationally recognised symbol of Brand Ireland, Bono could not resist getting involved when the Northern Irish peace process put Irish affairs in the global spotlight for the first sustained spell since the hunger-strikes. Since virtually all Irish-nationalist opinion, along with the British government and a substantial chunk of 'moderate unionism' in the North, was united in favour of the process and of the Good Friday Agreement that emerged from it; since elite figures in the American diaspora were on board, and Bill Clinton himself had shown strong, indeed disproportionately obsessive, devotion to resolving these Irish troubles; since there were no popular mobilisations in support of the agreement, North, South or among the Irish abroad (with their reputation for untrustworthy, uncompromising nationalism), and thus a dearth of images of enthusiasm; and since U2 had spent, by common consent, several years in the credibility doldrums with media-savvy political gestures in place of interesting musical ones (notably in Sarajevo – see Chapter 3) – for all these reasons and more, it was all too predictable that Bono would turn up for a photo opportunity at some allegedly crucial moment in the whole affair.

That moment came during the referendum campaign on the Good Friday Agreement. In May 1998, separate, simultaneous ballots were held in Northern Ireland and the Republic of Ireland to approve the new institutional arrangements for governing Northern Ireland. The result was never in doubt – more than 90 per cent of voters in the South voted Yes, and the referendum was approved by 71 per cent of voters in the North, with the opposition coming mainly from diehard Protestant supporters of the union with Britain ('unionists') who opposed the agreement as a concession to IRA terrorists and a step toward a united Ireland. The main political ambition of the British and Irish governments, and of most others on the Yes side, was to see the No vote in the North beaten into a minority not merely of the whole electorate, but even of the traditional unionist side; this sort of sectarian arithmetic had no bearing on whether the referendum would be passed or not, but it might conceivably affect the credibility of the institutions to follow it, themselves reliant on power-sharing via further sectarian arithmetic. The leader of the then-largest unionist party, David Trimble, was supporting the agreement, which had arisen largely through negotiations that aimed at including Sinn Fein, the IRA's political wing, in the process and in future governing arrangements for Northern Ireland. But the convenient fiction adopted for the occasion was that the agreement was a settlement between 'moderate unionism', embodied by Trimble, and 'moderate nationalism', embodied by the leader of the North's Social Democratic and Labour Party, John Hume.

The extent to which this was a fiction would be shown within very few years, with both men and their parties consigned to the political margins by the electorate. But it was already obvious at the time to anyone who was paying attention to reality, particularly to the extraordinary efforts that had been made by the Sinn Fein leadership to bring militant republicans and the community that supported them into the political process – without a split that would have seen a return to large-scale violence.

Nonetheless, it was to the convenient fiction rather than the extraordinary reality that Bono lent his support. According to a biography of Trimble, Bono himself was looking for a chance to visibly 'bring the two sides together'. As Bono told the writer, Bono said to Hume: 'John, I don't feel that our value here is to reinforce you with the nationalist community … It's to reinforce Trimble with the Unionist community. If you can put something together, we'll be happy to interface.'[55]

And so it was that newspapers all over the world featured a picture of Bono interfacing: holding aloft the hands of two 'long-time enemies', Hume and Trimble, who he brought together on stage in front of a cheering, mostly young crowd. 'I would like to introduce you to two men who are making history, two men who have taken a leap of faith out of the past and into the future,' he declaimed. Bono wasn't the only one who deliberately mistook these two increasingly irrelevant men for the heroes of 'the future' – the same was done by that reliably misguided body, the Nobel Peace Prize committee – and it would be churlish to deny they played a considerable role in the Northern Irish peace process. They were widely regarded as the acceptable faces of the process, and Hume in particular had played an honourable role over much of the previous decade by insisting that the key to the process was involving Sinn Fein and its supporters rather than attempting, as in so many previous attempts at agreement, to marginalise them.

But as the summary photo-op of the whole affair, the crowning achievement of the peace process, the Bono–Hume–Trimble moment was bullshit, and it seems it was bullshit of Bono's excreting. Speaking before the concert, the singer had reinforced his 'triumph of the moderates' message: '… to vote "no" is to play into the hands of extremists who have had their day. Their day is over, as far as we are concerned. We are in the next century.'[56] A few years into the real, as opposed to the imagined, 'next century', the former IRA man Martin McGuinness was the North's deputy first minister, serving beside the Protestant bigot the Rev. Ian Paisley, who had opposed the Good Friday Agreement: two of Bono's hated twentieth-century 'extremists', going so amiably about the business of governing Northern Ireland that the press corps dubbed them the Chuckle Brothers, after a pair of British slapstick comedians.

Bono and U2 continued in subsequent years to distort the reality of that 1998 intervention. In their magisterial 2006 'autobiography', *U2 by U2*, they incorrectly state that the referendum was on a knife-edge – Bono says 'the signs were not good', and Edge says it was 'won by a very small margin, two or three points', only after a Yes swing prompted by the concert. The actual margin in the North was more than 42 per cent. (In the same book Bono adds ignorance to distortion when he goes on to misidentify the republican dissident group who bombed the centre of Omagh town a few months later as the 'Continuity IRA', when anyone in Ireland who had been paying attention at all knew it was the 'Real IRA' – though even those paying attention might have found it hard to explain the precise distinction between the two republican splinter groups.[57])

In another interview for international consumption several years after the fact, Bono called that moment 'the greatest honor of my life in Ireland', and called Hume and Trimble, rather ridiculously, 'the two opposing leaders in the conflict'. He added: 'People tell me that rock concert and that staged photograph pushed the people into ratifying the peace agreement. I'd like to think that's true.'[58] No doubt he would *love* to think it's true. However, the 'people' telling Bono that must surely be extreme sycophants even by rock standards: of all the myths peddled by Bono's supporters, this surely is among the most obviously and egregiously untrue, refuted by a minute's fact-checking.

By 2012 the myth of Bono the Peacemaker had grown to absurd proportions, with his close adviser Jamie Drummond telling BBC viewers that for 'most of the Nineties Bono was very involved in campaigning on Northern Ireland'.[59] This notion would come as a great surprise to anyone who was actually involved in the peace process there, and one would like to imagine that Drummond's ludicrous assertion would embarrass even Bono himself.

The famous Hume–Trimble photo-op, and the subsequent fate of its two political subjects, is sometimes cited as evidence of the 'Curse of Bono'. It is of course nothing of the sort. Cynical people might argue that it is just another example of the extent to which Bono remained a conventional-thinking opportunist who could spot the shortest distance between himself and some great global publicity. Perhaps, unlikely though it seems, he was too dense to see the underlying political reality, and the inevitable ascent and key role of Sinn Fein on the Catholic-nationalist side and Paisley's Democratic Unionist Party on the Protestant-unionist side; it's more likely that he was smart enough to ignore it, because he was never going to be able to get it into a photograph.

WHERE THE CHEATS HAVE NO SHAME: TAX TROUBLES

The desire to make lots and lots of money – just so as not to be tempted to succumb to the love of it, naturally – and the desire to visibly embody All That is Good, especially in Ireland, need not come into conflict as far as Bono was concerned. Despite Mother's shortcomings, U2 were routinely praised extravagantly in the Irish media for their 'commitment to maintaining their base' in Dublin – Ireland was so gloomy for much of the 1980s and 1990s that staying there seemed counter-intuitive. The economic benefits enumerated for Ireland of having the band continue to live, record and run their businesses from their home city were never especially impressive, however.[60] They were a big rock band, but that didn't make them a particularly big business in terms of, say, employment, and no one could say if they actually attracted a large number of tourists to the city, though many visitors who came did make a pilgrimage to add graffiti to their old Windmill Lane base.

The fact is that Bono and the rest of the gang had very good reason for maintaining their base in Dublin. As an Irish journalist pithily noted: 'Up until 2006 U2 enjoyed extraordinarily favourable tax treatment in Ireland.'[61] Ireland has famously had, since 1969, an artists' tax exemption, whereby Irish residents' earnings from artistic work – published work, that is, not performance – were not liable to tax. This exemption was established by the notorious politician Charles Haughey, when he was minister of finance. Suspicions about how Haughey funded his lavish lifestyle trailed him through his career, and finally caught up with him in his final years in the 1990s, when a long trail of secret payments to him was revealed; the artists' tax exemption, however, was one of the reasons that Haughey went to his grave with a ringing postscript to an epitaph that was otherwise that of a scoundrel: 'But he was a great patron of the arts'. The artists' exemption not only protected the meagre earnings of most Irish artists, but turned Ireland into a minor tax for various foreign rock stars and best-selling writers, from Def Leppard to Frederick Forsyth. Many British artists positively went native, making films and records in Ireland and engaging cheerfully with Irish public life. Given the aggressive business mentality of U2 and McGuinness, it would be surprising if this exemption were not part of the attraction of remaining in Dublin through all their years of international superstardom.

As with any tax break, those who renewed it annually and those who benefited from it could make a case for the artists' tax exemption, even as it hugely assisted a handful of super-rich artists, for bringing various ancillary benefits to the state – such as the prospect that you might meet Elvis Costello at a party or see Irvine Welsh in the supermarket. It certainly had the effect of encouraging artistic production in the country, if that can be counted as a benefit. 'However,' a journalist wrote, 'the exemption for artistic income was costing the state tens of millions of euros in forgone tax.'[62] Just thirty artists accounted for nearly 60 per cent of what was theoretically lost.[63] It must be said that this was small beer compared to what was sacrificed for various non-artistic corporate tax breaks, and what was 'forgone' with the low rate of tax on corporate profits that had attracted so many multinational corporations to Ireland. Artists were a convenient scapegoat for Ireland's tax-haven status, which in reality had little enough to do with the arts. But throughout the period of the Celtic Tiger, perhaps because in the celebrity magazines artists were so visible among Ireland's conspicuously rich consumers, the artists' tax exemption came under populist pressure. Bono's name figured frequently in the discussion, its defenders forced to defend him, as in this newspaper report from a parliamentary committee hearing: 'An artist like U2 lead singer Bono is "priceless" and, if he left, Ireland would lose an extraordinary economic advantage, David Kavanagh of the Irish Playwrights and Screenwriters Guild said.'[64] A Green member of parliament defended the scheme, saying 'personalities such as Bono [and others] may earn large amounts of money in a particular calendar year but perhaps not earn money in the previous year or the year after'.[65] This parliamentarian displayed remarkably little understanding of how U2's financial affairs might be organised: the last year in which Bono failed to 'earn money', and plenty of it, was in the 1970s. On letters pages and radio phone-ins, Bono was the national poster-boy for undeserving tax-exempt artists.

Thus it was that, in 2006, the Irish government capped the exemption for any given individual at €250,000 annually – a threshold that would be a distant dream for the vast majority of writers, painters and musicians, but one that was of immediate concern to U2. (The cap would later be cut still further.) The group responded quickly by relocating U2's music-publishing arm to Amsterdam, where its royalties would be taxed at just 5 per cent, an arrangement the Rolling Stones had been enjoying for years. The news of U2's new Dutch location emerged in August of that year to some general outrage in the media and among the public at large, mindful especially of Bono's whiter-than-white image.

The band initially said nothing in public. The local grapevine suggested that if the move to the Netherlands both saved money *and* caused public embarrassment to Bono because of his apparent hypocrisy after all his calls for government spending on the Third World's poor, it would be counted as a win–win proposition by other members of the band. This glee at the reeling-in of Bono's ego would be enjoyed most, we heard, by drummer Larry Mullen Jr, who was annoyed at Bono's 'humanitarian' globe-trotting, particularly the photo-ops with the despised George W. Bush and Tony Blair (see Chapters 2 and 3). But those were mere rumours.

Commentators picked up the public mood and entered the vacuum left by the band's silence, with the most savage criticism directed at U2 in Ireland since at least the 1980s. Under the headline, 'When the Band Has No Shame', the by-no-means-leftist Hugh Linehan of the *Irish Times* recalled Leona Helmsley's famous dictum that 'only the little people pay taxes', and continued by attacking U2:

> When a special guest showed up for one of the band's Croke Park concerts last year, the singer welcomed him from the stage. 'I am aware An Taoiseach [prime minster] Bertie Ahern is in the crowd here tonight,' he announced.

'He has promised to give 0.7 per cent of our GDP to Africa and I urge him not to break that promise.' He added understandingly that: 'I know it's hard to build a hospital in Abuja, Nigeria, when you need to build hospitals here.' The crowd booed bad, mean Bertie and cheered the sainted Bono. Would the little people do the same today?

Even if you've never had much time for U2's particular brand of bombastic stadium rock, you have to respect Bono for the amount of sheer energy he has expended on the Make Poverty History campaign. Remarkably, he has managed for most of the time to be pretty self-deprecating about it – no easy trick. As critics of the campaign have pointed out, it's a bit, well, rich to be lecturing middle-income taxpayers about their government's responsibilities, while you're jetting around the world from one glamorous pad to another, meanwhile getting a third of your income tax-free. But if a key focus of your campaign is to raise the Irish Government's level of overseas aid to 0.7 per cent of GNP, then it doesn't look good if, after more than 20 years of tax-freeloading, you jump ship to avoid paying what many would see as your fair share.[66]

The Irish-born comedian Graham Norton, a popular presenter on British TV, joined the chorus of criticism: 'People like Bono really annoy me. He goes to hell and back to avoid paying tax. He has a special accountant. He works out Irish tax loopholes. And then he's asking me to buy a well for an African village. Tarmac a road or pay for a school, you tight-wad!'[67]

Even a top Irish concert promoter who had previously worked with the band, Jim Aiken, metaphorically burned any remaining boats he might have hoped to berth in U2's harbour by stating publicly that 'U2 are arch-capitalists – arch-capitalists – but it looks as though they're not.' He added: 'I believe the ultimate charity donation is to pay your taxes in the country where you live.'[68]

U2, of course, continued to pay many taxes in Ireland, a country that conveniently continued to have some of the lowest personal and corporate tax rates in Europe. But, however unfairly, no longer would most people believe that their status as Irish tax-residents arose from anything more patriotic than the bottom line. U2's complex multiple businesses were just doing their own version of the corporate tax-avoidance manoeuvre described memorably in the *New York Times*, when reporting how a company such as Google uses it, as 'Double Irish with a Dutch sandwich.'[69]

Even a reliably establishment journalist such as Matt Cooper could write: 'Critics of U2 pointed out that the band and its members had been able to increase their wealth dramatically over the previous two decades by reinvesting the tax-free profits they had accrued in such a favourable environment. Having made such a fortune already, how much more did they need?'[70] Activists pointed out that, globally, the use of offshore tax havens by rich individuals had a huge cost in terms of lost taxation to governments in the developed and developing worlds.

However, all this criticism was somewhat dulled by Ireland's general air of prosperity. In 2006 the Irish exchequer was awash in funds gained from taxing a still-booming economy, and what we were soon to learn was a dangerously bubbling property market. The outrage about U2's tax move was tempered by a sense of satisfaction with the government, not least for the fact that it had forced Bono and the boys into its Dutch move by capping the inequitable artists' tax exemption to ensure its benefits were enjoyed most by those who needed them most.

Bono was nonetheless sufficiently riled by the criticism that he eventually responded to it, while in Cork in 2007 to receive an honorary degree. 'Our tax has always been not just to the letter of the law but to the spirit of the law', he said. 'This country's prosperity came out of tax innovation so it would be sort of churlish to criticise U2 for what we were encouraged to do and what brought all of these companies in the first place.'[71]

Bono had no choice but to drawl a defence that cast U2 as just another corporate entity doing what corporate entities do. U2, we were forced to conclude, was a company like any other. But if this was a little painful for him, at least in 2007 when he said it there was still an honest, if somewhat blinkered, case to be made that 'tax innovation' had indeed been broadly beneficial to the Irish economy, leading to initiatives such as the Irish Financial Services Centre, where more than a quarter of the world's hedge funds had offices. It wouldn't be long before that case began to unravel horribly.

MR BONO: DEEPENING CRITICISM

The morality of U2's tax moves was suddenly under attack again in early 2009, due to a combination of economic hard times and an extremely clever campaign by global-justice activists in Ireland, timed to coincide with U2's need to show their faces to promote a new album, *No Line on the Horizon*. Singer Paul O'Toole – dressed vaguely like Bono, in leather trousers and sunglasses – stood outside the Irish department of finance, singing U2 songs with lyrics adjusted for the occasion by activist Sheila Killian:

> I want to run, my money to hide
> I want to build paper walls and keep it inside

> I want to seek shelter from income tax pain
> Where the accounts have no names ...[72]

The campaigners were hoping to make a modest point about how tax shelters undermine efforts to build a more equitable distribution of resources around the world. When the handful of well-behaved activists on the street confronted the arriving minister for finance, Brian Lenihan, with their complaints, he seemed almost pleased that a little heat had been diverted from his role in wrecking the Irish economy and financial system. 'You'll have to take that up with Mr Bono', he said with a discernible smile. (The only other recorded instance, by the way, of an Irish public figure calling the singer 'Mr Bono' came when the archbishop of Dublin, Diarmuid Martin, introduced him in 1999 to Pope John Paul II – who proceeded to try on Bono's sunglasses.[73] Archbishop Martin also mispronounced Bono's name, so he was 'Mr Bone-o'.[74])

The global attention won by the small musical publicity stunt in February 2009 was beyond the wildest dreams of the activists who organised it: for days afterwards they traded stories of the far-flung newspapers that had reported their protest. Indeed, it was so successful in garnering publicity – all the coverage highlighting the Bono angle – that some of the NGOs that had lent their names to the 'Debt and Development Coalition' responsible for the action began to get cold feet: Bono's ONE organisation, by then the main vehicle for his global campaigning work (see Chapter 3), was well connected, and with government cuts hitting their budgets they may have been worried about alienating a source of support, or they may have seen Bono as still an ally in anti-poverty campaigns more broadly.

Bono was shrewd enough not to attack directly a group of global-justice campaigners for taking his name in vain. His response came quickly, more in sorrow than in anger, on the front page of the following Friday's edition of the *Irish Times* – an edition that was festooned with publicity and special offers relating to the new album. When he might have expected to be revelling in hometown pride, Bono was instead answering vaguely difficult questions – albeit facing no real challenge with his answers.

Part of his answer was evasive, and carried more than a hint of 'don't blame me': 'I can't speak up without betraying my relationship with the band – so you take the shit', he said, implying the others were to blame, and prompting knowing nods from those who had suspected that the tax move hadn't been his idea and that his bandmates would scarcely worry if it caused him embarrassment. But he was not going to let it lie there: he was 'hurt' and 'stung' by the criticism, he said, and was prepared to return to his robust 'all the corporate entities were doing it' defence, with some 'it was broadly good for Ireland' thrown in:

> I can understand how people outside the country wouldn't understand how Ireland got to its prosperity, but everybody in Ireland knows that there are some very clever people in the Government and in the Revenue who created a financial architecture that prospered the entire nation – it was a way of attracting people to this country who wouldn't normally do business here. And the financial services brought billions of dollars every year directly to the exchequer.[75]

Helping rich foreign companies avoid taxes was indeed part of the story of the Irish boom. But it is revealing that in 2009 Bono was peddling the same line as in 2007 – 'this is how the country got rich' – without any acknowledgment of something else that 'everybody in Ireland knows': now that this get-rich-quick scheme had collapsed, Ireland was getting poor as precipitously quickly as any country in the developed world, at least until Greece started to unravel. Bono actually appeared to believe he was justifying U2's tax-avoidance by referring to the Irish 'financial architecture' that by early 2009 was justly regarded as a national scandal. Even the reliably middle-of-the-road Irish journalist Matt Cooper was taken aback that anyone in Ireland in 2009 could talk about the country's 'financial architecture' like it was a good thing: 'Unfortunately, it was clear already that much of this 'financial architecture' had been built on very flimsy foundations and created many of the problems we are currently experiencing today.' Bono, Cooper wrote, 'is a citizen of the world as much as Ireland but when he comes home he might be best advised to just shut up and sing.'[76]

And it's not only the Irish who might want to tell Bono to shut up. Credible research suggests that Ireland's 'financial architecture' and 'innovation' – i.e. the exceptionally light-touch regulation and low-tax regime that brought so many murky funds to the Irish Financial Services Centre – were partly responsible not only for Ireland's crisis, but for the chaos that gripped global finance in 2008, because its shadowy banking system had significant connections to virtually every important economy on earth.[77]

Bono had no idea, it seems. Clearly upset, he had more to say to the *Irish Times*, addressing his critics as though they themselves routinely benefited from shifting their money around various offshore tax havens:

> What's actually hypocritical is the idea that then you couldn't use a financial services centre in Holland. The real question people need to ask about

Ireland's tax policy is: 'Was the nation a net gain benefactor [*sic*]?' and of course it was – hugely so. So there was no hypocrisy for me – we're just part of a system that has benefited the nation greatly …'[78]

By Bono's increasingly belligerent and shockingly out-of-touch logic, then, tax avoidance was an act of patriotism, even when he was taking money out of the country, because as an international activity it was broadly to Ireland's benefit. Drummer Larry Mullen Jr, not always a reliable ally of the man whose ass he had gazed at across a thousand stages for thirty-plus years, showed similarly touchy out-of-touchness when he whined about dirty looks at Dublin Airport: there was 'a new resentment of rich people in this country … We have experienced [a situation] where coming in and out of the country at certain times is made more difficult than it should be – not only for us, but for a lot of wealthy people … The better-off [are] being sort of humiliated.' Without the entrepreneurial rich, Mullen concluded with accidental accuracy, 'we'd be in a very, very different state'.[79]

The Edge's response was much more low-key, and relegated to the last paragraph of the news story: 'it's our own private thing. We do business all over the world and we are totally tax compliant.'[80] No one had accused U2 of being anything other than 'tax compliant': the point of the campaigning around the issue was to highlight the myriad injustices that lurk fully within the category of tax compliance, rather than outside its boundaries.

As on the issue of Northern Ireland, Bono was capable of engaging in the odd bout of selective revisionism when it came to the Irish economy, and financial services in particular. So two years later, in 2011, he told a typically soft and sympathetic interviewer from *Hot Press* how exercised he was about the 'privatising profit, socialising risk' policies being pursued in his home country since 2008:

> if ever anti-globalisation protesters wanted to point to an incident of unfairness and injustice, they just have to look at what's happened to Ireland in relation to the bank bailout, where the people are paying the price for private sector greed. Ireland's public debt and finances actually weren't in bad shape, but it was the private sector that brought this problem.

He added, unnecessarily: 'I'm all for the private sector, and for people making profit …'[81]

Bono's reputation in Ireland is a complex matter, and not something that can readily be measured. Not long after the tax controversy, he came in the top five in a web poll to determine 'Ireland's Greatest' – but when it came to the final TV vote on the vexed question of who was the greatest

Irish person ever, he trailed behind.[82] The tax issue clearly did him 'reputational damage', but for many people it did no more than provide a hard, factual reason for the soft, emotional dislike he aroused. Some anti-Bono graffiti sprang up around Dublin, mostly referring to the tax issue, like the doggerel in Clanbrassil Street that mocked both his financial status and physical stature: 'Bono is a jerk / He never had to work / He doesn't pay his tax / He always wears stacks.' But none were so expressive as the spray-painted phrase that appeared on a wall in the inner city, using a word of dubious provenance but undoubted resonance, one that is practically unique to that locale: 'Bono is a poxbottle.'[83]

Lest the gutsy campaigners who drew U2's tax avoidance to the public's attention have been in any doubt about where they stood with Bono's high-profile ONE campaign, its executive director Jamie Drummond wrote to the *Irish Times* from London, spelling out his views (without mentioning, for the benefit of those who might not be aware of the provenance of ONE, that Bono was effectively his sponsor). In a short letter defending both Bono and the Netherlands, he managed to call the protest 'utterly wrong', 'misguided', 'deeply unfair', 'deeply inaccurate' and an example of 'self-defeating PR stunts'.[84] Hard-pressed activists and the struggling NGOs behind them would have been forgiven for reading 'self-defeating' as a threat from such a big player in the global anti-poverty business.

Tax avoidance has, nonetheless, attached itself to Bono like no other negative, as when protesters at Britain's famed Glastonbury music festival in 2011 inflated a giant balloon with the question 'U Pay Tax 2?' A spokesman for the Art Uncut campaign said: 'U2's multimillion-euro tax dodge is depriving the Irish people at a time when they desperately need income to offset the Irish government's savage austerity programme. Tax nestling in the band's bank account should be helping to keep open the hospitals, schools and libraries that are closing all over Ireland.'[85] The protest was quickly shut down by festival security, with Bono offering a typical response: 'I'm all for protests. I've been protesting all of my life [*sic*]. I'm glad they got the chance to have their say. But, as it happens, what they're protesting about is wrong.'[86] Presumably he meant they were wrong to protest.

In 2012, when Burmese leader Aung San Suu Kyi came to Dublin, Bono was at the forefront of the welcome, leading Bob Geldof to joke from the stage at a welcoming concert that after an afternoon with Bono she might prefer to revert to house arrest. But this sort of joking gave way to a more bitter attack on Bono from singer Sinead O'Connor, who blamed Bono (whom she called 'Bozo') and Geldof for inviting her to sing 'Nothing Compares 2 U' at the Aung San Suu Kyi concert only on the condition that she refrain from making any statement from the stage. (There was no evidence, she admitted later, that this silencing instruction came from either or both of the men.) O'Connor refused to appear at the concert, and one of her many angry tweets on the subject declared, as her ultimate punch-line: 'I pay my taxes in Ireland Bozo.'[87]

PROPERTY BARON: THE CORPORATE BONO

Again, U2's defenders would be quick to correct the implication of the idiosyncratic O'Connor: 'Bozo' and the rest of them did indeed pay taxes in Ireland. Still, it is striking that, in all the controversy that has dogged Bono on this issue since 2006, he and his advisers have not seen fit simply to document the extent of his annual contribution to the Irish exchequer. (Bono's personal taxes, like his charitable contributions, are obviously a private matter, to be made public only if he chooses to do so, and have never been revealed by any journalist.) Perhaps one reason for silence on this question is that such documentation would be far from simple, and might entail explaining exactly why the most profitable band in the history of popular music has been involved in such a litany of loss-making companies; all that red ink coincidentally minimises the profits to be subjected even to Ireland's internationally low 12.5 per cent rate of corporation tax.

The most common words used again and again by journalists who have attempted to research U2's 'financial architecture' are 'opaque' and 'web'.[88] The most well-known company associated with the band is Paul McGuinness's profitable Principle Management, which has handled the band's contracts and tours (and those of very, very few other acts) for decades. The key company for the band members for most of U2's history is another one – not, apparently, the one called U2 Ltd, but its parent company, a holding entity called Not Us Ltd, whose directors are the four band members. Not Us makes payments to the band members and has been described as 'at the centre of the U2 money web … but only manager Paul McGuinness and a few clever accountants could understand how it functions'.[89] The oddly named Not Us first came to prominence in 1995 when the Irish regulator, the Companies Office, threatened to strike it off the companies register for failure to file returns: it was one of several U2 companies thus threatened, including Mother Records, and '[t]he band were known to be embarrassed by the publicity surrounding this lapse'.[90] In the 1990s, Bloomberg has reported, 'U2 used nonexecutive directors who were resident in an offshore tax haven to limit the amount paid by the four band members'.[91]

Bono has had a long list of other company directorships in Ireland, most but not all in conjunction with his bandmates. Some of them, such as his spell as a director of Media Lab Europe – a trendy millennial attempt, funded by the Irish state, to import a version of Nicholas Negroponte's academic-business partnership for high-tech innovation, the MIT Media Lab, to a location near Dublin's Guinness brewery – may be largely symbolic and PR-oriented. (In the case of Media Lab Europe, the PR turned ugly quite quickly, but Bono wasn't really caught in the crossfire as the Irish government bailed out and Negroponte's crew left town.) However, the list predominantly consists of various U2 entities, some with cool musical and U2-ish names, and others that sound more off-the-shelf: 'Kitchen Recordings, Lakehaven, Lorijudd Investments, Mother Records, Mother Music … Ravencrest, Remond, Straypass, the Fair City Trust and Thengel'.[92]

Because of the band's global reach and structure, the publicly available records of U2's companies in Ireland tell us only part of the story about their finances, and even less about Bono's personal money pot. Indeed, the details about what these Irish companies do are not merely baffling, they are also quite thin. Much of the activity of some of these companies appears, to the untrained eye, to have consisted of making loans to one another. For example, the accounts for 2003 show Not Us Ltd owing €4.7 million to U2 Ltd, then described as the band's 'master-tape manufacturing subsidiary'.[93] (Yes, U2 had a company of their own just to create 'masters', the definitive final mix of a record from which copies are then pressed and otherwise copied.) Perhaps the master-tape business had been poor, or maybe it was something to do with this debt, but 'oddly [U2 Ltd] had accumulated losses of €3 million back [in 2004] … leading to a "fundamental uncertainty" notification from the auditors'.[94] The journalist who wrote those words, quoting from the bedazzling accounts of how these two companies alone further kicked money back and forth to each other in 2005, concluded: 'Confused? Presumably you should be.'[95]

Corporate matters were somewhat simplified, apparently, after the notorious Dutch move in 2006, when millions of euros in inter-company loans were written off.[96] U2 Ltd's balance moved into the black, and its activity began to be described in its Irish-filed accounts as 'the creation, protection and licensing of intellectual property' rather than making master-tapes; its turnover shrank dramatically, from €20 million to €3 million, between 2007 and 2010. Whatever the exact purpose of this company within the U2 empire, U2 Ltd is of some interest because it has visibly paid tax in Ireland on its profits in recent years. In 2009, the year of the biggest Bono tax controversy, it coughed up a not-very-whopping €144,000 in corporation tax: that's Ireland's 12.5 per cent corporate-tax rate on about €1.15 million in profits. (By way of comparison, Google Ireland declared €47.5

million in pre-tax profits in the same year.) But this was positively bleeding cash to the taxman compared to what happened in 2010: as U2, the band, were on the largest-grossing tour in music history, U2 Ltd's profits plummeted to just over €130,000, and thus its corporation-tax bill was a mere €16,500; though this is by no means to suggest that this was the only tax paid that year by U2 and its members, it is damnably difficult to document the rest. Poor old Not Us Ltd, meanwhile, was still in the red, with accumulated losses of €3.8 million, though these losses had been cut considerably since 2005.[97] With eight other Irish companies also still doing the band's business, and further entities passing their money around the world from bases elsewhere, it was and is difficult to put these sums in a global context. As an Irish financial journalist explained: 'Not Us is not obliged to furnish complete accounts, and its abridged returns do not contain details of income and expenditure. It is thought that the majority of U2's money is stored in trusts and partnerships. Neither the U2 partnership nor Princus Investment Trust, a pension scheme vehicle, has to file public accounts.'[98] (There is more about what is known about Bono's own portfolio and profile as an investor outside Ireland in Chapters 2 and 3: compared to U2's Irish 'web', only partly described above, they are blessedly simple.)

Losing money hasn't been limited to the various U2 entities that crowd their accountants' shelves. Among Bono's most publicly visible loss-makers has been Brushfield Ltd, and then the Clarence Partnership, through which entities he, The Edge and a varying cast of others have operated the Clarence Hotel in Dublin's city centre since 1992. This stolidly attractive Victorian edifice on the Liffey quayside, made over in the 1930s with Arts and Crafts touches such as the lovely little wood-panelled octagonal bar, was a slowly decaying two-star 'relic of old decency' when the surrounding Temple Bar area began to be transformed in the 1980s, first by arty gentrifiers taking advantage of cheap short-lease rents while the city waited to build a bus terminal, and then by tax breaks and other subsidies when prime minister Charles Haughey and his property-developer pals decided to abandon the bus-station idea and build a touristy 'cultural quarter'. It was probably inevitable in this context that someone would push the Clarence upmarket, reducing the number of rooms, popping a penthouse on top, putting in a fancy restaurant, and creating what would come to be called a 'boutique hotel'. What is more remarkable is that in the midst of the Celtic Tiger period, one of the most dramatic economic booms the developed world has ever seen – with nearly 10 per cent annual growth for six years in the late 1990s and further rapid expansion up to 2008 – Bono and his fellow investors in the Clarence were somehow unable to make it profitable most years. The exceptions were in 2006, when the tide of red ink was stemmed by the 'brave decision on the part of U2 to forego the loans given to Brushfield over the years, which – when the various entities are totted up – come close to €18m', and again in the 2010 accounts when, in another transaction, the hotel was able to waive almost all of a €770,000 lease payment to the Clarence Partnership itself.[99] Bono's partners by 2010 were reduced to The Edge and a controversial duo of property developers, Paddy McKillen and Derek Quinlan.

A man shouldn't be judged by the corporate company he keeps, but it is an inescapable fact that complex financing for the Clarence companies had been provided over the years by Anglo Irish Bank, which came to be known as a casino for developers and as the foremost exemplar and destroyer of Ireland's 'financial architecture'. The bank, described frequently after 2008 as 'Ireland's most toxic' – itself no mean distinction given the reckless lending throughout the Irish financial system – was a favourite source of seemingly bottomless money for property investments. In July 2012, long after the catastrophically indebted bank had been bailed out by the state, then wound up into a state-owned entity called the Irish Bank Resolution Corporation, criminal charges were at last brought against some of Anglo Irish's senior executives.

There was another kind of architecture at play, however. The Clarence became more than a footnote in Bono's complex financial arrangements, more than a stylish location that he tried to publicise with tricks like lighting up a cigarette in its lobby in defiance of the then-new smoking ban, when its U2 owners decided to gut both the building itself and a set of older neighbouring buildings to create a much bigger luxury hotel. Designed by that unequalled creator of neoliberalism's architectural icons, the Briton Norman Foster, the new, improved Clarence would be topped with what looked for all the world like a giant flying saucer that had aimed to land on the river but missed; it was the symbol of Bono's unearthly ego that Dublin had been awaiting for decades. Neighbouring businesses, initially worried about being dwarfed by the new monstrosity that utterly changed the scale of its immediate streetscape, were largely cajoled into acquiescence, and Dublin City Council approved the project in 2007. The state planning authority, however, was not so sure: its senior inspector called the scheme 'conceptually brilliant but contextually illiterate' (this was only half-right, since it mistook exhibitionist flamboyance for 'brilliance') and recommended its rejection. Other bodies chimed in opposition, as the *Irish Times* reported: 'The Department of the Environment argued that the "exceptional circumstances that might warrant the … demolition of protected structures have not been demonstrated". Dublin City Council's conservation architect Clare Hogan said the demolition of all but the facades would render the protected structures "meaningless".[100] Bono and his fellow developers, for their part, threatened that failure to gain approval might force them to sell the property, which might then be developed as – those of a sensitive disposition should look away now – 'a down-market budget hotel'.[101]

The planning board rejected its inspector's rejection, and in 2008 the plan got the go-ahead by a seven-to-one vote. About the best thing that can be said for the collapse that has decimated the Irish economy since that time is that it has put grandiose plans like the one that would have ruined the Clarence and its quayfront on indefinite hold, with Edge himself admitting early in 2009, in what might have been but probably wasn't a Yeatsian allusion, that such plans were 'being looked at with a much colder eye'.[102]

It wasn't just the Clarence plan he was speaking of. A couple of miles east along the Liffey, U2 had long been working on another building project with a similar mix of grandiosity, vulgarity and questionable connections. This time, in addition to Anglo Irish, Bono and the boys were working with the soon-to-be-discredited Dublin Docklands Development Authority (DDDA) to produce a skyline-piercing tower nearer where the river runs into the Irish Sea. This is not the place to tell the full story of the DDDA, set up by the state and then, naturally, devoted to the interests of property developers and financiers who were busy 'transforming' the old docks area into subsidised and, when the crash came, soon-to-be-vacant offices and apartments. The DDDA was in the happy position of being simultaneously developer, virtual financier (through intimate connections to Anglo Irish) and planning authority for the area under its remit. The consequences have been disastrous.

That was all to be revealed later, however. In the glory days of 2002 the DDDA and U2 announced a swap whereby the band would allow the authority to buy U2's studio site on Hanover Quay in exchange for a future penthouse studio in a tower, the U2 Tower, at Britain Quay, further from the city centre. At the announcement of the plans, Bono provided a moment that should be treasured by connoisseurs of historical irony: he stood on a platform provided by the DDDA and lamented that, in the past, the city of Dublin had been 'defaced and vandalised' through 'corruption and cronyism'. More observant Dubliners had already begun to notice how well the DDDA fitted that pattern, but Bono was pleased to say that the DDDA people 'know what they are doing' and that their plans constituted 'the best thing for the city'. He added: 'This city was a very, very beautiful city. Now with imagination it is being remade and the new Dublin is something I'm really excited about'.[103] The U2 Tower, he said, would be finished by about 2005.

The fiasco that followed was, in fairness, largely out of Bono's hands, but it put his remarks about the DDDA's competence into some perspective. The design of the tower was the subject of an international competition – with Adam Clayton as the band's man on the panel – that raised hundreds of thousands of euros in entry fees, then fell into disarray with misplaced entries, audits, reviews, and an eventual winner that included among its architects none other than the brother-in-law of Paul McGuinness. And just when it seemed that the outrage about the selection of that design for a sixty-metre-tall twisting tower couldn't get any more outrageous, the construction tender was awarded to a consortium that included the members of U2, which then quietly shelved the selected plan in 2007 in favour of a design two or three times taller, but perhaps a bit simpler in construction – slanting this time, rather than twisting, with an egg-shaped recording-studio on top – from none other than Norman Foster, again.

Then that plan, too, was suspended indefinitely in late 2008. In 2011 the DDDA, under new leadership that was labouring to clean the veritable Augean stables of 'corruption and cronyism' that had marked its two-decade history, quietly handed over the vacant U2 Tower site to a new, post-crash state 'bad bank' in part-settlement of its debts.[104] A few months later the Irish government announced that the DDDA was being wound up.

The U2 Tower debacle didn't cost Bono and the boys serious money, not by their standards: whereas they wrote off €18 million in loans to various Clarence-related entities, U2's share in the losses of the company behind the tower were less than a tenth of that amount.[105] But in the eyes of much of the Irish public, like the controversies over the Clarence Hotel and their tax arrangements that ran more or less simultaneously, it knocked them off any remaining moral high ground and located them firmly in a metaphorical ivory tower – since they never managed to build the real one. They were just another set of jumped-up property speculators, more of the well-connected bubble-blowers who cost the country so dear, and who got so full of themselves they thought they could leave a couple of U2-shaped scars on their home city and expect people to admire the view. Lucky for us, U2 didn't get their tower and spaceship; lucky for them, when the crash came, they had other sources of income.

AFTER THE DELUGE: IRELAND IN CONTEXT

Was he humbled? You must be thinking of a different Bono. Of course it helps that a summary of the sort presented in the last few pages is still almost unimaginable in most of the Irish media, where Bono remained an honoured celebrity right into 2013, as this book was going to press.

In moments over recent years it appeared that Bono might even be trying to learn something about how the crisis had played out in his home country. In the 2011 *Hot Press* interview cited above, he agreed that the Irish state paying off the (mostly foreign) bondholders in the banks that had destroyed the Irish economy was 'an affront … an injustice to the Irish people'. (He is invariably allowed to generalise about these topics without any reference to his own historic business connections, such as with Anglo.) He continued:

> I'm not an expert on Irish politics or the economy, not because I'm not interested but just because I've been so busy and so elsewhere on various projects, but there's an idea going around for a referendum on the subject of what we should do about the bondholders. There's two pieces: the sovereign debt and the private piece. It would be a very sophisticated thing indeed should the Irish people demand a chance to debate and argue, and finally decide themselves, on what will in the end be a decision that will affect their children and grandchildren. And surely this would also bolster the Government as they seek to reorganise, because they would have a very clear mandate on it. There's a deep unfairness there.[106]

This sort of vague talk about separating private and sovereign debt, and finding a way to strengthen the government's hand in negotiations with the EU and IMF bodies overseeing Ireland's bailout, was commonplace in Irish punditry by 2011; but at least the quote shows that he had begun to recover from the tin-ear that plagued his defensive public comments in 2009, when he had notoriously praised the country's 'financial architecture' at precisely the wrong moment. This was Bono restored to something like his previous status as outspoken advocate of conventional wisdom.

In other public pronouncements, however, it was clearer how perfectly that conventional wisdom was synced with the desires and priorities of global capital. In 2010, Bono used the occasion of a speech to the American Ireland Fund banquet in New York – fundraising for an admired U2-backed music charity back home – to make something of a spontaneous State of the Irish Nation address.[107] That section of his fifteen-minute speech is a typical collection of vaguely crowd-pleasing essentialist generalisations about the Irish character, plus some pandering to Irish-America for its noble role, together with quite specific nostrums about what the country needs in its hour of crisis. It even opens with some archetypal making of his own origins-myth: the 'two-up, two-down' house in Ballymun, in 'the bleak and beleaguered Sixties and Seventies'.

'I mean the Irish are European physically, but spiritually we're American. Or maybe Americans are spiritually Irish, I don't know', he told the crowd. 'On an emotional note, the rise out of despair of the Sixties and Seventies that I was born into would not have happened without investment by American companies: Intel, Microsoft, Dell. A lot of us badgered our friends at Google to set up their offices outside of America in Dublin and they did. As did Facebook. And they're pleased they did.' (It is interesting that he claims credit for Google's move to Dublin, but uses more circumspect language about Facebook, perhaps because he was known as a significant investor in the latter.)

This time he's not mentioning the hedge funds, the 'financial architecture'. No, the Irish devotion to innovation no longer has to do with devising tax shelters for multinationals: it's all about software. And hardware. And the spiritual gifts they bring.

> Irish people are great entrepreneurs and great technologists, not just because we're a smart, young, well-educated workforce, but actually probably for more un-obvious reasons. Like … our bolshie, anarchic approach to life. We're not buttoned down to tradition, we don't respond well to orders … We challenge accepted mores. This can be bad, in that we stay up too late and drink too much wine at your dinner parties. But this is very good, if you want to hire us to write software for the twenty-first century. It helps to think differently.

He couldn't resist one small bow to Wall Street, perhaps because of someone he had seen in the audience. 'So take note, Dow Jones. You want executives in your company who think differently and are smart, educated, well turned-out' – he pauses vaguely – 'the Irish.'

Much of this was a speech he could have made twenty years earlier. But even Bono could not completely ignore the elephant in the room. 'We may have blown up …' He suddenly thought better about using the first-person pronoun, even in plural form.

> It might have blown up, in our face. The economic bubble. And burst in our face. And we have made terrible mistakes that cost us what can't be counted. But do not rule us out. Do not make the mistake of thinking we'll roll over easily. We can take a punch, or ten, or twenty, but we can return them. We are relentless, we don't give up, and we're coming back.

He proceeded to indulge in a borderline-racist riff on the violence of Irish national sports: Gaelic football 'makes American football look like synchronised swimming'; and as for hurling: 'imagine giving fifteen Irish men wooden sticks, fifteen men whose idea of fun is beating the shit out of each other for an hour or so.' It is safe to say that there were no Gaelic games at Bono's childhood schools: this dismissal of hurling – in reality fast, skilful, often elegant, only occasionally violent – would on its own disqualify him from being taken seriously in several Irish counties.[108]

'What I'm trying to get across is not how hard we are, but how vulnerable we are at this time. And I'm going to say it: we need your help. But', he added, addressing some of the people perhaps most responsible for the global crisis, 'the rate of return on investment will be considerable.'

If anything could sum up Bono's relationship with Ireland better than his serving it up, seasoned with stereotype, for the profitable delectation of US multinationals, it might just be his eagerness to be honoured by the country's historic oppressor – and the historic oppressor of many of the other countries with which he expresses his cod-solidarity. In 2012, he attended the 'Royal Academy Awards', part of the 'diamond jubilee' celebration for Britain's queen, Elizabeth. With the by now familiar syntax in which he sort-of constructs himself as 'the Irish', he took to the podium to shower her with praise for her 2011 visit to the Republic: 'Truth be told, the Irish are more fond of revolt than deference. But I wanted to take this opportunity to acknowledge the extraordinary magic that you made on your trip to Ireland last year.' Then he laid it on thick in the receiving line: 'I hope you know really at a deep level what this meant to a lot of people ... Did you have fun at all, or was it all work?' He praised her too for speaking a few words of the Irish language, which he called 'Gaelic', as the British often do. 'And the Queen spoke Gaelic. I can't even speak Gaelic!'[109] The latter statement is almost certainly true, given his upbringing and education, in which the Irish language would have been present but a low priority, at best. The queen, however, had haltingly spoken just five words of Irish, stingy even by her travelling standards, and, prior to Bono's outburst, only the over-excitable Irish media and political elite had been so extravagantly impressed.

But perhaps all of Bono's praise was mere payback for the events of a few years before, when Bono, citizen of a republic, was made Knight of the Most Excellent Order of the British Empire, an honour many decent Britons have chosen to refuse. He joked his way through the 2007 ceremony with the British ambassador in Dublin, telling reporters: 'You have permission to call me anything you want – except Sir, all right? Lord of lords, your demigodness, that'll do.'[110] Indeed he could not be called 'Sir', a privilege reserved for the queen's subjects within the British commonwealth: the common British-newspaper ascription of 'Sir' to Bob Geldof is mistaken, though that error appears so frequently that it presumably does not arouse complaint or correction from Geldof himself. Bono, in any case, spurned the unachievable 'Sir' but accepted the honour gratefully, posing for photographs in his full silly splendour, making a peace sign while displaying in its open box the jewels of what Eamonn McCann rightly calls 'a bauble signifying association with the rape of continents'.

But it would be wrong to imagine that, among most of his Irish peers, this sort of behaviour brings odium upon Bono. He is, in this respect as in so many others, a perfect representative of a class that has long since made its peace with imperialism in all its forms and facets. As McCann writes:

> Let us reflect on the fact that not one of a large and representative sample of Dublin writers, film-makers, business executives and freelance celebrities who assembled in the U2-owned Clarence Hotel to mark the pop-singer's acceptance of this token of imperial approval managed to summon the half-ounce of self-respect it would have taken to stand up and shout, 'Shame!'[111]

2 AFRICA

DO THEY KNOW IT'S CHRISTMAS? BAND AID AND BEYOND

Bono's emergence and status as perhaps the world's leading 'advocate' for Africa is deeply strange, its history so contingent that it may be pointless to seek its origins in his Dublin youth, or anywhere else besides the 1984 phone call from acquaintance Bob Geldof asking him to take part in the recording of a charity single by 'Band Aid', the dreadful, plodding, patronising and very, very white 'Do They Know It's Christmas?'

Prior to that time, the only evidence of Bono's concern for the world's brown-skinned peoples had come in a pair of songs released earlier in the same year: 'MLK', with words of no great relevance to the man with those initials, and 'Pride (In the Name of Love)', in which Bono bellows vaguely Christian lyrics that give way to a specific evocation of the assassination of Martin Luther King. The latter song has been proved by the passing years to be one of the most powerful U2 tunes, borrowing King's martyrdom to boost its pounding affective climax. But the song's soaring generalities also highlight the thinness of Bono's early, right-on politics: the extent of the research behind it can perhaps be gauged by the lyric, 'Early morning, April 4 / Shot rings out in the Memphis sky' – King was in fact shot in the early evening. Years later Bono himself rather dismissed his lyrics as being unworthy of their subject, 'just a load of vowel sounds ganging up on a great man';[1] but that hasn't stopped him singing 'Pride' ad infinitum, including, with its erroneous lyric corrected, as the obvious passing-of-the-torch moment at the Obama Lincoln Memorial gig. (Bono's capacity to deliver this moment, more than any ethnic box-ticking, accounts for U2's presence at a concert where the Obama handlers wanted King's shadow to be shaped in just such a vague, inoffensive way; according to Bono, and to his disappointment, not long before the gig the Obama organisers scrapped plans to play the 'I have a dream' speech itself as a lead-in to U2.[2])

Why was the young Bono so interested, however vaguely, in King, and where does that interest fit into his wider politics? To some extent, attraction to King would have come as standard for a 'self-righteous student of non-violence' in the Ireland of the 1970s and 1980s. The Christian pacifism of Bono and many others in his time and place may be seen at least in part as a convenient stick with which to beat the forces then waging violent resistance against British rule in Northern Ireland. Why oh why couldn't Northern Catholic-nationalists have stuck to strictly peaceful means of protest when faced with, first, discrimination and disenfranchisement, and then with violent oppression and ethnic cleansing in 1968–70? The existence of a tradition of nonviolence somewhere else in the world – however small that tradition might be on a planet of violent conflict – was enough, it seemed, to condemn any Irish person who had taken up arms. It helped that, in the 1960s prelude to the Troubles, the nonviolent Northern Ireland Civil Rights Association had deliberately appropriated some of the rhetoric of King's American struggle, right down to singing 'We Shall Overcome'. By taking up arms, the IRA and its supporters – a young Bono might conclude from the safe distance of Dublin – had turned their backs on this man of peace and all he represented.

But there is more, of course, to the place of Africa in Bono's cultural make-up than a vague embrace of (some forms of) African-American resistance, and indeed more than a vague post-punk rejection of the most African-American elements of rock 'n' roll (see pp. 64–67). Ireland – Catholic Ireland in particular, though not exclusively – had a long and profound relationship with Africa through missionary and charitable work. This is most often parodied in reminiscences about the little blue collection boxes found in countless shops and schools with pictures of the 'black babies' that your pennies would help; but hundreds of Irish priests and nuns had involved themselves in African societies at a deeper level, for better and worse, and many of them eventually came home. Brian Friel's famed 1990 play *Dancing at Lughnasa* – a Tony Award-winning Broadway hit, later a film, and probably the most widely discussed Irish drama of its time – features such a priest, Father Jack Mundy, just returned to his family in Donegal from Uganda, seemingly addled by the sun and full of suspect heterodoxies, especially about sexuality. Friel was not the first to draw upon the longstanding stereotype. This archetypal figure, symbolic of Africa as somewhere entirely strange and 'other', somewhere you go to help but then are yourself possessed and changed, may perhaps be viewed as something of a template for the way people in Ireland have come to view the peculiarly Irish trajectories of Geldof and Bono.

In addition to this history of missionaries, with all its shading, Ireland had other unique connections with decolonising Africa. The first foreign deployment of the army of independent Ireland – under the auspices of the United Nations – occurred in 1960: it was to the Congo, and a messier conflict than the Irish 'peacekeepers' may have been prepared for as they came under attack from Katanga secessionists. Twenty-six Irish soldiers were killed.

Ireland also had, in the 1970s and 1980s, a surprisingly strong African solidarity campaign, in the form of the Irish Anti-Apartheid Movement – one of the largest anti-apartheid movements per capita in the non-African world. The reasons for this strength were complex. The presence of South African exile Kader Asmal of the ANC, teaching law at Trinity College Dublin, was certainly a significant factor. (Asmal became a government minister in post-apartheid South Africa.) The proximity of Britain, where there was already a strong campaign when Asmal set up the Irish group in the mid 1960s, was also a boost. Ireland, too, had thousands of missionaries, and migrants, in South Africa.[3] Finally, in explaining the strength of anti-apartheid politics in Ireland, you cannot discount the importance of a self-styled national liberation struggle in the North of Ireland: on the one hand, supporters of the IRA liked to emphasise its common ground with the ANC; on the other hand, radical and liberal opponents of the IRA liked to be able to show that they weren't against national liberation and anti-discrimination struggles per se. (For similar reasons there was a strong, albeit smaller, Central America solidarity movement in Ireland, and in 1984 the active and tacit support for the South African and Central American struggles combined to forge, without Bono, a huge demonstration against the visit of Ronald Reagan to Ireland.) Eamonn McCann used to joke that the supporters of only the most faraway struggles had applied an 'oppressometer' to the various situations to determine that Northern Ireland did not merit the forms of resistance that they endorsed, however regretfully, when they were used in warmer climes.

The anti-apartheid movement could frequently mobilise hundreds and even thousands of people, and had cross-class support, including no shortage of leading politicians; it served as something of an antidote to any view that saw Africans simply as recipients of Western aid, without agency of their own. In 1984, before Bob Geldof conceived Band Aid, and then Live Aid, workers in a Dublin grocery store were forced off their jobs for following the advice of their union by refusing to handle South African produce. The 'Dunnes strikers' stayed out for two-and-a-half years, and became an international cause célèbre. Eventually support came from Bono, who invited them to join the chorus on Steve Van Zandt's 1985 boycott-anthem, 'Sun City' – as in 'I, I, I ain't gonna play Sun Cit-eh' and, better yet, 'Nah nah nah nah nah nah nah, nah-nah-nah yeah'.[4]

It is extraordinary, given that rich and complex set of connections with Africa, that an Irishman like Geldof could come up with nothing better for Band Aid, his effort to raise funds to relieve the Ethiopian famine, than the stupid, banal and offensive song 'Do They Know It's Christmas?', its title alone standing as surely one of the most absurdly patronising sentiments in the history of patronising sentimentality, in the name of charity or otherwise. The song itself, sung on the charity single by a succession of top British and Irish acts, describes, in a series of clichés, the joy of Christmas at home and the suffering of Africans, and asks if the unfortunate latter even 'know it's Christmas-time at all'. (It is faint praise indeed to suggest that Bono himself might have done better: he was probably at the height of his artistic powers at this time, while Geldof had already fallen from his own more modest perch.)

The absurdly successful Band Aid single marked the beginning of Bono's long and largely deferential association with Geldof. (In the acknowledgments to a recent book, Bono calls him 'My Lord Bob Geldof'.[5]) But despite U2's enormous international success by the time it was recorded in November 1984, and despite his compatriot being in charge, Bono has employed the story of the star-studded recording session rather self-pityingly, to emphasise U2's exclusion from insular British pop circles – something of a sensitive subject, because U2 have rarely been English critical favourites. 'Seriously, it was like a blow-drying convention. And we were an Irish rock band who had broken America. People … were just staring at us, as if to say, "You don't look like pop stars." '[6]

Geldof said in a 2012 interview that, of all the stars he approached, 'the one who was most reluctant to do the record was this kid I knew from Ireland, Bono'.[7] Geldof may be exaggerating for the sake of historical irony, but Bono himself has acknowledged some specific hesitation. In Bono's telling, he arrived at the London recording studio, had a read of the 'really good' lyrics of the song, and thought 'the only line I'm not going to sing is that one: *Tonight, thank God, it's them instead of you.*'[8] (The italics and the strange punctuation of the lyric, which casts 'thank God' as an aside rather than an imperative, come from the Bono-approved source material; that punctuation makes no sense, since this section of the song is an injunction to pray.)

This controversial line was of course to be the one that Geldof chose for Bono:

So I walked up to Bob and he said, 'Listen, I want you to sing this fucking line here.' I said: 'Just please don't tell me it's this line.' He said: 'That's the very line.' 'I can't sing that, Bob.' 'Can't sing the fucking line? What do you mean you can't sing the line?' I told him I didn't want to sing the line. He said, 'This is not about what you want, OK? This is about what these people need.' I was too young to say, 'This is about what you want.' But it was his show and I was happy to be in it.[9]

It's a typical Bono story, ostensibly self-mocking, but it all works to underline his essential if sometimes accidental genius: 'It's the most biting line, and actually reveals how selfish a mindset we all have underneath. I think Bob was trying to be honest and raw and self-accusatory. Rather than sing, "We're lucky it's not us" he was saying: "Well, when you say that, you mean 'lucky it's them'. Now look at it. Now look at yourself."'[10]

It's questionable how many people were inspired to look at themselves by the line Bono sang in this Christmas hit, but as far as Bono was concerned, he came good. 'I kind of did an impersonation of Bruce Springsteen, that was really what was in my mind.'[11] Given Bono's rather different vocal range from, and technical superiority to, Springsteen as a singer, it seems an odd claim, like he's making an excuse for inserting such overt emotionalism into what he depicts as the smooth English setting. Certainly the line sounds more like a distilled version of himself rather than of anyone else. Perhaps his memory was playing tricks when he recorded those recollections some twenty years after the fact, and he was thinking of the following year's 'Sun City', when he actually did have to work out how to do a non-imitative imitation of Springsteen, singing the same line as 'the Boss' when it came around a second time in the song: 'We're stabbing our brothers and sisters in the back' – a line that one might perhaps regard as prophetic.

In any case, Bono cannot be blamed for the sins of Geldof and his appalling Band Aid song. It just so happens that Geldof's lyrical vision – in which Africans are 'they', literally 'the other ones'; Africa itself is essentialised as a nightmarish place of undifferentiated poverty ('where nothing ever grows, no rain or rivers flow'); and Westerners are cast as their saviours, the people who will give them both physical sustenance and spiritual uplift ('Let them know it's Christmas time') – bears a striking resemblance to the dominant themes of Bono's African work in the decades that followed.

BAD: AT LIVE AID

The Live Aid concert, staged simultaneously in London and Philadelphia in July 1985, is sometimes depicted as U2's breakthrough moment. This is an exaggeration, at least. U2 were already big stars, already *Rolling Stone*'s 'band of the decade', as their place in the day's line-up attests. They were the first band onstage at Wembley after the Philly stage had got started up, and thus had a role in underlining the transatlantic link for the audience in the US, where they were so popular. And they were followed in London only by a handful of the biggest, longer-established acts in Britain: Dire Straits, Queen, David Bowie, the Who, Elton John, Paul McCartney. A measure of their standing is that U2's young members were the only musicians born in the 1960s, or anywhere near that decade, to get close to the business end of that event.

It might nonetheless be fairly regarded as Bono's personal breakthrough to a mass audience, as in: 'Did you see what that singer from the Irish band did at Live Aid?' The cameras loved his dramatic preening, even to the point of following him during the instrumental break of 'Sunday Bloody Sunday', when he pulled one cameraman over, apparently to get the best shot of his bandmates, but with his antics ensuring that there was in fact no shot of his bandmates.[12] Not then and not later: there was hardly a moment in the band's eighteen-minute spell onstage when Bono was not in the camera's gaze, usually alone, and the climax came during 'Bad', when he leapt two levels down to the edge of the audience barrier, got three young women pulled from the heaving crowd, then embraced one of them in a sort-of slow dance – the woman's back getting more camera time than did, say, drummer Larry Mullen Jr.[13]

What's striking in retrospect is that, in those eighteen minutes, the man who later attached Africa so definitively to his image makes no effort to connect with the African mission of Live Aid, much less the Ethiopian famine for which the event was intended to raise relief funds. If it were not for the familiar dark silhouette of Africa on the stage backdrop, you could not differentiate this from any other performance – despite the fact that each of the songs U2 performed lent itself so well to a preaching break. 'Sunday Bloody Sunday' was rattled through efficiently, and referred, at least explicitly, to nothing more than familiar Irish war-weariness (see Chapter 1); the only significant ad lib was 'We are so sick of it.'

It was U2's plan, however, to perform 'Pride (In the Name of Love)' at Live Aid, thus at least making an African-American connection via Martin Luther King. Bono blew that plan to pieces with his long foray off the stage during 'Bad', plus the snippets of Lou Reed and the Rolling Stones he dropped into the song's greatly extended coda – no sign on this occasion, thank God, of 'Candle in the Wind'. There was no time, as a result of all the carry-on, for another song in their allotted slot, though there was no visible hint of Bono being told this officially as he breezed offstage, leaving the rest of the band still playing, over and over and over, the repeating figure that is the distinctive mark of 'Bad'.

The walk-off, with a wave and a white towel around his shoulders, like he was Elvis with an anonymous backing group, must have been the crowning insult for the rest of U2, who had already spent part of the long, long song wondering where on earth he had gone and if they should simply abandon their vamping.[14] It is well-established U2 lore that they fought with Bono backstage afterwards, and, we're told, an allegedly chastened Bono joined the rest of them in brooding for days – though it is hard to believe that the length of their brood is anything other than their memories enjoying some literary licence – about the career disaster they had brought upon themselves with this chaotic and self-indulgent performance.[15]

Except, of course, that they had done nothing of the sort, as they eventually discovered. Bono summed up the experience years later: 'Crap sound, crap haircuts and we didn't end up playing the hit "Pride (In The Name Of Love)" because the singer fucked off into the crowd – band wanted to fire me as a result – and it turned out to be one of the best days of our life. Explain that. Ask God, he probably knows.'[16] God's knowledge presumably rests, like everyone else's, on Bono's barrier-breaking huggy-dance down at the edge of the crowd, the moment when the whole event seemed that little bit less like some self-congratulatory rock-star extravaganza, what Frank Zappa famously called 'the biggest cocaine-money-laundering scheme of all time' and a 'show-business-oriented bogus charity event',[17] and more like the natural fusion of music and love, or something like that.

Bono's description of that moment in a twenty-first-century TV interview is only slightly more ridiculous than much of the hyperbole that burst out around it at the time: 'I didn't know that when I was holding on to her I'd be holding on to the rest of the world.'[18] (In a franker moment he recalled: 'I'd gone AWOL to try and find a television moment and forgot about the song.'[19]) It tells us all too much about the delusions fostered by Live Aid that an embrace between a rich rock star and a London fan could be constructed as somehow symbolising the unity of the world in this moment, a unity somehow connected to providing relief to the absent, hungry 'they' living in the dark continent outlined behind the stage. The idea that the girl in the crowd had been singled out for 'rescue' by him from an allegedly dangerous crush grew over the years, and added further messianic significance to the moment; in fact he had often pulled women from audiences to dance with them.[20]

Bono made his fame at Live Aid, but he was not responsible for the event as a whole, and this is not the place to consider all its pretensions, failures and ramifications. However, Bono's moment of glory – hidden from the sight of most of the audience at Wembley Stadium but carried around the world to the (exaggerated) hundreds of millions of live television viewers – is worth dwelling on, because it can distil the meaning of so many of the charitable impulses he would surrender to over the following decades. Here is a moment that is ostensibly about making connections, about transcending segregation, about giving something of oneself. But it is ultimately so easy, so smug, so self-satisfied and exhibitionist; any connection made lasts a moment, if that, and then the generous 'giver' is returned to security and comfort, feeling better about himself; the segregation returns, nothing of significance really changes. Except perhaps the reputation and self-image of the giver, who now believes himself capable of embracing the world.

Bono, it hardly needs to be added, then went to Africa.

INTO ETHIOPIA: DISCOVERING AFRICA AND THE BLUES

It should be said, all the same, that Bono's first trip to Africa looks positively modest and self-effacing at this distance. There is considerable debate within development organisations about the usefulness or otherwise of the armies of young and unskilled volunteers who descend on poor countries looking to help however they can – which usually isn't very much – and maybe to brush up their resumés in the process. The best and worst that can be said about twenty-five-year-old Bono and his twenty-four-year-old wife Ali in Ethiopia in the autumn of 1985 is that they appear to have been unexceptional troops in such an army – in his words, 'going under the wire, as regular volunteers'.[21]

While it is true that not every volunteer returns from Africa to publish a slim limited-edition volume of photos that sells for £1,000,[22] Bono's six weeks in Ethiopia were so low-key that they don't figure at all in Eamon Dunphy's 1987 band biography. They are described by Bono in some detail, however, in the 2006 book *U2 by U2*. His and Ali's trip was arranged by World Vision, a California-based evangelical charity that has come in for criticism over the years for its marketing of 'child-sponsorship' as a means of fundraising. Bono didn't discuss either that marketing issue or the Christian connection; and though the heavy emphasis on children in his account of the trip may remind the reader of the disproportionate use of kids in most famine-relief publicity, it should be noted, in fairness, that 'we were put in charge [!] of an orphanage in north Ethiopia, in a feeding station at Ajibar', so children were at the heart of their work.[23]

What is more striking is that, two decades after the fact, Bono still seemed quite impressed by the impact made by his young self.

[T]here was a lot of waiting around in the camps, not just by the children but also by the adults. So we developed a repeating educational programme with various one-act plays and songs to spread information on health, hygiene and other issues … in an entertaining way. One was called *The Labour Play*, it was about giving birth … We would teach the kids a song and they would go round the camp singing it and educate their parents … I learned some of the language and wrote simple songs … So the children would sing *We can't eat the seeds because they're for next year / If we plant them right there will be no more tears*. It wasn't poetry but it sold the idea. I still remember the tune. I have heard that some of the ideas lived on after we left. I hope that is true.[24]

We can only assume the facts laid out in his telling are true. The significance with which he imbues them is more revealing: Bono, despite all the careful work he had done in the interim in African-development circles, appeared fully comfortable with the idea that two childless young urban Europeans could make such a lasting impression on the childbirth and agricultural practices of rural Ethiopians, a shockingly colonial notion. (By his own account, his language-acquisition skills appear to have been truly amazing – 'I learned some of the language and wrote simple songs' – though they have not surfaced in his later life.)

In among all the talk of being 'humbled' by the dignity and struck by the 'regal faces' of the natives, of the one boy whose suffering he has taken with him all through the years, Bono did, at the end of his recollection, partly transcend the merely charitable and pictorial:

The thing I came away with in the end was a sense that there was a structural side to this poverty. There had been a civil war in Ethiopia as well as the natural calamity that had caused this particular famine but the story of starvation and poverty in Africa is not always war and natural disaster. A lot of it is corruption, as I discovered later, and not just theirs but our corrupt relationship with Africa – trade agreements and the like, old debts we keep making them pay. My awareness of all this started on that trip.[25]

Apart from the somewhat confusing conflation of what he learned then and what he 'discovered later', and apart from the fact that he doesn't appear to have acted on any of this knowledge about Africa for many years, this is a fairly unimpeachable piece of quick analysis. The likelihood that it is something other than post-facto rationalisation is supported by other evidence that he was drawn at this time toward leftish analysis of international relations – namely his work with Amnesty and trips to Central

America (see Chapter 3). Indeed, his capacity to speak the language of global justice while advancing policies that do little to advance it might be regarded as the central political fact of Bono's subsequent career.

Interestingly, in reality and in the flow of his recollections, he came straight back from what he would later call 'the terrible beauty that is Africa' to find himself immersed in the African-American heritage of rock 'n' roll, of which he had been so ignorant. The story of his enlightenment is another typical Bono mix of self-mockery and self-aggrandisement, since the person who took the trouble to turn him on to the blues was none other than Keith Richards, one of the genre's most famous white interpreters.

In his telling, having been invited into a Rolling Stones recording session, Bono shocks Richards and Mick Jagger by his ignorance of musical history.

> That is when I realized that U2 had no tradition, we were from outer space. There were no roots to our music, no blues, no gospel, no country – we were post-punk. Our starting points were the *NME*, Joy Division, Kraftwerk, Penetration and The Buzzcocks … Keith said, 'You don't know the blues?' I said, 'Not only do I not know the blues, I object to it.' He was taken aback. 'What do you mean?' I told him, 'Anyone who ever played the blues, where I came from, it was just twelve-bar laziness and it meant they were fresh out of original ideas.' … Sometime over the next few hours, Keith got hold of some vinyl and put on some John Lee Hooker and Robert Johnson. I was already in awe of Keith just as a songwriter and a rock figure; that he was taking time out to turn me on to the blues was something I was never going to forget. He played me these records and it sounded like the end of the world – more punk rock than anything I'd grown up on.[26]

The rhetorical disdain for his young self in Bono's twenty-first-century recollection of events in 1985 is almost overwhelmed by the residual contempt for Irish traditional music – not even referenced as a potential 'root' – and for the rather rich tradition of Irish blues-playing. And the story's punch-line is that Bono was, again, such a brilliantly quick learner that he went back to his hotel 'with my head in a spin' and wrote a blues song, 'Silver and Gold', for the *Sun City* anti-apartheid album.[27]

Neither the intolerably mannered version of the song that Bono contributed to that album – with help from Richards and Ron Wood – nor the bombastic approach to it by U2 released three years later, in the 1988 album and film project *Rattle and Hum*, would mark 'Silver and Gold' as among Bono's finest achievements. Nonetheless it is one of his most interesting lyrics – typically sloppily structured, but mixing the story of the slave trade with that of apartheid. It refers to 'the captains and the kings' (a phrase previously borrowed from Kipling in Brendan Behan's devastating anti-imperialist ballad of that name, so Bono *had* actually listened to some Irish music), and makes a rather pointed plea for economic sanctions against South Africa: 'Hit where it hurts: silver and gold.' In his preaching break during the song in *Rattle and Hum* he explicitly suggests that the song sympathises with the impulse to armed revolt: 'This is a song written about a man in a shanty town outside of Johannesburg. A man who's sick and tired of looking down the barrel of white South Africa. A man who is at the point where he is ready to take up arms against his oppressor.'[28]

In the *Rattle and Hum* documentary, this onstage speech comes just a few minutes before the 'fuck the revolution' speech about Irish America in 'Sunday Bloody Sunday', which (as noted in Chapter 1) pours angry scorn on those who support a faraway rebellion of which they have little immediate knowledge. Any irony in this juxtaposition is apparently lost on Bono and the film-makers.

It is an interesting coincidence, at least, that Bono came to an appreciation of African-American music, and to an attempt to write in a blues idiom, just after visiting Africa, and in the course of his first African 'advocacy' work. Indeed, for the next several years, which delivered unprecedented levels of success, the aesthetic explorations would take precedence over the humanitarian – U2 weren't even able to take part in the star-studded Amnesty International 'Human Rights Now' roadshow that played in Zimbabwe and Ivory Coast in 1988, though they had performed on Amnesty's short US 'Conspiracy of Hope' tour in 1986. The outcome of the bluesy musical experiments was, eventually, that embarrassing *Rattle and Hum* film, in racial terms a cornucopia of clichés, from its (mostly) black-and-white cinematography, Harlem gospel choir and street singer to the spectacle of B. B. King turning up to lavish praise on Bono's lyrics for 'When Love Comes to Town'. The film's less overtly racialised clichés of 'discovering America' – staring out over the darkening Mississippi, playing in the Sun studios in Memphis, visiting Graceland – are no less ridiculous.

Rattle and Hum, directed by a Frenchman but heavily crafted by U2 themselves, also features a few familiar signifiers of 'real' Ireland, not least the camera swooping across the sea, up some cliffs and along forty shades of grey sward – this is arty black-and-white, remember – behind its opening credits. A recent scholarly book suggests the film could be 'regarded as a problematic and flawed attempt by the band to "un-whiten" its sound and to intertwine the two authenticities of blackness and Irishness,'[29] to become, in the words of Dexys Midnight Runners, Celtic Soul Brothers – and perhaps also to justify their overt and oft-criticised

Christian spirituality by connecting it to the critically reputable sounds of African-American religiosity.

The nature of their effort was, in any case, something quite different from what Bono's teacher Keith and the rest of the Rolling Stones had done in the early 1960s. When the Stones visited the Chess Records studio in Chicago in 1964, it was, after all, still producing R&B hits. The U2 pastiche of African-American musical history was so thin and disconnected from contemporary reality that Bono was reduced, in the lyrics of 'Angel of Harlem', to singing that he heard Billie Holiday on New York's black-pop radio station WBLS – not out of the question since the station had a 'classics' slot in the weekend graveyard shift, but not exactly representative of its output.[30] The reference sounds like Bono simply stringing together signifiers of blackness. (By contrast, the Clash famously came to New York in the early 1980s to hear their own music being played on the likes of WBLS.)

Paul McGuinness's later concession that *Rattle and Hum* 'became a little too self-reverent' as the band moulded it in post-production considerably understates its faults, despite some powerful concert footage.[31] He remained partly defiant nonetheless: 'We sold twelve million copies of the record so that is the kind of failure I can live with.'[32]

The band came to see this late-1980s period of earnest, conspicuous roots-hunting in America as a dead end, or at best, in Bono's words, 'a necessary part of our development', its role in the ultimately glorious U2 narrative summarised instrumentally, as it were, by the singer: 'Listening to black music helped us get the groove ready for *Achtung Baby*.'[33]

But actually it's hard to hear direct black-American sources even when U2 eventually get their groove on. U2 had their black moment not, as their predecessors had done, to find sexy ass-shaking sounds. 'The U2 fascination with African America was more to do with furthering their brand of "caring rock", drawing on a mix of African-American political struggles (most notably the civil rights movement) and a respect for musical traditions, than with reproducing any racialized sexual essentialism.'[34] The Irish academic authors quoted here, Noel McLaughlin and Martin McLoone, seem to credit U2 for not adopting 'racialized sexual essentialism'. They're right insofar as there is rarely anything sexy about U2. But one might well counter that a white rock group playing the blues (or a semblance of it) to show that they cared about something-or-other is at least as silly and patronising as playing the blues to show that they were sexually potent and could boogie.

Bono's artistic turn after this period from soulful truth-seeker to arch Euro-postmodernist is considered in Chapter 3. It is fair to say, in any case, that Africa and humanitarian causes in general became a relatively low priority for him for much of the 1990s. He did not even travel to Africa again until a U2 concert in Cape Town in 1998. He did, however, make a further, quiet return to African-American music in 1995, recording a Marvin Gaye cover for *Inner City Blues*, an ultimately low-profile Motown tribute album to the singer, who was then eleven years dead. Bono's choice? What else but 'Save the Children', to which he contributed a maudlin vocal – his version never achieves anything like Gaye's spiritual lift-off – and an even more maudlin video, directed by South African–born Earle Sebastian, in which Bono sits outside a peepshow in a New York red-light district and gazes sadly at the mostly black low-life unfolding around him, contemplating the tragedy of the poor brown people.[35] Both its name and its gaze strongly prefigure much of what was to follow once Bono got engaged – or 're-engaged', though that risks overstating his previous efforts – in humanitarian work.

'I'M NOT A CHEAP DATE': THE DEBT CAMPAIGN

That re-engagement only became very public early in 1999, when he put his name to a creditable editorial for the British *Guardian* newspaper under the faux-innocent headline 'World debt angers me'. In fact, the editorial didn't read as especially angry, even when it claimed to be: 'Live Aid raised $200 million for Africa. Anger is the only response on realising that that sum is spent every week by the poorest countries of Africa – on debt service.' That's a good point made clearly, and the emphasis throughout the article is on reason and persuasion in the name of debt cancellation, suggesting there was fault on both sides of the global divide, and showering flattery on leading politicians, 'a unique set of players, who I believe are ready to face the implications of their own script' – Blair, Brown, Schroeder, Clinton. He pointedly shouts out to the *Wall Street Journal* and the Adam Smith Institute for their words of support for debt relief, along with another economist previously regarded as right-wing: 'Jeffrey Sachs, formerly the architect of "shock therapy" ultra-monetarist reforms in post-Soviet Russia, argued that the first fundamental need for the poorest countries is that their debts should be "cancelled outright".'[36] It's his first public mention of the man who would be his guru and partner for many years to come.

For all the occasional outbursts of 'caring' that had dotted his career prior to this article (they are discussed further in Chapter 3), it should be recalled that this opinion piece calling on governments to embrace debt cancellation marked his real coming-out as a serious campaigner. (There is evidence of him being quietly involved in debt campaigning for some months prior to the editorial.) He arrived, full-grown, via what must have seemed at the time like a canny invitation from the Jubilee 2000 campaign, a mostly British-based coalition that sought to mobilise popular and political support for debt cancellation to mark the millennium, and in response to a widespread belief, shared within the UN, that the World Bank and IMF needed reform to make them more supportive of global development. Led by Catholic and Anglican relief agencies, it included groups from across the spectrum of Africa-oriented development organisations, from the traditionally radical to the gently charitable. By 1999 Jubilee 2000 had been running for several years and had already gathered tens of thousands of protesters at the 1998 G8 meeting in Birmingham, England. Bono's op-ed was published a few days before another global leaders' summit, this time in Bonn.

It is no criticism of Bono to point out that his first foray into serious campaigning was a leap into an existing campaign with considerable infrastructure, and that in backing it he put out a moderate message designed to appeal across the political spectrum, just as he would continue to do for all the years to come. Perhaps it does, however, cast some doubt on the image of a man drawn impulsively and inexorably by his great love and anger into political involvement.

Bono's timing was that of a politician, and had been carefully planned with his Jubilee 2000 adviser Jamie Drummond, a posh Londoner and former Christian Aid worker who had convinced him to join the campaign.[37] The op-ed was followed the next day by a speech from the stage at the televised ceremony of the Brit Awards, for pop music, in London: Drummond had convinced the Brits' organisers to allow Bono to raise the debt issue in the context of giving a 'special award' to Muhammad Ali, who was in the audience and supportive of the campaign.[38] After the televisual moment came the politics: the British chancellor of the exchequer, Gordon Brown, was happy two days later to tie himself to the campaign, making a plea before the G7 summit in Bonn for more debt relief, as the press reported: 'Mr Brown praised the efforts of Jubilee 2000 and celebrities, including singer Bono …'[39] This was within three days of Bono's first prominent public pronouncements on the matter! Two glaring facts emerge from this sequence of events: (1) Bono, far from afflicting the powerful with his outburst, was part of a coordinated effort between campaigners and the British government to advance the debt-relief agenda and present Britain as an enlightened global leader on the issue – a partnership that would re-emerge some years later; and (2) anyone would get a taste for campaigning if their first effort went this well.

Bono went into global action on the debt question, with scant regard for his bandmates: McGuinness acknowledged wryly that 'there were times when they were left waiting because Bono was meeting the Pope'.[40] His main focus was on the United States, on the basis that for the US to cancel the debt owed to it by the poorest countries would be important in itself and would set an example for others. He later recalled: 'The best phone call I ever made in my opinion was to the most extraordinary woman in the world: Eunice Kennedy Shriver … A legend and a lesson in civic duty. All the Kennedys are …'[41] Again, he was pushing an open door. 'She told me to ring her son Bobby [Shriver], which I did. And he immediately put the family Filofax to work for me … his brother-in-law Arnold Schwarzenegger had a lot of Republican friends.'[42] Shriver, he has said, 'knew, from his family's experience, just how many layers of body armour we would have to get through to find a beating heart in America's body politic'.[43] The body-armour metaphor was perhaps a little unfortunate in relation to the Kennedys, but you know what he means.

Shriver's Filofax didn't merely contain key party-political contacts. Shriver, then in his mid-forties and a Kennedy in all but name, was not only nephew to Jack, Bobby and Ted; he was a successful corporate lawyer who had, just a few years earlier, worked in a venture-capitalist firm, James D. Wolfensohn Inc. – the selfsame Jim Wolfensohn whom Clinton had appointed as president of the World Bank in 1995. Before he had even switched on the vaunted charisma, Bono had direct entry to virtually every office not only in Washington, but on Wall Street as well.

Bono's love-bombing of America's most powerful political family bore bipartisan dividends. From the autumn of 1999, Bono rather impressively devoted much of his time, into the following year, to working his way through America's corridors of power in search of legislation that would deliver bilateral debt relief. He had the smooth Shriver by his side, and for extra Republican appeal, he teamed up with a friend of Schwarzenegger, representative John Kasich of Ohio, later to become governor of that state. Knowing that he needed to beef up the economic aspects of his arguments, Bono sought out the somewhat notorious mainstream economist he had cited in his *Guardian* article, Jeffrey Sachs – the man he had accurately labelled as the author of 'shock-doctrine' rapid privatisation of the Russian economy – and ended up sitting in on some of Sachs's classes at Harvard's Kennedy School of Government. The two men soon became close. And Bono made a special target of the economics team in the Clinton administration, slowly but surely charming his way into the office of an initially hesitant treasury secretary, Larry Summers (Bono's incarnation as a Washington lobbyist is discussed further in Chapter 3).

Ultimately the Clinton White House was especially susceptible to his charms. Writing in 2005, James Traub of the *New York Times* revealed in unlikely detail how Bono had convinced Clinton's chief economic adviser, Gene Sperling, to join the crusade:

> One Sunday morning that fall [of 1999], Bono called to ask Sperling if he could come to his office in the West Wing. There he put his hand on top of a giant stack of papers Sperling was working through and said: 'I bet that most of the things in this pile feel more urgent than debt relief. But I want you to think of one thing: Ten years from now, is there anything you'll feel more proud of than getting debt relief for the poorest countries?' Bono understood something about people like Sperling: that in their heart of hearts, the chastened New Democrats of the Clinton administration yearned for morally resounding acts, but that they needed political cover, and they needed permission – the feeling that the thing could and must be done. When Bono left, Sperling called a treasury official and said that he wanted to insert something on debt relief into a speech Clinton was about to give at the World Bank.[44]

Traub does not say which of the two men is his source for this tale, which resembles nothing so much as a clip from Aaron Sorkin's pragmatic-liberal fantasia, *The West Wing*. Bono's own story of how he persuaded the administration to adopt his policy is that he convinced Bill Clinton directly by suggesting obliquely to him that the leader of the Free World needed a big millennium vision for the end of 1999.[45] In truth, for all the dramatic recollections, the White House had already been committed before Bono's arrival to two-thirds debt reduction for the poorest countries through a World Bank plan.[46] The additional cost of Bono's plan would be relatively trivial in the context of the federal budget – not much more than $100 million, and even that sum was largely theoretical, since everyone knew that the poor countries were never going to be able to pay all their debts anyway.

Clinton's support for even such a modest measure was not enough, however. Congress had to be convinced. Washington insiders noted the rapid proliferation of photos-with-Bono on the walls of countless members of Congress, though it has been suggested it was the vast population of congressional staffers – well-educated under-forties, the U2 generation personified – who drove his progress through those corridors. Bono's most famous conquest during his time in the capital, because it seemed the unlikeliest, was the right-wing North Carolina senator, Jesse Helms, whose deserved reputation as a racist, homophobe and xenophobe was less important than his role as chair of the senate foreign relations committee. Speaking about it some years later, Bono described their meeting in September 2000:

> I went into his office in the Senate to find out why they were blocking debt cancellation and after talking for some time to really get under the hood of the issues, he became quite emotional, even tearful about Africa. It was clear beneath the tough skin of this old cold warrior was a heart that could be moved. It was front page of the *Wall Street Journal*: Jesse Helms Brought to Tears by Stories of African Children. [Bono neglects to mention that he was the named source for that item.[47]] People couldn't believe this had happened. As I was leaving he wrapped his arms around me and gave me a blessing like an ancient Jewish patriarch to his son. I was very moved … God was on the move.[48]

It may take a strong stomach to picture this encounter. The fact that Bono conferred anti-poverty credibility on such a hateful character is indeed distasteful. But it is surely rather unjust to criticise Bono – as some on the Left do – simply for his repulsive associates. After all, if he had achieved something of real and revolutionary impact for Africa's poor, then a little unmerited burnishing of previously bad reputations would be a small price to pay, wouldn't it?

Moralising about Bono's guilt-by-association with these characters diverts attention from just how little was at stake in reality, especially in the early phase of this campaigning. Put simply, while some in Washington were certainly opposed on principle – 'ideologically', if you like – to forgiving debts, no one could claim that substantial Western material interests were at risk if the debt were written off. Unlike the debates that whirled around Latin American and Asian debt in the 1980s, or around Irish or Greek debt after 2008, no major First World banks, or indeed governments, were in danger if the US, the UK, other states and multilateral institutions decided to forget about what a few of the world's poorest countries owed them. The upside was at least potentially just what Bono and supportive neoliberal economists such as Jeffrey Sachs promised: African economies, freed from some of their onerous, odious debt, in a better position to provide stability and infrastructure for foreign investment. Moves toward debt relief in the poorest parts of Africa wouldn't discommode the global economy, though they were unlikely to do it much good either; and once you factored in the feel-good glow that Bono conferred, it counted as a win–win for many of the major players. And debt relief often, of course, came with strings attached, as the small number of lucky recipient countries were monitored for necessary 'reforms', often involving opening up their public services to privatisation by foreign firms – the sorts of things that rendered them ever-friendlier for foreign capital. Why, really, would Jesse Helms or Jeffrey Sachs be imagined to have any serious problem with any of that?

That is not to say that the Jubilee 2000 campaign was pointless or worthless, or that the NGOs that had worked for many years to build it were cynical or misguided, or wrong to adopt the media-friendly Bono. However, the small good they achieved in gaining some debt cancellation – the US Congress in 2000 eventually forgave just half the US debt owed by the poorest African countries – and making the issue a public concern should be weighed against the publicity boost that was given to some of the most viciously destructive forces in the world. History tells us that, as they were being hugged by Bono for dropping a few pennies to the poor, his friends in the Washington–Wall Street axis were gorging themselves on the fruits of massive and newly unregulated financial spec-ulation, all the while running up unpayable debts that would eventually dwarf those they were so magnanimously forgiving in Africa – these debts have been estimated as running into trillions of dollars, compared to the hundreds of millions under discussion to be 'forgiven' in Africa. (Those First-World debts were happily socialised after 2008 without any need for rock-star lobbying: the bank bailout in Bono's native Ireland alone saw the government assume responsibility for more than €300 billion in private debt, and it has actually had to pay back tens of billions of euros of that debt already.)

Among liberals there was, it is true, some grumbling when, from 2001, Bono's friendly persuasion started to provide 'caring' cover for a Republican White House rather than a Democratic one. But such grumbling is a mere artefact of the partisan divide in the US, where the distinction between the two parties hides the fact that they have few substantial differences. What substantially divided the likes of Summers and Sperling, on the one hand, and Bush treasury secretary Paul O'Neill, on the other, that should have rendered O'Neill ineligible for an African safari with Bono? In reality, the differences were scant, and if Bono could charm one side, why not the other?

O'Neill was a more literally rapacious capitalist than most of his peers: before his spell in cabinet he had run the ecologically devastating Alcoa aluminium company, a scourge of landscapes and water supplies with its mining and processing operations around the world. O'Neill has said he initially refused to meet Bono: 'I thought he was just some pop star who wanted to use me.'[49] Perish the thought. But Bono soon got access to

O'Neill, as to everyone else. By June 2001 Bono was sufficiently defensive about his charm offensive with the widely despised new administration to whine: 'It's much more glamorous to be on the barricades with your handkerchief over your nose than it is to have a bowler and a briefcase and go to work ... But ... that's the way to get the work done. It's uncool. It's incredibly unhip. But it's the way to get it done.'[50]

If Bono was suffering a glamour deficit, he at least had what few on the barricades could aspire to: the adoring screams of his fans to comfort him, as U2 continued to tour. It was reported that he would hop on a plane immediately after a gig and dash to Washington for meetings first thing in the morning. The Bush White House increasingly liked the cut of his jib. Condoleezza Rice, then serving as national security adviser, later told the *New York Times* that the administration had been working on ways to 'rebuild a consensus about foreign assistance'.

> Rice was surprised to learn that Bono took the hard-headed view that 'there's a responsibility for the recipient' as well as for the donor. In fact, Bono championed a new paradigm [*sic*] in which aid would be conditioned not only on need but on demonstrated capacity to use that aid effectively – which was precisely the kind of reform the administration had been thinking of.[51]

Leaving aside the nonsense about Bono's startling new paradigm under which aid should be spent 'effectively', it's not hard to translate this from *Times*-speak. The White House was pleased that Bono was on board with the sort of 'conditionalities' on aid that First World governments and institutions had been demanding from developing countries for decades.

After 9/11, it perhaps became a little harder to sell development assistance in Washington. However, Rice and secretary of state Colin Powell were keen to ensure that US foreign policy was seen to have a non-military dimension, and Bono and others were frequently heard to conjoin the 'war on terror' with a 'war on poverty': as the *New York Times* put it, paraphrasing Bono's argument, 'fragile states could not be allowed to become failed states, as Afghanistan had been.'[52] In early 2002, the White House called in Jamie Drummond, the English Jubilee 2000 campaigner who was by now something like what officials might call Bono's 'policy guy', both an adviser and a representative.

> ... Drummond recalls, he was 'summoned to Washington and asked not to leave.' In a series of closed-door meetings, he says, he worked with White

House officials on the details of an aid program based on the principles Bono had proposed ... But the administration wanted something from Bono in return – his imprimatur. [Rice said:] 'It's great to have a person who would not normally be identified with the president's development agenda as part of it.'[53]

It probably did no harm that, in the midst of all this talking, Bono appeared on the cover of *Time* magazine flashing the inside of a jacket that appeared to be lined with the Stars and Stripes. The giant text read: 'Can Bono Save the World?'[54]

In May 2002 Bono's schedule and that of Treasury Secretary O'Neill collided for ten days as they palled around Africa on what was described as a fact-finding mission, to press coverage that initially seemed as much bemused as impressed, the rock star and the cabinet member being some people's idea of an odd couple. Appearances can be deceiving, however: despite the quarter-century difference in age, the men proved to have a lot in common. They bonded over plans for improving African drinking water, and O'Neill successfully 'tried to impress on Bono the liberating power of the global market', explaining as they visited factories 'that Africa would benefit more from even a modest expansion of trade than from a radical increase in aid'.[55] Bono later recalled that O'Neill constantly told him 'the future of Africa is in the hands of business and commerce. And I knew that to be sort of true, but not as much as I needed to ...'[56] Thus, in Bono's own version of the trip, it helped convert him to a fuller embrace of market principles as a solution to poverty. The *Washington Post*, firmly in 'impressed' mode, said the trip signalled a 'momentous alliance between liberals and conservatives to launch a fresh assault on global poverty'.[57] Once again, the media cast Bono at the centre of an unlikely conciliation story.

Bono's oft-quoted joke about that trip, 'I'm not a cheap date', would prove somewhat embarrassing, however, as the Bush administration slid backwards on even the relatively modest development-aid targets that had been agreed; meanwhile, O'Neill's enthusiasms fell on the president's deaf ears, and he was fired a few months after their African trip.

Economist Robert Pollin responded to the Bono–O'Neill trip with a devastating analysis of the neoliberal assumptions that both men, despite their alleged differences, took for granted. Pollin pointed out that it was precisely the insistence on free and open markets in the developing world that had inhibited growth there, compared to an earlier period when 'developmental states' had been allowed to pursue their own industrial and trade policies with an emphasis on domestic development. Assuming even the most enormous increase in aid envisaged by Bono, Pollin showed that 'Bono plus Paul O'Neill' neoliberalism was actually costing poor and moderate-income countries $375 billion annually, compared to the growth they might have enjoyed by embracing the policies (and thus the growth rates) of the pre-neoliberal 1960s and 1970s.[58] Such simple but profoundly political mathematics was literally beyond the bounds of Bono's thinking, as he stuck firmly within the corporate Washington consensus about which O'Neill was educating him.

During and after this time, Bono would steadfastly insist that the political assistance, the imprimatur he had rendered to the Republican White House had been worthwhile, and the reason he could say that with any credibility was what he saw as crucial progress on AIDS.

HEARING AIDS: PROGRESS AND COSTS ON HIV

Bono had been aware of the persuasive power of AIDS among some American conservatives before Bush took office. In one account of his famous September 2000 meeting with Jesse Helms, he recalled that his explanations of debt weren't getting anywhere. So 'I started talking about Scripture. I talked about AIDS as the leprosy of our age.' The senator's eyes began to well up as Bono explained that 'married women and children were dying of AIDS, and governments burdened by debt couldn't do a thing about it.[59]

When George W. Bush came to office in January 2001, Bush used the same arguments on him and his officials. Helms helped get Bono a meeting with Bush: Bono brought the president an Irish Bible and talked to him about all of the Good Book's injunctions to help the poor.[60]

In an interview with CBS News in 2005, Bono appears to take credit for getting the US Christian Right involved with the AIDS issue.

> I was very angry that [conservative Christians] were not involved more in the AIDS emergency. I was saying, 'This is the leprosy that we read about in the New Testament, you know. Christ hung out with the lepers. But you're ignoring the AIDS emergency ... How can you?' And, you know, they said, 'Well, you're right, actually. We have been. And we're sorry. We'll get involved.' And they did.[61]

Even allowing for the simplifications of a TV soundbite, Bono's imaginary exchange with 'conservative Christians' – in which he speaks to them collectively, 'angry' like a prophet, and they apologise and repent – seems just a tad egomaniacal. However, if there is one set of achievements about which Bono can be justifiably puffed-up, it is his role – and that of the organisation he helped to establish in 2002, the awkwardly named DATA (Debt AIDS Trade Africa) – in lobbying for funding for the provision of anti-retroviral drugs for people with HIV in Africa. This was by no means the solo effort his quote might suggest, but his work among US Christians, including a short 'Heart of America' bus tour to photo-op the grassroots in 2002, did help to produce, in 2003, President Bush's five-year 'Pepfar' (the President's Emergency Plan for AIDS Relief). This was promised as $15 billion over five years, and it delivered on that promise. Funding for African AIDS became a rare 'political safe zone' in Washington.[62] Again, you can always argue, accurately, that the problem needed more money than that, but alongside other efforts by DATA and its successor, the ONE campaign, in seeking care for Africans with AIDS, there was tangible good done for hundreds of thousands of people – some of whom would spontaneously tell visitors that they got the drugs that saved their lives 'from Bono'. It would be foolish to deny these achievements, even while recognising that, in a celebrity- and media-driven culture, the distribution of the credit for them may be somewhat distorted.

But if we are giving credit to Bono, we should also see if there are items in the debit column on this issue. What were some of the costs of the particular form of his campaigning on AIDS? They are significant, though of course no one can pretend to measure them against the lives saved by the work in which he played a part.

Firstly, when the Christian Right boarded the Bono AIDS bandwagon, they didn't leave their sexual morality at home. Bono had appealed to them precisely by emphasising the sexual innocence of so many of Africa's HIV-positive people ('married women and children'), and the aid, when it came through Pepfar, reflected that emphasis. As the New York Times put it, in an otherwise favourable profile, Bono did not

> see fit to remonstrate with [Bush official Randall] Tobias over the damage that may have been done by the AIDS program's ideologically inspired guidelines: a requirement that one-third of prevention funds go to programs promoting abstinence and sexual fidelity, stringent restrictions on the use of condoms and even a demand that groups receiving funds must formally oppose prostitution. An editorial in The Economist characterized Pepfar as 'too much morality, too little sense.'[63]

The Bush AIDS funding didn't explicitly reject condoms, but suggested limiting their use to 'at risk' groups, meaning gay men and prostitutes, rather than, say, married couples, among whom a great deal of HIV transmission was happening. On the ground in Africa, organisations perceived the Americans as hostile to condoms, and stopped promoting them in the hope of attracting and keeping US funding.[64]

As the *New York Times* article goes on to note, the Bush administration was less generous with international efforts against AIDS, such as the multilateral 'Global Fund', where it couldn't make the moral rules. Helping Africans with AIDS became, for Bush and his like, a matter of saving women and children – and, even then, with hesitation over condom promotion – rather than of standing up for the rights of all people to vital healthcare.

Moreover, Bono's emphasis on 'innocent victims' may have largely worked for Africa, where HIV was so often heterosexually transmitted, but it may also have been counter-productive for advancing the cause of the less photogenic millions of people with AIDS elsewhere in the world. That meant predominantly (as the subtitle of Nancy Stoller's 1997 book on AIDS politics calls them) the 'queers, whores and junkies' who had built a global movement in the face of devastating prejudice in the first two decades of the disease's spread. Even in Africa, gay men are far more likely to be HIV-positive than straight men, and a recent report suggests that sexual minorities may be the losers in the long run: the American evangelical Christians that Bono encouraged into Africa are 'colonizing' and 'transforming' sexual politics in several countries on the continent, with homosexual and reproductive rights under threat.[65]

It is also impossible to evaluate Bush's Pepfar fully without noting that, in the next paragraph of the State of the Union speech in which the president announced his AIDS plan, he spoke of his intention to invade Iraq. The two issues were clearly conjoined by Bush, under the ever-flexible auspices of humanitarianism. (There is much more about Iraq in Chapter 3.)

If Bono chose to make conservative allies and arguments in working to treat AIDS, his organisation DATA was also conservative in other ways. Like the Global Fund to Treat AIDS, TB and Malaria (to give it its full name), DATA chose to work in cooperation with First World pharmaceutical companies, paying the full prices for their products, rather than directly challenging their medical patents, as Nelson Mandela, among others, had demanded and attempted. This meant that, for some years, those companies made substantial profits from the AIDS spending that poured into Africa. This sort of 'constructive engagement' with Big Pharma has been controversial, but activists have honest differences about it, many agreeing to cooperate with the companies. Over the years the relevant organisations have moved matters along gradually to the point where generic drugs from India are playing a substantial role in African AIDS treatment.

Then there was something that would become a recurring theme: the fondness of Bono and his organisation for declaring victory, over the heads of other AIDS activists. Thus, for example, the $15 billion over five years announced in 2003 for Bush's Pepfar was considered inadequate by most of the organisations that campaigned for such funding, but their disappointment was drowned out by a Bono-led chorus of praise. Again, there is a tactical argument that can be made in defence of Bono's approach: that 'victories' are encouraging for activists and helpfully stroke the egos of politicians and officials. (The first Pepfar actually spent more than $15 billion, and considerably more money was won for the next five-year plan in 2008, after all.) But some campaigners feared that this sort of 'pragmatism', the embodiment of Bono's briefcase-over-barricades line, had been elevated to a principle, at the expense of making enough noise about the fundamental rights of all people to decent, free healthcare, and the incapacity or unwillingness of the West to address those rights.

Finally, there are the most profound philosophical questions about how the West is constructed by this sort of activism as the dispenser of all that is good. Africa, rather than being a real and varied place, is transformed into a project for Western conscience, a sort of vocation – with or without religious connotations. A wealth of powerful insights, some by African scholars, have mercilessly criticised the political and value structures in which Bono's brand of celebrity humanitarianism is situated, on AIDS and other matters. In their view, it is not excessive to label Bono's activity 'cognitive imperialism', which 'constructs Africa as an eternal lack, and narrates its future as westerners' good deed to be done'.[66]

Zambian free-market, anti-aid economist Dambisa Moyo has sparked the ire of Bono's campaign group by writing that the 'pop-culture of aid', firmly located within the entertainment industry, has strengthened the popular misconception that aid is the solution to African poverty.[67] Other scholars, who may not share Moyo's general outlook, are nonetheless harsh on over-simplified campaigns that ignore the obvious – namely, decades of historical failures of aid as a spur to really significant development in Africa, where hundreds of millions of people remain desperately poor.

Researcher Audrey Bryan, who has examined how Bono and Geldof are portrayed in Irish schoolbooks, draws conclusions that are valid well beyond the texts she studies:

> While ostensibly *about* the lives of those whom they seek to uplift and save, discourses of high profile Western benevolence, concern and compassion actively position 'our guys' as *the* stars of the development show, while the objects of national (and Northern) benevolence merely function as the

backdrop to a story which is *really* about 'us.' In other words, the trope of celebrity humanitarian functions as a redemption fantasy ... wherein inhabitants of the Global South are discursively positioned as the backdrop against which 'global good guys' can enhance their sense of themselves, and the reputation of the nation they represent, with insufficient attention to their own participation in relations of domination.[68]

These dissenting voices may be varied, but they are not isolated, at least in the low-profile realm of scholarship. In 2008 the *Journal of Pan African Studies* devoted almost an entire issue to highly critical research concerning Bono's '(Product) RED' campaign. (See pp. 87–101.)

Finnish scholar Riina Yrjölä has written some of the most densely powerful critiques of how the words of Bono and Geldof 'elaborate a colonial imaginary' about Africa: 'these discourses not only serve a purpose in the maintenance of hegemonic Western activity in Africa, but are also instrumental in constructing consensus for the existing world order, where the global South is, and remains, in a subordinate position to the West.'[69]

Bono constructs 'moral geographies and world views'.[70] At a 'national prayer breakfast' in Washington, for example, he said: 'I truly believe that when the history books will be written, our age will be remembered for three things: the war on terror, the digital revolution and what we did – or did not do – to put the fire out in Africa. History, like God, is watching what we do.'[71] 'We', the embodiment of 'our age', are assumed to be Western actors. In another interview he said that, just as the post-war Marshall Plan had defended Europe against 'Sovietism' in the Cold War, aiding Africa would help combat Islamism, creating 'a bulwark against the extremism of our age in what I call the Hot War. This makes sense, not just as a moral imperative, but as a political and a strategic one.'[72]

Such words, according to Yrjölä, reflect 'colonial rescue narratives cloaked with religious language of crusades and inscriptions of Western self-mastery'. In them, ' "Africa" becomes located ... outside Western modernity, freedom and civilisation, rendering the continent as a central battleground between good and evil.'[73] All of this is of course familiar from the history of colonial 'civilising missions' and the opposition to them. From the Crusades to the Iraq War, the West, as many writers have pointed out, is almost always portrayed as improving and assisting native peoples, even while it is killing them.

Yrjölä notes that most discussions of celebrity humanitarianism display a 'trained incapacity ... or unwillingness to acknowledge the wider global exchanges of this activity, and the power relations embedded in the celebrity humanitarian representations and their aesthetic insights'[74] – in other words, what other agendas, hierarchies and status quos are being rein-forced under the flag of 'humanitarianism', whether in combating AIDS or invading Iraq.

Humanitarianism, she writes, 'has become the key way to frame con-temporary world politics – an essential expression of what is meant by "international community" and the contemporary world order behind it',[75] rather than more social justice-oriented goals such as workers' or women's rights. Hence, this is not 'a politically neutral change but rather a political project in its own right, a policing practice that advances some objectives while neglecting others … They signal a historic transition to a mode of world governance in which humanitarianism and development operate as key practices … As a consequence, all traces of the political become excised'.[76] One side of such a 'policing practice' is that Western 'humani-tarians' may claim to enforce, say, the political rights of the Libyan rebels while simultaneously neglecting, for example, those of the Bahrainis; they may privilege women's rights in Afghanistan but ignore workers' rights in Indonesia – and resource limitations are only part of the reason behind why some cases are selected over others. At the same time, humanitarian-ism and development are often treated as universal moral goods, somehow beyond the real and conflicted operation of politics in the societies where they operate.

Celebrity humanitarianism is one component of this. Yrjölä and other scholars locate its rise within a wider shift in global governance in the neo-liberal period, one 'that brings northern governments, NGOs and global celebrities together'. Celebrity politics, other scholars conclude, are part of a new 'expert–celebrity' axis, and function 'to convince electorates that they are being well governed'.[77] This new mode of governance, in which celebrities act as 'significant emotional proxies',[78] the caring face of the global technocracy, has already become so ingrained that most people have forgotten to question the fundamental legitimacy of the likes of Bono as a spokesperson for Africa or anywhere else. Indeed, Bono himself has often been the most likely to raise questions about who he is to talk; in a disarming reflex, he has, as researchers Philip Drake and Michael Higgins put it, 'moments in which he seems to temporarily concede to doubts con-cerning his right to speak, which are then followed by transitions in which he reconciles his celebrity position with his holding the political stage'.[79] We are repeatedly and reassuringly invited to conclude that nobody is more sceptical about Bono than Bono himself. The events of 2005 firmly established, however, that this was not in fact the case.

MAKING HISTORY: THE SCOTTISH SUMMIT

Disquiet about the elevation of Bono to more than merely the figurehead of a movement for Africa was bubbling under the surface of the global-justice community by the time the G8 summit meeting had convened at Gleneagles, near Edinburgh, in the summer of 2005.

In the aftermath of that summit, that disquiet had crystallised into the most coherent critique yet seen of his brand of celebrity humanitarianism, which came to be seen even by some of his erstwhile allies as a form of PR for Western governments. Bono, it seemed, was less an advocate for the world's poor than an apologist for leaders like Tony Blair, who used Bono and his campaign to legitimise their inaction, inadequate action and downright damaging action in relation to poverty. In the meantime, Bono had helped to reduce the question of global inequality and impoverishment to, simply, 'Africa'.

To understand how this set of realisations began to dawn, to the point where campaigners were openly accusing Bono of 'hijacking' their work, it is necessary to look in some detail at events in the run-up to July 2005 and at the summit itself, as well as at the central role Bono played in them. With Geldof – also involved with DATA – by his side, Bono was at the forefront of the Make Poverty History campaign and the Live 8 concerts designed to encourage a 'better deal' for Africa from the gathered heads of government at Gleneagles. After those statesmen emerged with an agreement of sorts on debt and aid, it was no exaggeration to say, as the *New York Times* did subsequently, that 'Bono's own embrace of the package was treated with a solemnity worthy of a Security Council resolution'.[80]

To untangle what happened that July, it is important to recall the warm relationship between Bono and the Blair-and-Brown-led British government, which dated back to the Jubilee 2000 campaign. Alex de Waal, a respected human-rights activist and writer, argues that, at a London breakfast meeting in 2003, Bono and Geldof had shrewdly 'bounced' Blair all the way into their agenda on Africa, 'frogmarching' him into making a statement of support and a pledge to establish a 'commission on Africa' after the prime minister had 'charmed' various NGO leaders without making 'a single concession on substance'.[81] With due respect to de Waal, who paints a vivid picture of supine British charity bosses quietly 'munch[ing] pastries' while being rendered irrelevant by the more vigorous Irishmen, it seems unlikely that Blair regarded Geldof's insistent demand for a 'commission on Africa' as requiring a major policy concession – it was more like a nice PR suggestion. As Blair himself later recalled with pride, he stocked the commission with 'high-quality people' who wouldn't entertain any 'rubbish about not being able to govern because of the wicked colonial past'.[82] It's hardly surprising that the 'high-quality people' didn't bore him with postcolonial 'rubbish': that commission was described by Professor Paul Cammack, an analyst of global political economy, as a 'web of bankers, industrialists and political leaders with connections to the IMF and the World Bank, all committed to spreading the gospel of free market capitalism'.[83]

Blair, in any case, was well aware of the political benefits that both he and President Bush had already reaped by being seen to cooperate with Bono. In May of 2004 Blair paid a chummy visit to Bono at his home in Dublin. Four months later Bono spoke at the annual conference of Blair's Labour Party, saying: 'I'm fond of Tony Blair and Gordon Brown. They are kind of the John and Paul of the global development stage ...' He urged them to 'finish what they started' in ending global poverty.[84] At the end of June 2005, a few days before the summit, Bono told ABC News: 'Remember today that this president committed to try and get all African kids into school ... Bill Clinton did an incredible thing on starting this debt cancellation. He deserves real credit. And now, President Bush deserves credit for finishing it out.'[85] Then, a few days later, he joined Blair for a meeting in 10 Downing Street with the main negotiators from all the G8 countries. As *Time* magazine described it breathlessly, it was another West Wingy moment: 'Bono asked them to "please go that bit further", reminding them that "in 20 years, this week is one of the things you'll be most proud of in your lives." Says Blair: "These are all pretty hard-bitten people who have worked in international relations a long time, but they were very, very enthused by that spirit." '[86] Bono was so close to the centres of power that it was his helpful suggestion that resulted in the summit ending, unusually, with a formal signing ceremony.[87]

To read Blair's memoirs – not, it must be noted, an entirely reliable source – is to understand clearly that he regarded Bono as a dependable ally, and Geldof as merely a rather more incendiary one. Bono, he writes, 'had an absolutely natural gift for politicking', and 'could have been a president or prime minister standing on his head'.[88] When it came to bringing Bush on board with commitments on African debt in 2005, 'I knew Bono would be an important person to see George'.[89] Political scientist John Street summarises Blair's account as putting 'Geldof and Bono close to the centre of the story of the policy change, but significantly [it] assigns them the role of presenting that policy, rather than [of] crafting it ...'[90]

The alliance extended beyond lobbying the Americans and selling policy to the public, to include putting discontented activists in their place. Blair, who is quite open in his contempt for most campaigners, reveals how delighted he was to have the Irish duo aboard, in whatever capacity, when he comes to describe the first stirrings of NGO dissatisfaction with the proposals that emerged from the summit:

> I did the press conference in the garden of the hotel. There was the usual nonsense from some NGO bloke about how we had all let Africa down, and the usual riposte from Bob who basically tore the bloke's head off for being so negative and followed him down the path from the press area, shouting abuse as only an irate Irishman can.[91]

Bono, meanwhile, summed up emotionally at the end of the summit: 'The world spoke, and the politicians listened.' The assembled press broke into spontaneous applause.[92]

Geldof and Bono would both be more cautious in assessing the outcome of the fateful 2005 G8 summit in subsequent years, but by that time the cameras were elsewhere. By declaring victory in the full glare of publicity, they had done their bit for Blair, Brown and Bush.

Unfortunately, the Make Poverty History campaign as a whole had managed to get itself caught up in the Irishmen's hatred of 'negativity' even before this capitulation: thus the main mass gathering in Edinburgh was billed officially as a 'walk' to 'welcome' the global politicians attending, rather than a protest. This was quite a 'rebranding' of the relationship between campaigners and the G8, whose encounters had previously been bracingly confrontational, and it was widely seen in retrospect as an ingenious manoeuvre by the British government to deflate protest and political debate. That summer Make Poverty History, with its millions of little white plastic bracelets distributed across Britain, was so mainstream that some critics were calling it 'a PR exercise for the government', with Britain presented as if 'it were literally leading the world in ending poverty'.[93] (This was scarcely surprising, since Bono himself had declared that to be the case.) Britain's corporate newspapers rallied with their typical nationalism, treating Blair and Brown as the leaders of the campaign, and happily 'made themselves into campaigning tools';[94] even the *Financial Times* gave a prize to the campaign's online petition and 'virtual rally' (g8rally.com), which featured nice cartoon images of Geldof and Bono.

A scholar who was broadly sympathetic to the goals of Make Poverty History, Kate Nash, nonetheless concluded:

> Although Make Poverty History was hugely successful in constructing a public space for its claims and in mobilizing popular sentiment for its aims, then, it is generally agreed that, ultimately, it was a terrible failure ... it failed to achieve any of its concrete aims in changing global economic

policy, and it surely also failed to achieve genuine cosmopolitan solidarity across state borders.[95]

This should hardly come as a surprise given the campaign's insistence, against all evidence to the contrary, on presenting heads of Western governments as essentially, or at least potentially, benevolent actors who could be persuaded by dint of morality to do the right thing. Nash concedes that the campaign descended into 'narcissistic sentimentalism', and acknowledges the absence of African voices.

> African intellectuals were critical of the campaign, in contrast to those Africans represented as the grateful recipients of 'our' help. Across the focal points of the campaign, criticism was virtually uniformly identified with cynicism and not permitted. In this respect, critics of Make Poverty History are the embodied Other of its apparently universally inclusive 'we', who are rightfully angry about the continuing existence of global poverty and who want to see it ended, excluded in order to make the universal 'we' possible.[96]

The critic who got most publicity in Britain, because of the element of celebrity cat-fight, was Blur singer Damon Albarn, who had worked previously with musicians from Mali. He criticised the British Live 8 concert for its lack of black artists: 'If you are holding a party on behalf of people, then surely you don't shut the door on them.' The BBC reported:

> Live 8 treated Africa like it was 'a failing, ill, sick, tired place', [Albarn] said.
> 'My personal experience of Africa is that yes, I have witnessed all those things there.
> 'But it's incredibly sophisticated – the society and the structure of people's lives is as sophisticated, if not more sophisticated in some ways, than in the West.'[97]

However, once the summit was finished, and as Blair's gleeful account of Geldof versus the 'NGO bloke' indicates, trenchant criticism of Bono, Geldof and the G8 outcome came from experienced workers in the development sector. Some representatives of charitable organisations, including the World Development Movement, Christian Aid and Action Aid, however compromised they may have been themselves by their relationships with states and with elite donors, were remarkably unstinting in their attacks on the whole fiasco (though Oxfam, which had been steering Make Poverty History alongside the celebrities, was notably tepid in its auto-critique). Before the end of 2005, the London *Independent* was running a headline that read, 'Celebrities "Hijacked" Poverty Campaign, Say Furious Charities'. Dave Timms of the World Development Movement said, 'some of the real issues became overshadowed by the hype':

> There are celebrities who really didn't seem to know what they were talking about and Bob Geldof's comments after the G8 were very unhelpful, because they made people think everything had been achieved … There was some progress on debt but we have yet to see any of those pledges translated into a penny for the poorer countries and there was no progress on trade. The other problem we had was that the Labour Government managed to get into a position where they said that they were partners with the movement, when in fact there are many issues, for instance on trade deals, where we disagree strongly.[98]

It was true that much of the Make Poverty History coalition had made clear its opposition to the sort of 'free-trade' conditions of trade deals that emerged at Gleneagles. Furthermore, Richard Miller of Action Aid pointed out that, from 2005 'up to 2008 almost all of the aid increase will be Iraqi and Nigerian debt relief, most of which wasn't being serviced' anyway.[99]

It's not clear how much Bono and Geldof had themselves actually been fooled by this sort of shifty accounting, including the jumbling-up of aid and debt relief; perhaps, invested so deeply in a 'successful' summit, they had simply chosen to ignore it. Campaigners said they had already briefed the two Irishmen based on leaks from negotiators that the numbers from the summit agreement were bogus, but the celebrities chose not to say any of this in their summary statements. Certainly it should have been clear enough to them even as the summit agreement was being announced, as Blair's gleeful tale of Geldof's excoriation of a disgruntled activist makes obvious. No sooner had the celebrities endorsed the summit statement than an NGO press officer was heard to shout down his phone, 'They've shafted us!'[100] South African activist Kumi Naidoo, who chaired the global umbrella group of which Make Poverty History was a part, responded quickly and directly to Bono's assertion that 'the world spoke, and the politicians listened'. Naidoo said: 'The people have roared but the G8 has whispered.'[101]

In the regret-filled autumn of 2005, Britain's *Red Pepper* magazine featured another couple of thousand words of campaigners who seemed to curse themselves for ever having gone near Geldof and Bono. Charles Abugre of Christian Aid said: 'The campaign has been too superficial … Numbers have been more important than politics and we have placed too much emphasis on celebrities with strong connections to those in power. Consequently, a serious occasion was turned into a celebration of celebrities.' Senegalese economist Demba Moussa Dembele, of the African Forum on Alternatives, said: 'People must not be fooled by the celebrities: Africa got nothing.'

It might be more accurate to say that what little it got came at a very high price:

> [D]espite agreeing that 'poor countries should be free to determine their own economic policies', only Britain had announced [before the summit] it would no longer tie overseas aid to free market reforms – a promise it would instantly break in the G8 debt deal. The US, in contrast, had made it immediately clear at Gleneagles that aid increases would require 'reciprocal liberalisation' by developing countries. Worse, as Yifat Susskind, associate director of the US-based women's human rights organisation, Madre, explains, Bush's 'millennium challenge account', specifically praised by Bono and Geldof, 'explicitly ties aid to cooperation in the US's "war on terror"'.[102]

The deceptions and betrayals inherent in the 2005 G8 'deal' for the global poor, and for Africa in particular, are too numerous to count here. Few people now seriously claim that it achieved anything of significance – unless you count creating brief and false popular expectations of the caring role of political elites as an achievement. But the controversy surrounding it played an important role in opening up the differences between rock-star philanthropists, on the one hand, and the genuine global-justice movement, on the other. In Britain, in particular, the attacks on Geldof and Bono by popular *Guardian* columnist George Monbiot – including one headlined 'Bards of the Powerful' – sowed unprecedented discontent, at least among an engaged minority, with the dominant celebrity-humanitarian discourse:

> I have yet to read a statement by either rock star that suggests a critique of power. They appear to believe that a consensus can be achieved between the powerful and the powerless, that they can assemble a great global chorus of rich and poor to sing from the same sheet. They do not seem to understand that, while the G8 maintains its grip on the instruments of global governance, a shared anthem of peace and love is about as meaningful as the old Coca-Cola ad. [Monbiot is presumably referring to the vaguely hippy 'I'd like to teach the world to sing' advertisement of 1971.]
>
> … Bono and Geldof are … lending legitimacy to power. From the point of view of men like Bush and Blair, the deal is straightforward: we let these

hairy people share a platform with us, we make a few cost-free gestures, and in return we receive their praise and capture their fans. The sanctity of our collaborators rubs off on us.[103]

It was significant that Bono's man, DATA boss Jamie Drummond, saw fit to fight back, and slapped down the Left in the process. He wrote to the *Guardian*:

> For too long a righteous handful on the left has felt it owned development policy, helping to perpetuate mainstream indifference and holding back the scale and ambition necessary to actually achieve the enormous goals of making poverty history. Bob and Bono are doing something far more significant and strategic: making these issues massive and mainstream so power must come to the people, not the other way round.[104]

Whatever Drummond meant by that last phrase – that the people must not come to power? – it was obvious that there would now be a sort of parting of the ways, in Britain at least, between Bono and traditional global-development activists. But there was something else that Bono and his crew had presumably noticed in the course of 'making these issues massive and mainstream': Make Poverty History had sold something like 15 million wristbands. That was a lot of people who were willing to wear their hearts just below their sleeves. And there was also the burgeoning corporate support they had enjoyed in the course of their campaigning – Live 8 sponsors included 'Nestlé, accused by activists of exploiting the HIV/Aids epidemic in Africa to sell more milk substitute products to infected mothers; Rio Tinto, the world's largest mining corporation, widely condemned for its longstanding record of human rights and environmental abuses across the global South; and Britain's biggest arms manufacturer, BAE Systems'.[105] All this pointed the way to a new(ish) model for conjoining commercial consumption with pseudo-activism.

SEEING (RED): SHOPPING AS ACTIVISM

How funny it was, after Drummond's parting shot at the Left, that Bono's new project, launched in 2006, conspicuously expropriated the colour red, both exploiting it and stripping it of its traditional political meaning. Mind you, Bono's (RED)[106] was and is primarily a phenomenon of the US, where red doesn't always signify 'communist' or 'socialist' – 'red states' are the ones that vote for the right-wing Republican Party. But since (RED) was co-founded by that scion of the Kennedys, Bobby Shriver, the Republican association can only be accidental. No, we must assume (RED) is simply the colour of alarm, a global stop sign, rather than an act of political appropriation.

(RED) is nothing more or less than a brand for sale, one that is licensed to a number of corporate 'partners' – initial ones were American Express, Apple, Emporio Armani, Converse, Gap and Motorola, and many others have come and gone – so they can stick it on a product or product range, with the promise that a part of the profits will go directly to the Global Fund, for the purpose of buying HIV drugs for Africans. It is a simple enough idea, and the Global Fund, while occasionally controversial, is certainly a reputable international body outside Bono's control: it gets a large majority of its funding from governments, as well as a substantial wedge from the Bill and Melinda Gates Foundation.

Still, what (RED) raises from its corporate partners and from direct contributions to the fund through its website – less than $200 million in total after six years, as of the Global Fund's last published spreadsheet, downloaded in August 2012 – is small change in the context not only of the organisation it is funding (the (RED) money has comprised less than 0.8 per cent of the Global Fund's income since 2001), but also of the multi-billion-dollar sums being tossed around in Bono's previous lobbying work in Washington and points beyond. (It also pales in comparison to U2's latest two-year tour gross of $736,137,344.[107]) Why has Bono expended so much time and effort, for so little return, in this particular piece of branding, and what does it signify?

To begin to understand it, perhaps it is worth noting where the idea allegedly originated. As Bono recalled in 2007, when it was still acceptable to refer in public to Bill Clinton's now notorious deregulating treasury secretary, the guru of a Goldman Sachs generation, as 'the great Robert Rubin', he was the man.[108] Rubin advised him in 2004 about his exertions for Africa, 'You'll never get this issue out there unless you market it like Nike.'[109] Bono's story doesn't mention paying the great Rubin for this startling advice, and Bono presumably did not do so, though Rubin was, at the time, one of the world's priciest, and (it turns out) worst, advisers: Rubin was hired out of the White House by Citigroup to advise its top executives in 1999; when he announced his resignation in January 2009, he had been paid $126 million in cash and stocks over the decade, and Citigroup had posted losses of $65 billion.[110]

Still, once Bono and Shriver took Rubin's advice, what did marketing 'it' like Nike mean in practice? Basically, selling stuff coated with a thin layer of conscience, and perhaps a little guilt-relief, and taking some of the proceeds for AIDS in Africa. It's easy to mock (RED) and its partners for offering up such classic slogans of cause-related marketing as 'Desire and

Virtue: Together at Last', or 'Be a Good-Looking Samaritan', or 'Smart Case, Smart Cause' for a branded iPad cover. It is even easier to moralise about the ugly juxtapositions of extreme poverty and excessive consumption that lie just barely below the (RED) surface. For many people, the mere fact that someone can pay $200 for giant headphones – Beats, by Dr Dre – that not only shut out the noise of the world but also flaunt a tiny charitable dona-tion (the promo-copy for the Beats explicitly names an amount: $5) is itself an obscenity, just another symptom of a brand-mad consumerist culture in a terribly sick world. But for many other people, pricy branded products are a pretty cool fact of life, and the idea that they signify something mean-ingful to the purchaser is a given, not even especially new: even hippies argued over Levis, Lee and Wrangler; African-American schoolyards were riven in the early 1970s by a division between Pro-Keds and Converse foot-wear factions that was as highly charged as the split between supporters of Muhammad Ali and Joe Frazier.

Surely, turning that sort of market power to work for the genuine good of people is something like the sort of 'judo' that Bono is prone to talk about, leveraging the strength of an opponent to defeat … something-or-other.

Maybe, but probably not. Again, the small good achieved by (RED) comes at a high price, in principle as well as in practice. One of the many dangers that may arise when social services of various sorts are privatised is that their operation becomes more immune to scrutiny, hidden behind obscuring layers that aren't amenable to cleaning via freedom-of-informa-tion laws. As legal scholar Sarah Dadush has spelled out in great detail, (RED) is typical in this regard: words like 'transparency' and 'accountabil-ity' are thrown around in its promotional copy, but only in regard to the Global Fund, not to the operation of (RED) itself, which is a model of opacity.[111] How much money from your purchase of a (RED) product goes to the Global Fund? They don't have to tell you, though, as noted above with the Beats headphones, they sometimes do. How much money do the corporate partners pay (RED) to use the brand – money that, after all, they have to make somewhere, perhaps hidden in the price of products? They don't tell you. What are (RED)'s own salaries and overheads? Nope, sorry, that's not public information. How much money does each of the corporate partners pass on to the Global Fund? Erm, let's see – there's just a total figure, with no breakdown by company (though Apple does claim to have chipped in more than a quarter of the total[112]). How does (RED) select partners? Are there criteria in terms of, say, labour practices (hello Gap and Nike), ecological sustainability, political or charitable profile? Or just a bidding war? Yes, you guessed it: that's a secret too, though once a company is in there are guidelines and (RED) gets to vet any of a company's (RED) ad copy. The website says up to half a company's 'profits' on a particular product get donated, but who measures that, and what if a company says it didn't make a profit on its (RED) line, however much of it got purchased? They don't have to tell you any of that either, though (RED) told Dadush that its licensing agreements do stipulate a minimum dona-tion.[113] How much? Ah, that would be telling.

Legally speaking, (RED) is neither a charity nor a registered charita-ble fundraiser, but is instead the property of a limited-liability company called The Persuaders, registered in Delaware. (The small US state is the legal home to half the Fortune 500 because of its business-friendly legal, taxation and regulatory environment.) Contracts between The Persuaders and its corporate partners are entirely secret. The money the company takes in from its partners must be considerable, because Dadush could write in 2010, based on her research and a 2009 interview with its chief executive officer Susan Smith Ellis, that '[l]ittle information is available concerning Red's overhead costs, other than that the organization has an estimated staff of twenty-two and has offices in New York and London … One would assume that staff members receive competitive salaries, as a number of them came from the marketing divisions of the Partners in the private sector.'[114]

With its first CEO being Shriver himself, and his successor from 2007 being the Madison Avenue marketing hotshot Ellis, this sort of size, status and accommodation suggests an annual budget of many millions of dollars. (Those London offices are in the premises of the city's most politi-cally connected PR agency, Freud Communications, so that 'overhead' may be paid in kind rather than cash.[115]) Bono has never been remunerated for his (RED) work, it seems.

Meanwhile, the Global Fund, despite being the (largest) beneficiary of (RED) and the alleged reason for its existence, apparently has no control over it. But it's not complaining: as one analyst explains, 'Red is a mecha-nism for the Fund to outsource a significant portion of its private-sector fundraising efforts.'[116]

But if (RED) is a small 'win' for the Global Fund, it is hard to imagine it as anything other than a big one for its participating partners. It is an undisputed fact that far more money is spent by the partners in advertis-ing their (RED)-branded products than ever reaches anyone in Africa: the widely publicised 2007 analysis by *Advertising Age* magazine that estimated a $100 million (RED) marketing spend, compared to $18 million raised for the Global Fund, was never refuted in any detail by the campaign, though its huge disproportion is presumably partly a function of its reflecting the campaign's first year and the publicity needs of any start-up.[117] Given that *any* (RED) product effectively benefits from the advertising of *all* (RED) products, and from all the Bono-led generic marketing of the brand – the partners can apparently void the contracts if Bono ceases to be involved[118] – they clearly get serious bang for their buck. The fact that much of this money flows into the coffers of media companies selling their advertising space can't do any harm for the sort of press coverage (RED) gets.

For a marketing student, (RED) is probably quite exciting, a new thing, a transcendent brand that unites Apple mp3 players and Dell laptops, Converse shoes and Nike shoelaces – though never directly competing products: one thing we know about the agreements is that a company's contract with (RED) buys it exclusivity against its competitors for the agreed product. But for anyone serious about global affairs, (RED) is clearly just another example of corporate-social-responsibility whitewashing ((RED) washing?), whereby not only do particular companies get injected with the purifying Bono medicine, but transnational consumer capitalism as a whole is furnished with conspicuous evidence of its vital role in making the world a better place, at a cost of peanuts.

Among other charities there is real concern that people who have been invited to tinker with their conspicuous consumption so that it benefits poor, sick people will reckon, when invited to make a direct donation to a charitable cause, that no, actually, they don't have to, because they gave at the Gap. And Starbucks. And the Apple Store. And got a T-shirt, a mocha latte and an iPod Nano in the bargain. (Recall that Bono publicised (RED) by going on a televised shopping spree with Oprah Winfrey, who called him 'the reigning king of hope'.) And so, increasingly, the practice of giving is sucked into the cash nexus of 'philanthrocapitalism'.

Among the baldest statements of the benefits for the corporate partners, and for wealthy consumers, came from one of those nice people in the credit-card industry, where charitable partnerships are a growing practice. Laura Powers-Freeling, head of the UK consumer-card business for American Express, was interviewed by the *Guardian*, and she told how delighted she was (a 'red carpet' was mentioned, with no pun apparently intended) to meet Bono:

> Powers-Freeling says the company, more often associated with power lunches than global poverty, had an immediate meeting of minds with the singer. 'It was an interesting moment for us because one of the things we at American Express have been observing for a while is this trend towards what we now call the conscience consumer. The people saying, "I have to spend money anyway, so if there's a way of using the power of my purse for good, great, but I don't want to give up anything to do so." '[119]

Needless to say, she had an absurdly precise number for Britain's 'conscience consumers', whose conscience extends to not giving anything up: 1.5 million, 'expected to swell to 3.9 million within three years'. And Powers-Freeling told journalist Jane Martinson that she saw the Amex (RED) card as a means of growing her company's business beyond the business-lunch market into that growing conscientious space:

> To reach these people, Amex has decided to change the way it markets itself for its new scarlet-hued card. Although it has spent money on advertising in papers such as this one [the *Guardian*], it has eschewed more traditional means of launching new cards through direct mail and television advertising. Instead, it has used the association with rock stars and charities to spread the word, be it through the internet and blogs, or via other 'viral' marketing.
>
> The involvement of U2's lead singer is a key part of the company's aim to be 'cool and sexy', terms not normally associated with a piece of plastic. More than a month after the launch of RED at the World Economic Forum's annual meeting in Davos, the head of Amex UK is still singing the rock star's praises. 'Bono said this beautiful thing in Davos. He said that this card – he was holding it up – is not about what you have, it's about who you are.'[120]

Researcher Nathan Farrell has written that Bono and (RED) are 'part of a network of business interests … ideologically driven by a belief that market methods can provide solutions to problems such as the African AIDS epidemic'.[121] This perhaps gives the 'network', summed up by that beautiful Bono moment at Davos, an unwarranted benefit of the doubt, in ascribing a genuine 'belief' to them collectively, rather than the sort of unbridled cynicism displayed above by Powers-Freeling, whom Farrell quotes. Nonetheless, Farrell argues powerfully and persuasively that 'the (RED) campaign has sought to construct AIDS in a manner consistent with the ideological views with which it is underpinned' – that is, as a problem to be solved by the depoliticised application of Western cash.[122] Its mission is presented as a simple and unproblematic moral imperative to assist an undifferentiated continent, while research suggests its shoppers have only the vaguest idea of the 'good cause' they're supporting.[123]

In addition, as a corporate marketing campaign, (RED) must generally avoid being the bearer of bad news. Thus, in 2012, its website (joinred. com) highlighted the decline in the number of babies born HIV-positive – 'Fighting for an AIDS-free generation', those innocents beloved of the

Christian Right – but not the continuing increase in the number of people who have been diagnosed with the disease.

As Lisa Ann Ponte and Stefano Richey point out, (RED) markets itself not with the usual images of passive African sufferers – though it might be argued that they are implied, being so embedded in Western consciousness – but by avoiding them in favour of sexy Western consumers. Occasionally, a happy African appears, as in the famous Amex (RED)-card advertisement in which supermodel Gisele Bundchen reaches behind her to sort-of embrace (without looking at him) Masai warrior Keseme Ole Parsapaet; more often Africa is sexily suggested, a streak of face paint on Gwyneth Paltrow's white cheek. Bono himself, fashionable, brand-conscious, is part of the visual project:

> AIDS provides the quintessential cause as the outlet for RED's hard commerce approach to doing good, because – like fashion, rock music, or celebrity – it is about money, power and sex.
>
> While modern philanthropists have morphed into postmodern consumers, the stationary supporting cast is dragged back onto the development stage to justify this newest version of assistance, the 'rock man's burden' …
>
> … RED takes a new twist in which sexuality is being reclaimed by the West as healthy. Bono provides the healthy and sexy body to contrast with the 'African woman dying from sex' body. In the role of the totemic celebrity, he redeems sex, while reclaiming masculinity, and restoring a social hierarchy where cool, rich, white men save poor, voiceless African women and children. All of this is managed within a discourse of concern, care and ethics … The complex scripts of race, gender and global economic inequality are ignored with justifications that 'AIDS is an emergency' and thus normal rules do not apply. At the same time the 'normality' of consumption, and the social and environmental relations of trade and production that underpin poverty, inequality and disease, are not questioned.[124]

Another devastating critique appeared in medical journal the *Lancet*. The authors note that the (RED) website features an 'impact calculator' to measure how your purchase helps in Africa. (This is, by the way, the nearest (RED) gets to transparency about how much money gets through from any given purchase.) But they wonder where you'll find a deeper analysis of the role of global capitalism and its built-in inequalities:

> There is no impact calculator tabulating the relational injustice of the economic institutions that privilege some (largely middle and upper class, and in developed countries) consumers able to buy (RED) while increasing

risk and vulnerability to HIV and other diseases among those unable to afford even life's necessities. The implacable logic of this injustice is hidden in high-gloss advertisements in which looking good (fashion), making good (profit), and doing good (charity) become a feelgood endorsement of an unhealthy status quo. The seemingly just consumer supplants the just citizen and social justice itself is commodified.[125]

These authors conclude that we should 'be wary of the 21st century's new *noblesse oblige* that replaces the efficiency of tax-funded programmes and transfers in improving health equity with a consumption-driven "charitainment" model whose appearances can be as deceptive as they are appealing'. In a later follow-up retort to their critics, who defended (RED) on the strength of the funds and the awareness it raises, the *Lancet* authors add that, in the world of (RED), commodities 'seem disconnected from those who have produced them, and the resources on which their production is based. The HIV/AIDS pandemic, in turn, is disconnected from its historical and contemporary roots in the global economy and posited as a technical or medical problem for which there is a simple solution.'[126] That is to say, instead of asking what global social and economic structures ensure that such a deadly pandemic overwhelmingly affects poor and marginalised people, we simply rely on the same structures to fix it.

Since the money made by (RED) is so trivial in the greater scheme of things, and even in the budgetary arithmetic of the fund it supports, you could be forgiven for concluding that it exists precisely to send out this message – of a rootless crisis solvable firmly within the logic of commodity capitalism.

It might be objected that Bono's world-view isn't always limited to the peculiarly simplistic and paternalistic discourse of 'consumption for a cause' that arises, perhaps intrinsically, from a consumer marketing campaign such as (RED), crucial though his role has been in that campaign. We know, after all, that he is capable of speaking the language of 'justice, not charity', and of at least appearing to analyse the Western-led practices and relations that 'underpin poverty, inequality and disease' in Africa. So what did he do to disseminate a deeper set of ideas when he took over as editor at various major international publications?

EDITORIAL CONTROL: PRINTING THE MYTH

'I have no embarrassment at all. No shame.' Bono said so himself, disarmingly, in the 16 May 2006 edition of the London *Independent*, which he was credited with editing. He said it apropos of nothing much, in the course of an interview with comedian Eddie Izzard.[127] Nonetheless, it sums up as well as anything else could his capacity to take an opportunity like this and sink it in the mire of 'brand awareness' for (RED), rather than using it as a vehicle for developing a higher and deeper consciousness of global development issues.

The *Independent* should have been the perfect vehicle for the latter approach. Then still a part of Irish mogul Tony O'Reilly's Independent News and Media group, the most powerful chain of newspapers in Ireland, the English 'Indie' had a modest circulation among mostly left-liberal readers; and though its editor Simon Kellner had dragged it slightly downmarket, it still had a name for sharp and sophisticated reporting and analysis, not least through its two great writers on the Middle East, Robert Fisk and Patrick Cockburn. Its tabloid shape was used as a means of presenting strong pictures and graphics rather than as an excuse for dumbing-down. Its front page was generally used as a sort of poster for a story or stories inside, and didn't contain much text.

Bono-as-editor's front page was a strong one, though why he needed the fashionable artist Damien Hirst to come in and design this simple twist on the idea of a newspaper is unknown: it was soaked in red – or should that be (RED)? – and cried out in large letters, 'NO NEWS TODAY', with an asterisk to guide the eye to the small print at the bottom of the page: 'Just 6,500 Africans died today as a result of a preventable, treatable disease. (HIV/AIDS)'.

No mistake, this was a powerful message. In a world of death tolls, where fewer than half that number of fatalities in New York and Washington on 9/11 became the dominant fact of global affairs for several years thereafter, it is worth noting not only that thousands more people die each day, every day, of AIDS, but that in the eyes of the Western media this apparently does not constitute a story. Yet at the same time it must be admitted that it is the sort of impersonal statistic that makes readers glaze over; and in keeping with the (RED) message it both limits and overgeneralises the AIDS story to be about 'Africans', when in half the continent's countries it is not a huge problem, and when those dying are first and foremost individual people, not the inhabitants of a particular landmass.

Still, if Bono had stopped right there it would have been a good day's work. Indeed, given that millions more people glimpsed this front page than actually bought and read the paper, it might be said that, having produced a strong consciousness-raising cover, he achieved much of what he set out to achieve.

But there was another phrase on that front page: 'Genesis 1:27'. The text for that biblical verse does not appear, but it is easy even in this secular age to locate it: 'God created man in his own image, in the image of God he created him; male and female he created them.' It's a funny message to throw, unannotated, into the sea of unbelief that are the British public and, especially, the *Independent* readership. For most of them, the key argument for caring about the fate of unknown 'Africans' is not that they are images of God, but that they are human beings like ourselves. The idea of using this verse is dissonant not only because it attempts to smuggle faith into the discourse of a country where it is largely irrelevant, but because it brings to the fore a paternalistic relation, between an entity that creates and the 'them' who are his handiwork.

So who was God in this context? Well, given that journalists are likelier than most workers to characterise their boss, the editor, as 'God' – the most high, all seeing, all knowing, the final judge – then it's not much of a stretch – or perhaps it is! – to suggest that Bono, the creator of this day's newspaper, is at least auditioning for the role.

Certainly this edition of the *Independent*, largely given over to Africa and AIDS, created an image of a continent in dire need of an outside Saviour. On page after page, in stories, photographs and advertisements, Africans were presented as pathetic victims, often children: the pathos is laid on much thicker than would be acceptable in (RED)'s own upbeat promotional copy of celebrities, products and AIDS-free babies. Shockingly, from the front to the back of the paper, no Africans write about Africa. Only one is presented in an interview as having any agency at all: Nigerian finance minister Ngozi Okonjo-Iweala. Bono would not always be so neglectful of African voices in his work, but after the debate with Damon Albarn about Live 8 just ten months before, one would have expected a better showing, even if only for the sake of appearances for his sceptical British public, than this paternalistic presentation.

While there is some talk in Bono's *Independent* about Africa's need for fairer trade, there is nothing in the edition about the destruction wrought in Africa by the arms trade, though perhaps this is not surprising after BAE's kind sponsorship of Live 8 and the presence in many of the paper's advertising and editorial columns of (RED) partner Motorola, which in addition to its more familiar mobile phone line is also a military contractor, supplying high-tech communication systems. Nor is there any coverage of mineral exploitation in Africa – perhaps something else Motorola and Apple might be sensitive about, given the importance of central African coltan in manufacturing the electronic capacitors that are so vital in mobile-phone technology and other electronic devices.

Another missing story is the one that was convulsing Dublin on the day the paper appeared: forty-one Afghan men were on hunger- and thirst-strike inside historic, and touristic, St Patrick's Cathedral to prevent their deportation to the dangers of their home country. A photo of them had dominated the front page of the previous day's *Irish Times*. Since this story clearly involved the West's role in the suffering of people from the poorer world, and also involved poor people taking their own, desperate measures to defy a Western government's prescriptions, it obviously failed to fit Bono's world-view.

Bono himself was more than a figurehead as a reader flipped through the pages of his newspaper. He was present, conducting interviews, writing editorials – defending himself, undoubtedly, against the widespread criticism there had been on the British Left about the Make Poverty History fiasco (including in the *Independent*'s own 'hijacked by celebrities' story five months earlier). In his editorial, poignantly headlined 'I Am a Witness. What Can I Do?', he wrote (in prose that is both beyond parody and a stupidly ironic twist on a famous Yeats poem in which a poor man declares his love for a woman):

> I truly try to tread carefully as I walk over the dreams of dignity under my feet in our work for the terrible beauty that is the continent of Africa. I'm used to the custard pies. I've even learnt to like the taste of them. But before you are tempted to let fly with your understandable invective, allow me to contextualise.

He defends (RED)'s meet-you-at-the-shops strategy – 'as you lead your busy, businessy lives' – and again stands up to Left critics:

> On the far left, we will meet 'better dead than RED', a reaction to big business that is not wholly unjustified. But given the emergency that is Aids, I don't see this as selling out. I see this as ganging up on the problem. This emergency demands a radical centre, as well as a radical edge. Creeping up on the everyday. Making the difficult easy.

Then the punch-line: 'For anyone who thinks this means I'm going to retire to the boardroom and stop banging my fist on the door of No. 10 [Downing Street], I'm sorry to disappoint you.'[128]

The astonishing suggestion of fist-banging at his friend Tony's place, where the butler had surely glidingly admitted him without waiting for a knock, for meetings like the one with top G8 officials the previous July, is belied elsewhere in the paper, in his skin-crawlingly obsequious interview with Blair and Gordon Brown, his John and Paul. The most newsworthy aspect of this article was that he apparently got the two men, sworn enemies by this time, to share the same conference call.

Bono's hard-hitting line of questioning to Brown included: 'Chancellor, I've just got back from a trip to Washington, where your announcement of $15bn over 10 years for education for the poorest of the poor created a real reverberation. Are you worried that some of your other G8 partners and finance ministers are not coming up with new initiatives to match this?' Bono is still reverberating a few lines down when he turns to Blair: 'Prime Minister, I want to just take you to a more personal place in your trips to this terrible beauty that we call Africa now – to an inspiring moment, a person you have met, or a moment of despair.'[129] (They're all interchangeable, these African people and moments.)

The obsession with justifying Live 8 and Bono's premature declaration of victory, in partnership with Blair, turns up again in the newspaper's centre-spread, which is given over to a play-it-yourself board game called 'Gleneagles Crazy Golf', subtitled 'Will the G8 keep their word?' Sadly, the biggest move available in the game is 'Move Forward 3: *Independent* goes RED'.

Whether or not Bono's longstanding two-step with the British government could compensate him for the fact that so much of the British public steadfastly refused to dance with him, Bono could not resist taking part of his (RED) *Independent* across the Atlantic, where he was and is loved more unambivalently. So we've got Condoleezza Rice getting an entire article to name her 'ten best musical works'. Condi, it seems, is a 'big fan' of Bono and named 'anything' by U2 as number seven on her list, just ahead of Elton John's 'Rocket Man'. Cream's 'Sunshine of Your Love' is at number two (after Mozart): 'I love to work out to this song. Believe it or not I loved acid rock in college – and I still do.'

The *Independent* supplement features another hard-hitting interview, and a further hint of what was to come the following year when Bono got his hands on *Vanity Fair*. 'She's the bright young star breaking all the rules. He's the grand master whose influence on the way we dress is felt around the world. In a rare interview, STELLA McCARTNEY asks Giorgio Armani about fur, fashion and film – and why RED is his new favourite colour.'

The *Independent*'s associate editor, Paul Vallely, is a journalist who has done decent work reporting from Africa, worked for big development agencies, co-authored Blair's Commission for Africa report and various official Live 8 paraphernalia, and also happened to ghost-write two Bob Geldof books. (His assessments of Africa policy are presented regularly in the *Independent* without any of these biographical facts being noted. He is also a sort of moral philosopher who has, for example, sought to justify the prison at Guantánamo.) So his feature in Bono's *Independent* – 'Can rock stars change the world?' – was always going to end up with a soul-searching Yes. 'Oh all right then. But with a little help from their friends. Which includes all of us – fans, activists, politicians and now – as Project RED so clearly demonstrates – shoppers too.'[130]

BBC radio DJ Zane Lowe sang loudest from Bono's (RED) hymn sheet:

> The only thing people who are trying to make a difference can do is work alongside corporations. We're not going to abolish big business, people aren't going to stop drinking Starbucks and buying Nike, but you can say to them, 'There's a big difference you can make and if we find a way to make it easier for you, would you contribute?'[131]

The only thing, indeed. Two more signed opinion pieces, by Geldof and Niall Fitzgerald (chairman of Reuters, former chairman of Unilever), both advocate more or less neoliberal solutions to Africa's crisis, focusing on trade and investment. Geldof, like Bono in the Blair/Brown interview, does criticise in a few lines 'enforced liberalisation by the IMF, the World Bank or the EU'[13.2] – but frankly, if you blinked you'd miss such trenchant politics in the sea of (RED).

Bono's edition of the American style magazine *Vanity Fair*, a year later, is the same, only different: glitzier, more Hollywood, and very definitely more black. This time the brand is not simply (RED), it is, in huge capital letters, AFRICA. Africans and Africa, nonetheless, are objects rather than subjects: here's Bill Clinton on Nelson Mandela, Brad Pitt interviewing Desmond Tutu. The cover this time is a space for excess: twenty different covers, all shot by snapper-to-the-stars Annie Leibovitz, all used to display Bono's star-studded cast through a sort of celibate twist on *La Ronde*: a celebrity is shown speaking to another celebrity, then the latter appears on the next cover talking to yet another one. They're spreading the message about something, presumably the terrible beauty that is Africa; no one openly suggests it's a metaphor for the spread of AIDS, not when it's 'H.M. Queen Rania of Jordan' to Bono to Condi to Bush to Tutu to Brad Pitt, or Warren Buffett to Oprah to George Clooney.[133]

Notable among the cover stars, for a magazine that was planned for months before its July 2007 publication date, was Senator Barack Obama, with whom Bono was striking up yet another beautiful friendship (see Chapter 3). It is interesting, though, that inside the magazine, where Bono interviewed the whole crop of presidential candidates from both parties to get their views on Africa – although the replies read exactly like emailed statements – the one who most conspicuously kissed the Irishman's arse, saying he was going to make Bono's ONE campaign a key part of his own presidential run, was not Obama but the Southern Baptist preacher and former Arkansas governor Mike Huckabee.[134] Bono remained an attractive figure for much of the evangelical Right, and incidentally had his bases covered in the event of further political success for that wing of the Republican Party.

Although (RED) had already been widely criticised by this time, Bono's outing as editor for Africa received fawning coverage in other media, not least the *New York Times*, where Bono was presented as a rare missionary to the 'idle rich', who it seemed might otherwise have been unfamiliar with charitable causes such as African disease and poverty.[135] Not everyone was so impressed, however: the photographic image of Bono and regular *Vanity Fair* editor Graydon Carter discussing their Africa issue against the backdrop of the Manhattan skyline incensed at least one Nigerian woman, cited as typical by the two South African scholars who quoted her:

'Look', her finger wags wildly, as she did what the Nigerians refer to as the 'yabis', mock jabbing, and rap crying furiously … 'A-f-r-i-c-a?' she pauses, aghast. 'Look at this!' she points mockingly. 'What do you see? … What do you expect? Two white men. Two middle-aged white men at the helm of it. Where are the Africans?'[136]

Those scholars, Natasha Himmelman and Danai Mupotsa, write of 'wanting to love' this issue of *Vanity Fair* because it did, after all, feature some great African writers and artists, but finding it ultimately 'self congratulatory' and oblivious to its alleged subject, not least because neither it nor (RED) seemed to be marketed in Africa.[137]

Sociologist Zine Magubane, noting how Bono regularly deploys his Irishness as a signal of his understanding of colonialism, conflict, famine and development, says that even as his *Vanity Fair* chose to give strong emphasis to humanity's common ancestry in Africa hundreds of thousands of years ago, it denied equality to contemporary Africans:

[W]hile it appears to be bringing Africa up to the level of the West, indeed making Africa responsible for the genesis of the West, the ultimate effect of the discourse is a complete denial of coevalness. There is no possibility for communicative interaction because the salient parties – the 'small group of hungry Africans' [the original humans] have all died millennia ago. Their present day 'cousins' are atavistic throwbacks, awaiting the arrival of a Western savior … Africa's contribution came millennia ago in the form of a genetic gift given to the peoples and cultures that are destined to sail forth and make history. People living on the Continent today, must simply sit and wait, with the hope that someone will take pity on them and write them into history.[138]

The critique of Bono's *Vanity Fair* was largely confined to academic and blogging circles. By 2010, when Bono and Geldof 'edited' a special section of the *Toronto Globe and Mail*, it was striking how strongly that sort of critique had embedded itself among a larger community of readers. The two celebrities had sharpened up their act to the extent that they hired an actual Kenyan blogger, Ory Okolloh, to handle the online edition. Bono's big contribution was a deeply banal Barack Obama 'interview' (email again looked the likely medium for the paragraphs of familiar boilerplate, probably authored by an Obama speechwriter, though the introduction highlighted the men's meeting). Despite such efforts at relevance and respect for its subjects, before the edition had even appeared a local Canadian blog reported: 'Comments on the *Globe*'s post asking readers to send questions in to the stars have already been disabled because "an overwhelming number of readers were making offensive statements about other commenters and/or the individual or individuals mentioned in the story".'[139]

MORE BAGGAGE: SETTING THE AGENDA

There is no need to paint Bono as somehow awful in unique ways. Just as there are ways of interpreting his thoughts on our common African ancestors in ways that are different from – and more benign than – Magubane's analysis given above, representing them as something resembling racism, there is also room for honest differences about what really constitutes the best set of policies to promote African development and overcome the serious obstacles to it. Bono does, after all, regularly harness 'expert opinion', basing many of his arguments less on sentiment than on technocratic confidence that there is a way beyond political nostrums and polemical stances to sort out these problems. He is not necessarily either a fool or a knave, though at times he has seemed to deserve both labels.

But – fool, knave or neither – Bono has found himself so deeply invested in the nostrums of a Western elite conception of African development that he has been prepared to shout down an African to protect it. This example of his devotion to such a party line came in the summer of 2007. The occasion was a prestigious TED conference in Arusha, Tanzania, full of visiting Silicon Valley types, and the speaker was Ugandan journalist Andrew Mwenda, who had only recently been jailed, briefly, by his government. Mwenda was laying out his African perspective on the catastrophic failure of Western aid – it has made things worse, he said – and on the special problems created when development agencies work with African governments. Bono piped up from the floor, 'Bollocks!' And for the benefit of those present who had grown up removed from a British colonial vocabulary – at least one American blogger reported that he mentioned 'bullocks' – he added: 'That's bullshit.'[140]

When Mwenda invited the audience to name a country where international aid had led to development, Bono reportedly stuck up his hand and cited Ireland during the Famine[141] – which, if he really said it, would be taking postcolonial revisionism-in-the-name-of-reconciliation to brave new heights. The reports of his intervention are sketchy, so, to give Bono the benefit of the doubt: perhaps he was referring to the widespread historical view that the British government of 1845–46, led by Robert Peel, was more active in bringing famine relief to Ireland than its successor, which under John Russell took the view that the markets and nature should be allowed to take their course – a course that was catastrophic for the Irish people. This wouldn't have amounted to a case for international aid having promoted Irish development – especially since the British were actually governing Ireland at the time – but it would make some sense as a critique of free-market attitudes to relief.

Whatever rubbish Bono may or may not have spouted about Ireland – let's face it, deploying Irish history rhetorically is a reflex for him – it can be plausibly stated that in this Tanzanian TED debate, where he stood up for aid, debt relief and good governments against a view that development would only come from private investment, Bono was taking something like a leftish posture. He certainly thought so himself, calling Mwenda an African Margaret Thatcher.[142] Whether or not this was a fair characterisation of Mwenda, Africa is as entitled as anywhere else to its own Thatchers – and the failure of its own states and the Western multilateral institutions that have claimed to embrace the continent's interests might well lead some Africans to a rejection of states in favour of markets as a means to genuine development. But you don't have to think Bono was wrong, or even right but self-serving, in this argument to recognise that this was boorish behaviour. What kind of 'bollocks' does it take for a white European – a man with ready access to all the world's media and a speaking slot of his own still to come at the conference – to visit Africa and heckle any African speaker, let alone one as obviously qualified to speak as Mwenda? More important than the arrogance on display is the obvious strength of his personal commitment to the idea that Western aid is vital to Africa – hardly surprising, given that he is for many people the very embodiment of that idea. It was important enough to him that he risked embarrassment in the elite circles where this event was being discussed and blogged in order to make his point, loudly.

Did Bono do his sums and calculate that, on balance, Africa owes him? That is one explanation for an act that was more grotesque than his Arusha heckling. Late in the summer of 2010, Louis Vuitton released an advertisement for a limited-edition, monogrammed range of luggage, the Keepall 45, costing about $1,000 a piece. The ad shows Bono and his wife Ali Hewson striding across African grasslands carrying the bags, looking like they have just stepped off a tiny old-style propeller plane behind them. 'Every journey begins in Africa' says the ad's tagline, lest we be in any doubt which continent was signified by the presence of Bono.

The couple looks quietly glamorous – Ali shows a tiny shadow of cleavage – but deadly serious. This doesn't look like somewhere they've gone on vacation: there's nothing to be seen but grass, low mountains and sky. Surely we are being invited to imagine that a refugee camp or an orphanage, like the one they worked in all those years ago, is lurking just out of the shot, with children ready to be saved by the couple's amazing grace.

The only possible saving grace of the image itself is its obvious fakeness. It's been softened and coloured like nothing natural, giving it a retro look. A video available online of the photo-shoot – with Annie Leibovitz, natch – underlines the artifice, showing the plane being rolled in, its visible wheel sprayed to look muddy, while Bono and Ali roll up in a four-wheel drive to mwah-mwah with their favourite photographer.[143]

But nothing can save Bono from the plain and revolting fact that he used Africa as a prop for commercial purposes; that he directly exploited all that is known or believed about his relationship to that place and its people in order to help a multi-billion-dollar company sell expensive handbags. This was of course merely a variation of the (RED) shopping spree with Oprah, in which he did something rather similar; but the fact that this time the image is 'on location', somewhere on the Dark Continent, gives it a stench that makes his previous efforts seem positively perfumed.

The fact that he did this for Louis Vuitton lends added irony. As anyone interested in issues like African suffering and artistic freedom might have been expected to know, Vuitton's lawyers had since 2008 been suing a Danish artist, Nadia Plesner, who painted an image of a hungry-looking African child holding a recognisably Vuitton bag, the stark juxtaposition being part of her efforts to raise consciousness about Darfur. Vuitton was seeking to hit her for hundreds of thousands of euros for violating its intellectual-property rights, embodied in the logo on the bag, though happily, in May 2011 (many months after Bono posed for Vuitton), a court in the Hague lifted the injunction against Plesner showing her work, *Darfurnica*, and it appears the bad publicity convinced Vuitton to let the matter lie there.[144] There's also another reason that Louis Vuitton was not entirely unknown in Africa: in 2001 its parent company, LVMH, had entered into a retail partnership with that longstanding paragon of ethical employment and environmental practice on the continent, the De Beers diamond company.[145]

But the advertisement with Bono and Ali was more than simply another celebrity endorsement for Vuitton's vaguely humanistic Core Values campaign, to place alongside those from a motley assortment including Michael Phelps, Catherine Deneuve, Mikhail Gorbachev, Sean Connery, Francis Ford and Sofia Coppola, Andre Agassi and Steffi Graf.[146] Nor was it anything so simple as Bono cashing in on his association with Africa. No, it was the cementing of what the couple were bound to see, given their corporate position, as an important corporate relationship. Indeed, the image can be read, like a Renaissance painting fast-forwarded into the age of brands, for its commercial iconography: the ring means this, the bag means that, the direction of their eyes suggests the other thing: it's a veritable twenty-first-century version of the 'Arnolfini wedding' – Van Eyck's great, densely symbolic portrait of a couple taking their place in the world.

There is of course one crucial difference between the Van Eyck painting and the Leibovitz photograph: the decoding of the latter cannot be left as the preserve of an elite group of cognoscenti. For commercial reasons, its layers of meaning must be immediately unpacked for as many potential consumers as possible. Thus, no sooner had the advertisement appeared than Britain's *Daily Mail* was fed the necessary information, in order to exult in its synergies:

> [U]nlike other images in the Core Values series of advertisements … the pair are not wearing clothes made by Louis Vuitton. Instead, they are wearing Hewson's own organic and ethical label Edun, which she created in 2005 and aims to encourage trade in Africa. In fact it is the latest evidence of a love affair between the two brands – last year Louis Vuitton's parent company LVMH acquired a 49 per cent stake in Edun. And now they have joined forces to create a limited-edition version of Louis Vuitton's monogrammed Keepall 45 – carried by both Bono and Hewson in the new image. Each bag boasts a hand crafted charm created in Kenya for fairtrade jewellery label MADE, as well as a plaque with the inscription 'Every journey began in Africa.'[147]

The following day's New York *Daily News* website – perhaps having been deprived of the 'scoop' – was a tad more cynical about this corporate 'love affair' rendered in photographic flesh, headlining its report: 'Ad nauseum: How many messages can Bono, designer wife Ali Hewson and Louis Vuitton fit in one ad?'[148] (Both newspapers managed to get fairly important things wrong: Edun makes no promises about 'organic', despite what the *Mail* said, and Hewson is ostensibly the boss but is not the designer at Edun, despite what the *News* headline stated.)

It is, in any case, a funny twenty-first-century sort of love that consists of a massive multinational luxury-goods company (LVMH stands, dripping in excess, for Louis Vuitton Moët Hennessy) flaunting a few of the products of a company that had effectively become its near-subsidiary in exchange for a relatively rare and treasured celebrity endorsement. In the real world of the Hewson marriage, Bono and Ali had their own complex nexus of corporate entanglements, and teaming up to promote Edun and its new 'partner' was an essential step in trying to make them pay their way.

ANOTHER EDUN: ETHICAL BUSINESS

Ali Hewson, it should be said, is the object of remarkably little resentment and begrudgery in Ireland. On the contrary, she is liked for her 'ordinariness' – ordinary, that is, apart from her beauty, which isn't her fault, after all. She is even on the receiving end of popular sympathy for being, as Dubliners might put it, 'stuck with yer man'. One hugely and typically sympathetic – nay, gushing – Irish newspaper profile contrasted him tearing around town in a Maserati with her collecting the children from school in an old Volkswagen Golf.[149]

However, insofar as her business ventures are an extension of the Bono world-view, and a way of putting that world-view into action, then they are fair game for anyone seriously considering his place in contemporary global affairs. Moreover, Bono serves on the board of Ali's Edun, and it was one of the interests by which he introduced himself in his *Vanity Fair* editorial: 'the missus's clothing line that wants to inject some dignity through doing business with the continent where every street corner boasts an entrepreneur'.[150] (The rhetorical equation between Western capitalists and African street-traders is just another case of Bono chip-chipping away at his ideological work.)

Ali Hewson herself has connected Edun directly to her husband's activities: 'Bono was working on a macro level with governments and debt cancellation. We wanted to see how the policies translate to factories and the ordinary worker and their daily lives. It's such an incredible continent, so sexy and bright, and they want the jobs.'[151] Even her strange and troubling capacity to find an entire continent 'sexy' is an echo of Bono's own racially freighted words on a previous occasion to the same effect.[152]

If the success of Edun was meant to offer some index of 'how the policies translate', the answer thus far is 'not so well'. In an interview in 2011, six years after the company's foundation, Hewson noted that Edun is not a charity but a for-profit company: 'Only right now ... there are no profits, just to let you know – but it's a proper business.'[153] In August 2012 the online store at edun.com was full of garments at slashed prices that were still out of the reach of the vast majority of people.

But the problems with Edun go beyond mere business shortcomings. To begin to unravel them means starting not in Africa but in Ireland, where company accounts give some useful background on this particular investment vehicle (and help explain the screwy spelling of 'Edun'). They also reveal that Edun's partnership with Louis Vuitton is nothing unusual: in spite of the colossal piles of money he sits on, Bono rarely goes it alone when it comes to business. As we saw in Chapter 1, he partnered with sometimes-controversial property developers and financiers, but this was arguably to be expected when he was trying to run and expand a hotel. What is more surprising is to see the same pattern, with one of the same characters, in Ali Hewson's ethical start-ups.

Indeed, for whatever reason, Ali Hewson and The Edge emerged as the two shareholders in the musically named Lorijudd Ltd, through which Bono and The Edge had invested in the Clarence Hotel.[154] And, lo and behold, property developer Paddy McKillen, a partner at the Clarence, returned the compliment by taking a one-third stake in Nude Brands Ltd,[155] the London-based ethical, natural skincare company for which Ali was described as 'investor and muse'.[156] Bono also had a one-third stake in Nude, though he had stepped down as a director by 2010.

Although Ali and her Nude company had a famous legal clash with Stella McCartney over the use of the word 'nude', there was apparently no fighting over it in the Hewson family: Bono's brother Norman Hewson had been using the name Nude for many years for his struggling chain of healthy fast-food joints, which finally went to the wall in 2010. Norman was a shareholder in Ali's fashion company Edun (Nude backwards, you see) for its first few chaotic years, but had passed his share to Bono in time for the Louis Vuitton partnership.[157]

Fashion designer Stella McCartney, meanwhile, had backed (RED) on its launch, but the legal battle between Nude Brands Ltd and Stella McCartney Ltd (and its partners Yves St Laurent and L'Oreal) saw celebrity bloodletting on the old red carpet. To read the rather stylishly written judgment of the British High Court after Nude sought an injunction against the 2009 launch of 'Stellanude' perfume is to get a little education in the reality of 'ethical business'. The judge, Mr Justice Floyd, at times seems almost contemptuous of both sides: McCartney's company had actually approached Nude in 2008 seeking their agreement for the use of what might seem like a generic word, but after the initial refusal it seems some of the communication got garbled and Hewson's small company found itself, at the last minute, fighting in the High Court to block a multi-million-pound product launch.

McCartney's lawyers pointed out that Nude didn't even make perfume, so they were in no danger of confusion with a competing product. Nude countered that plans were afoot to market one, but the judge wrote sardonically: 'The evidence establishes that this is anything but imminent ...' (As of December 2012 there was still no fragrance from Nude.) Nude said that McCartney's relatively low-end perfume would damage its reputation among the upmarket customers for its pricy skincare products. The judge noted that Nude had already licensed its name to a Dior make-up range: 'The Dior licence shows that NBL are not able or concerned to protect the exclusive repute of the brand or prevent dilution. There are no quality control provisions in it.' The Dior stuff even contained (whisper it, your lordship) 'numerous synthetic ingredients'. Not that the judge was entirely convinced by Nude's own communion with Nature: 'Their products are marketed as being free of synthetic ingredients, although this is not always so as they include synthetic preservatives.'[158]

The judgment refusing the request for an injunction must have come as a harsh blow, and might have been regarded by Ali and Bono – in the same year as the big Irish tax controversy – as another exception to the maxim that all publicity is good publicity. Help, as always, was at hand. Some sixteen months after this humiliating legal encounter, in February 2011, the luxurious lads at LVMH were on hand again, this time to buy a 70 per cent controlling stake in Nude.[159] Ali Hewson and her original partner in the business, Irish businessman Bryan Meehan, remained the faces of the brand, but now it really was no more than a piece of a particularly gooey corporate pie.

Still, Nude was merely supposed to be vaguely ethical – selling Nature, not global development, though confusion would be understandable. Its mirror-cousin Edun, by contrast, was meant to typify a transformative new investment and production relationship with Africa. Things went very wrong very fast for Edun, and by 2009, plagued with what was described in the press as problems in the supply chain and quality control, Edun apparel was being sold in only sixty-seven stores worldwide, down from hundreds soon after the company's launch just a few years earlier.[160] That's where the experienced back-scratchers at LVMH stepped in, picking up 49 per cent of the company for €6 million, and, as noted above, picking up serious celebrity-endorsement power at the same time. LVMH also added its own pair of directors to the Edun board, including the boss himself, Mark Weber.[161] Edun remained, nonetheless, a substantial loss-maker: $8.7 million in the red in 2009 alone, then another $10.2 million in 2010, bringing accumulated losses to more than $38 million.[162] The 2011 losses were in a similar range, with the end-of-year accounts stating that the company was financed by shareholder loans totalling €28.8 million, up by nearly €10 million from 2010.[163]

Sure, LVMH had a plan, including a new designer. The only trouble was, part of the recovery plan for the beleaguered Edun was to produce more clothes, most of them in China, a few in Peru – out of Africa, anyway.

China? The world's press could scarcely believe it. Ali conducted apologetic interviews:

> 'I know, but their capability …' Hewson trails off, before recounting the conversation they had with LVMH CEO Mark Weber during negotiations. 'His thing was that if you're a business, you're going to have to be competitive and you have to be able to provide for demand. And deliver on time! Which was an issue before', she admits.[164]

You live and learn. Of course the beauty of being in ethical business to save Africa is that it doesn't really matter what happens anywhere else in the world: the press is remarkably uncurious about, say, labour conditions in the company's Chinese suppliers; merely breathing the word 'Africa' offers remarkable licence to do almost anything, anywhere, including trading on the continent's reputation to market products that don't actually provide jobs there. Hewson has insisted, just about plausibly, that Edun didn't really reduce production in Africa, but just added capacity elsewhere, and that by 2013 fully 40 per cent of Edun's business would be in Africa. At the time of writing, this very much remains to be seen. Edun does genuinely have, as it crows, a range of T-shirts already being entirely produced there.[165]

But enough about the struggling business and its various locations. What about the aesthetic? Very African indeed. As Ali Hewson explained, Edun's trendy Irish-born, Paris-based designer, Sharon Wauchob, worked in colours that 'are very influenced by the dusty kind of landscapes there' – there being, you know, 'Africa'. 'Even the way some of the clothes look like they've been worn before and sort of restitched. That's part of her way of thinking … to incorporate the continent, in a sense. She's very influenced by what's going on in Africa, but she also wants to keep it modern.'[166]

If you don't think there's already enough imperial contempt residing in the very idea of a European company and designer producing expensive clothes in China that are nonetheless 'African' because they look dusty and second-hand, then just dwell for a moment on the word 'but' in Hewson's last sentence: influenced by Africa, *but* modern. The language of equality and justice doesn't stand a chance, in the end, against the language of marketing and the legacy of colonial notions of modernity.

We've already heard how Bono hates losing money. But he and Ali can well afford to shed their cash on Edun: they can intone, like Charles Foster Kane, that at the rate they're losing money, they'll 'have to close this place in … sixty years'. They can insist that Edun is more than just a clothing line, that it is a company with a mission. And it so happens that, in Uganda, Edun has partnered its mission with that of the notorious American missionary charity, Invisible Children.

Invisible Children exists, by its own account, to encourage US military intervention in eastern and central Africa to destroy the Lord's Resistance Army, a paramilitary 'child army' led by the hated Joseph Kony. But Invisible Children has its own presence on the ground in Uganda, and Edun has joined forces with it for an agricultural training programme called the Cotton Conservation Initiative. Incredibly, the Edun website describes Invisible Children as 'a non-profit organization that develops social programs principally in North West Uganda … [Its] role is to implement the CCIU social programs, which are savings and loan schemes, adult literacy programs, and building water holes'.[167]

Was there really no one better to dig holes in Uganda than Invisible Children, a US-based NGO with right-wing and homophobic evangelical links and a cult-like social-media presence devoted to distorting the reality of African politics?[168] A group that has taken in tens of millions of dollars in donations, mostly in the United States, but that is, according to its own mission statement, far more concerned with raising money by making glossy 'consciousness-raising' videos than with social justice in Africa? A group whose videos, its *raison d'être*, have been credibly accused, even before they gained unavoidable attention in 2012, of manipulating facts and painting an image of feral African violence like something out of Conrad's *Heart of Darkness*?[169]

Apparently not, in the world of Bono and Ali and Edun. In the wake of Invisible Children's viral *Kony 2012* video, made by the idiosyncratic Invisible Children film-maker and spokesman Jason Russell – widely watched for its horrible depiction of the African warlord, but also widely discredited[170] – Bono jumped happily to the organisation's defence. His support was blogged on the website of his ONE campaign. 'Having just been in Gulu with Edun … this is particularly pertinent for me [Kony had not in fact been in Gulu or anywhere else in Uganda for six years.] …

Spreading like wildfire, and sparking a heated, fascinating, much needed debate, this is brilliant campaigning … Is there an Oscar for this kind of direction? Jason Russell deserves it.'[171]

Bono includes too the pro-forma language about the need for 'solutions owned and directed by the people of the region' (a belief hardly reflected in Edun's relocation of production to China), but the conclusion could scarcely be clearer. Twenty-seven years after he first went to Africa with the evangelical World Vision, twelve years after he first charmed the racist, homophobic, imperialist Christian Jesse Helms, Bono and his organisations were working on the ground and in the media to support an American right-wing, militarist agenda in Africa. It's no wonder that the company name is a misspelling of Eden.

3 THE WORLD

BEAUTIFUL DAY: KISSING CORPORATE ASS

Wherever two or three of the world's rich and powerful are gathered, there too shall you find Bono, telling them how good they are. But Bono does more than schmooze at places like Davos: he launches projects, he presents plans, he promotes causes – it's a lot of work being the world's leading humanitarian, but he makes sure he's there on merit.

Sometimes he does have to give way a little to the upstarts of the good-doing realm. Thus in the summer of 2006, when Rupert Murdoch held his annual three-day get-together for top News Corporation executives, in Pebble Beach, California, Tony Blair spoke on the first night, effectively presenting his credentials for the post-prime-ministerial career that he would officially kick off the following year; Bill Clinton gave the closing speech; and Bono had to squeeze his 'keynote' on 'The Power of One' somewhere in between. But he knew how to upstage the politicians: instead of speaking at the usual glass-and-steel venue, like the unimaginative Blair and Clinton, Bono dragged his Murdochian congregation to the old Mission church in nearby Carmel.[1]

Such is Bono's special status among the elite globalist sets of Bilderbergers and Trilateralists that he has, inevitably, come to the attention of American conspiracy theorists, who incoherently (even by their standards) paint him as a knowing 'frontman for genocide' through his connection to an obscure but deadly eugenics agenda that appears to be run by Bill Gates.[2] As usual, such ravings distract from serious consideration of Bono's place in the world and the service he provides to the powerful by dressing their work, individually and collectively, in humanitarian garb – a relationship that is right out in the open and can be viewed clearly without resort to conspiracy.

It is not just in Davos and Pebble Beach that Bono is a big draw, obviously. The exalted place of Bono and U2 in the rock 'n' roll pantheon has not been in doubt, at least in the United States, for at least a quarter-century. But it was interesting that, on the night that status was officially underlined at the Rock and Roll Hall of Fame, a leading American musician, making the induction speech, casually mocked Bono's famous role in the wider world and presented him, albeit jokingly, as a 'shyster'. Bruce Springsteen was supposed to be returning the favour that Bono had done for him six years earlier, when 'the Boss' was inducted – Bono made a very good if unexceptional speech in 1999 – and Springsteen in 2005 produced a veritable tour de force of backhanded compliments and faint praise, slyly capturing something of the special qualities of the U2 singer.[3]

The Springsteen speech was not at all overtly hostile, and paid plenty of blush-inducing compliments, especially to U2's 'sonic architecture' and spirituality: Springsteen and Bono, indeed, are known to be friendly.[4] But whereas, for example, Edge was 'a rare and true guitar original and one of the subtlest guitar heroes of all time', Bono was merely 'one of the great frontmen of the past twenty years'[5] – not a time-frame that presents the very toughest competition. And while he didn't stint when describing some of Bono's performing qualities, Springsteen disposed of all the Irishman's humanitarian work in one vague, overcooked sentence about 'ideals' and 'connection', and instead concentrated on Bono as huckster:

> Bono ... where do I begin? Jeans designer, soon-to-be World Bank operator [there were rumours at the time that President Bush might appoint Bono to the World Bank], just plain operator, seller of the Brooklyn Bridge – oh hold up, he played under the Brooklyn Bridge, that's right. Soon-to-be mastermind operator of the Bono burger franchise, where more than one million stories will be told by a crazy Irishman. Now I realize that it's a dirty job and somebody has to do it, but don't quit your day job yet, my friend.[6]

Springsteen went on: 'Shaman, shyster, one of the greatest and most endearingly naked messianic complexes in rock and roll.' (Then he had the decency to add: 'It takes one to know one, of course.') Springsteen, well known for eschewing commercial endorsements, moved to the climax of his speech with a devastating and funny story about how he had discovered, the previous year, that U2 had teamed up with Apple to make an iPod advertisement:

> Well ... there I was sitting down on the couch in my pyjamas with my eldest son. He was watching TV. I was doing one of my favorite things – I was

tallying up all the money I passed up in endorsements over the years and thinking of all the fun I could have had with it. Suddenly I hear 'Uno, dos, tres, catorce!' [the opening of 'Vertigo'] I look up. But instead of the silhouettes of the hippie wannabes bouncing around in the iPod commercial, I see my boys! Oh, my God! They sold out![7]

Springsteen then joked about his own 'insanely expensive lifestyle … I burn money, and that calls for huge amounts of cash flow. But I also have a ludicrous image of myself that keeps me from truly cashing in.' He recounted how he phoned his manager Jon Landau the next morning to find out how U2, also previously supposed to be above all that, had pulled off this stroke.

'They didn't take any money?! … Smart, wily Irish guys.' Anybody … anybody … can do an ad and take the money. But to do the ad and not take the money … that's smart. That's wily. I say, 'Jon, I want you to call up Bill Gates or whoever is behind this thing and float this: a red, white, and blue iPod signed by Bruce "the Boss" Springsteen. Now remember, no matter how much money he offers, don't take it!'[8]

The Boss iPod has yet to appear, of course. Springsteen's portrait of himself as a naif who didn't know his Gates from his Jobs was clearly a joke, but his decision to wind up his speech with a story that portrayed U2 as smart and wily corporate operators who had gone where he himself refused to go was a pointed one. Springsteen didn't need to spell it out: we were invited to consider the wiles of men who publicly proclaimed that no cash had changed hands for this ad, while at the same time getting their new record featured in a global advertising campaign that someone else was paying for. Then there was the special U2-branded iPod itself: it turns out that the band and Apple were sharing profits from that product.[9] Indeed, any arrangement whereby U2 weren't profiting from this arrangement would have been absurd and exploitative; but they managed to hide the simple business facts of how they were 'cashing in' behind their aura of cool integrity.

Reports of their prior purity were also somewhat exaggerated. While U2 music hadn't been used previously in product advertising, there were a number of commercial and charitable bodies that got licences: 'Beautiful Day', for example, was used as an opening theme for soccer-highlights shows in Britain and Denmark – it was quite an effective adrenalin hit when played over fast-moving clips of goals, saves and tackles – and the same song was used by the US TV network CBS to plug its autumn 2002 season, part of an arrangement by which CBS also screened a U2 concert film; the American ABC network had done something similar to the 2002 CBS arrangement, with varying music, back in 1997; U2's Super Bowl appearance in 2002 meant Rupert Murdoch's Fox TV and the National Football League could use the band's songs to promote the game; 'Electrical Storm' introduced the America's Cup yacht-racing on New Zealand television; and Bono's old child-sponsoring friends in World Vision used 'I Still Haven't Found What I'm Looking For' in Australian TV advertising.[10]

The October 2004 Apple arrangement, with the U2 iPod as its centrepiece and a couple of nice sweeteners – the release of 'Vertigo', and an unprecedented 'Complete U2 digital box-set' at a mere $149, exclusively on the iTunes store – was a key moment for both U2 and the tech company. The iPod was just three years old, the iTunes store barely eighteen months, and U2 were helping Apple ease an older demographic of potential customers into its vice-like grip: it was and is notoriously difficult for people who begin to use the Apple hardware and software to purchase, manage and listen to their music ever to escape to other companies' products. But both brands, U2 and Apple, had also managed to imbue themselves with aesthetic and moral properties that seemed to place them above such grubby market considerations.

Steve Jobs – who the previous year had sold a duplex apartment on Central Park West to Bono – made the iPod deal sound like an extension of fandom: 'U2 is one of the greatest bands in the world and we are floored to be working with them.' Bono, as is his wont, found the emotional connection, the feeling, in this moment: 'We want our audience to have a more intimate online relationship with the band, and Apple can help us do that. With iPod and iTunes, Apple has created a crossroads of art, commerce and technology which feels good for both musicians and fans.' The Edge chimed in with music to corporate ears: 'iPod and iTunes look like the future to me and it's good for everybody involved in music.'[11]

The iPod and iTunes were indeed 'the future', and surely that would have been the case with or without U2. But at a time when artists and consumers were beginning to question all sorts of things about iTunes in particular – its pricing structure, the digital-rights management it used to lock up the songs people purchased, the way it sustained and reproduced the old record-company relationships that painfully squeezed artists, the massive cut Apple took from every 99-cent song, the roughly 11 cents left for acts if they were lucky – here was the most ethical band in the business arriving on the scene to tell us very loudly that it 'feels good', it is good, for musicians, fans, everyone.

The reference to the way it 'feels' was presumably at least partly an indirect way of alluding to how bummed-out consumers were supposed to be feeling about illegally downloading music. (See pp. 117–120 for more on the file-sharing issue.) As the anti-industry activist group Downhill Battle put it in a parody ad: 'With iTunes I don't feel guilty when I download music – Apple and the record labels handle the screw job for me.'[12]

Bono, in fact, had endorsed iTunes on its fanfare-filled launch on Windows operating systems in 2003. He appeared behind Steve Jobs live on the big screen and declared, 'I'd like to teach the world to iTunes.' Calling Jobs 'the Dalai Lama of integration', Bono said: That's why I'm here, to kiss the corporate ass, and I don't kiss every corporate ass.'[13] (Even as of 2013, the number of corporate asses Bono has publicly kissed remains in the low double-digits, so he is indeed not especially promiscuous.)

Bono and U2 had a choice, and they made it. While other artists were fighting the labels and building alternative ways of reaching their audiences, one of the biggest acts in the business, with one of the most loyal followings, almost unparalleled resources and a reputation for idealistic innovation, chose to lend its support to a highly centralised, closed-source corporate system of delivering music that was using new technology to recapitulate the sins of the old. And they were well rewarded for kissing the corporate ass, both by Apple and by a largely compliant media that viewed the move as placing the band somewhere in the vicinity of the cutting edge – technologically and culturally, at least, if not musically. The decades-deep integration of the traditional mainstream media with the record companies' way of doing business, and rewarding journalists, shouldn't be underestimated in evaluating the media's love-affair with the industry and its apparent saviour, Apple, with U2 by its side.

It was no surprise when, two years later, Bono's (RED) featured an Apple iPod as one of the early products carrying the conscientious new brand.

WEALTH: DEFENDING PROPERTY

Bono and U2 were fully entitled to enter into commercial partnerships of their own choosing, and it was merely part of their ingenious capacity to read and manipulate the media environment that they (mostly) managed to enhance their credibility rather than attract disdain for doing so as profitably as they did.

U2 is in fact one of the few rock bands whose trajectory is taught affectionately in business schools. Manager Paul McGuinness has always been the focal point of the depiction of the band as hard-nosed commercial players. The portrait of his and their general acumen may be somewhat exaggerated – an Irish magazine was noting two decades ago that while U2 constituted 'a licence to print money, their boss [*sic*] has found it surprisingly difficult to make a penny anywhere else'.[14] (See pp. 119–23 for consideration of Bono's own more recent investment profile.) But McGuinness and the band members, as equal partners, took care of their own business very well indeed; from the early days the model whereby they partnered with a big player rather than taking risks by striking out on their own was firmly established. Their 1984 contract with Island Records gave them not only some of the biggest upfront payments (£2 million per album) in the business, but also a 10 per cent stake in the company and control of their own publishing. When Polygram bought Island in 1989, U2's shares netted them more than £20 million, and further tens of millions were guaranteed throughout the 1990s.[15]

The partnership with Apple, the industry's last best hope against illegal file-sharers, was in keeping with their earlier pattern of behaviour in another way, too. U2 had long cultivated a reputation for being tough operators when it came to their exclusive right to profit from their intellectual property and to decide who else would. The British Performing Rights Society (PRS) 'found themselves on the wrong end of a lawsuit over not letting U2 collect their own live-performance royalties', according to an Irish magazine report.[16] (The PRS normally takes it upon itself to collect money on behalf of songwriters from venues where any music covered by copyright is played; U2 reckoned they were getting a raw deal, and fought the PRS for improved terms.) American DJ Carter Alan, an early friend and champion of the band, found his efforts to publish a book of reminiscences of his time with them vigorously opposed, especially by McGuinness and Larry Mullen Jr – he was cast out of their favour for some time as a result of pressing ahead with his work.[17]

And, perhaps most notoriously, in 1991 an obscure American art-music band called Negativland came under legal attack for producing a record that appeared to be called 'U2': it featured a U-2 spy plane on its sleeve, and aurally it consisted of barely recognisable bits of 'I Still Haven't Found What I'm Looking For', including some snatches on kazoo, plus various speech recordings, including profane out-takes (from a tape that had circulated for years among radio insiders) of famed US presenter Casey Kasem losing his cool. The U2 connection came in a snippet in which the velvet-voiced Kasem was first introducing the young band to his American Top Forty audience: 'That's the letter U and the numeral 2 ...' Kasem proceeded to read from a script that required him to name all the band members, including those annoying nicknames, and he suddenly blew up at his production team: 'This is bullshit! Nobody cares – these guys are from England and who gives a shit? It's a lot of wasted names that don't mean diddly-shit!'[18]

The audience for Negativland's audio collage of Kasem, U2 and who-knows-what-else couldn't have been large, but it quickly came to include the lawyers at Island and Warner-Chappell Music, the music publisher that managed U2's copyrights for the band. Ten days after the record was released, they issued a 180-page lawsuit.[19] They initially got a temporary restraining order from a federal judge against the record, and, 'preferring retreat to total annihilation', Negativland and its tiny label SST complied with all their demands, which were couched in scary legalese about turning over every single copy of the record and all the material used to produce it to Island for immediate destruction, as well as assigning their copyright to Island.[20]

In an extraordinary postscript, a trendy California culture magazine, *Mondo*, assigned Negativland to interview The Edge in 1992 when he wanted to talk about the technology U2 were using on their Zoo TV tour. Not realising to whom he was talking, Edge happily discussed all the video-sampling U2's techies were doing, using random satellite-feed material, some of it with copyrights that clearly belonged to someone else, that was then mashed-up in different ways for their live audience – he explained that it was all perfectly legal in copyright terms because the collage effect made it essentially a new work. He was taken aback when Negativland took that assertion as a cue to introduce themselves, but nonetheless entered into a long and fascinating conversation, admitting that he and other members of U2 had gone along with the lawsuit because they were persuaded that Negativland had tried to present the record as though it were by U2 – and by the time they had a clearer picture, he said, it was too late to intervene. He added: 'I know you've really taken a kicking and I'm really sorry about how it's all come out. Island Records hasn't been affected, but we have gotten so much shit in the media about all this, and it's really annoying.'[21] Negativland have said on their website that they obtained information in 2003 that the case didn't in fact originate with Island but with Paul McGuinness, who got the Negativland record from a friend in the US and sent it on to Island's legal department, though Negativland's evidence for some elements of this claim appears to be second-hand at best.[22]

McGuinness has, in any case, been probably the music industry's most consistent copyright hawk in recent years, denouncing peer-to-peer file-sharing and music piracy at every opportunity. Bono has occasionally joined in. Even as *No Line on the Horizon* hit number one on the US album charts, Bono spoke to *USA Today* about how file-sharing was spoiling the sacredness of music – which is apparently measured in units sold – and he was offended:

Piracy grates on Bono, yet he's reluctant to lead a rebellion 'because people think people like me are overpaid and overnourished, and they're not wrong', the U2 singer says. 'What they're missing is, how does a songwriter get paid? There's no space for a Cole Porter in the modern age.

'It's not the place for rich rock stars to ask for more money, but somebody should fight for fellow artists, because this is madness. Music has become tap water, a utility, where for me it's a sacred thing, so I'm a little offended.'

The Internet has emasculated rather than liberated artists, he says, noting that the record industry has lost billions in value.

'From punk rock to hip-hop, from heavy metal to country, musicians walk along with a smile and jump like lemmings into the abyss', he says. 'The music business has been thrown to the dogs legislatively.'

That indifference will vanish once 'file-sharing of TV shows and movies becomes as easy as songs', Bono says. 'Somebody is going to call the cops.'[23]

Bono wasn't wrong about how the crackdown against piracy was to escalate as the sharing of video – already easy by 2009 – became more widespread. But he might have acknowledged how shrilly his own industry, and his manager in particular, had already been calling the cops for many years. His suggestion that the solution to the file-sharing problem would have to come 'legislatively' is also an interesting guide to his priorities.

Bono's concern with what states and law-enforcement agencies could do to protect the record industry was echoed in a January 2010 editorial he wrote for the *New York Times*. This was his particularly dreadful, almost unreadable preview article about the next decade, replete with plugs for his pals in Apple and elsewhere in America's corporate and state elite, and including the famous line from his perch high above the greatest economic and financial crisis in more than seventy years: 'Trust in capitalism – we'll find a way', by which he appears to identify himself ('we') with capitalism (which was at least honest). In the 2010s, Bono said, he wanted states to get serious about file-sharing: '[W]e know from America's noble effort to stop child pornography, not to mention China's ignoble effort to suppress online dissent, that it's perfectly possible to track content.'[24] Leaving aside his assessment of either the success or nobility of these Chinese and American efforts, Bono really appeared to believe that a massive government-led effort to identify, and presumably prosecute, individuals who share music was justified by what he called 'the lost receipts of the music industry'[25] (typically, of course, he skirts the US authorities' tracking of 'online dissent' in the name of fighting terrorism).

Bono even jokes in the column that he and his rich pals may not be the best people to lead the cavalry charge on the piracy issue. 'Note to self: Don't get over-rewarded rock stars on this bully pulpit [*sic*], or famous actors; find the next Cole Porter, if he/she hasn't already left to write jingles.'[26] He is quite fond of deploying Cole Porter metaphorically, but how likely is it really that the 'next' anyone would be happy to front for a campaign to protect an industry that has ensured that its rewards are increasingly restricted to a tiny minority of established artists, and executives, enjoying life up at its pinnacle?

Perhaps Bono's imagined invitation to such an imagined credible musical figure would be more persuasive if he shared, say, some financial advice with the next Cole Porter. U2's own finances, as discussed in Chapter 1, are notoriously difficult to read with the naked eye, but it was touching to see in an Irish magazine a few years ago that one U2 company, Not Us Ltd, had made 'pension contributions' on behalf of another, the then otherwise quiet Eventcorp Ltd, of more than €3.8 million. Another entity, the Princus Investment Trust, was recorded as having a pension surplus of a similar amount.[27]

ELEVATION: BUILDING A PORTFOLIO

Perhaps Bono reckoned he needed a better pension plan than that. For whatever reason, since 2004 Bono has not been content merely to leave his cash-pile in the care of investment managers. He has been for most of the last decade a co-founding managing director of a New York-based private-equity firm, Elevation Partners, a company with no visible ethical strings attached.

Although it is named after a U2 song, Bono is not especially noisy about Elevation. It didn't, for example, figure in the otherwise quite comprehensive introduction of himself and his organisations in *Vanity Fair*. But nor is he secretive about his involvement – there's a nice potted bio of him, complete with photo and an emphasis on U2's intellectual-property record, at elevation.com. And through his involvement Elevation has garnered enormous amounts of publicity, most of it undesirable, either because of the ostensibly unBono-like nature of its investments, or because of their poor performance. In 2010, for example, a Wall Street website gained a lot of publicity when it named Bono (personally, not his company, which wouldn't have got nearly as much publicity) as 'Worst Investor in America' because of flops including Palm and Forbes.[28] The tune changed somewhat in 2012, when the Facebook IPO appeared initially to earn Bono, and Elevation, a billion-dollar fortune in shares; but the tanking of Facebook stock in the subsequent weeks and months (when old shareholders like Bono were prohibited by agreement from unloading their fast-devaluing shares) again cast Bono in a bad light, both as an investor whose shares were rapidly losing worth, and as a party to an overpriced share flotation that seemed to offer exceptionally poor value to new entrants.

But hey, it's Bono's money, earned because millions of people love his music, and he is entitled to use it as he pleases. (Indeed, many people would be inclined to cut him some slack on the assumption that much of his personal fortune ends up going to 'good causes', though the evidence for that proposition is scant: we know plenty about the causes to which he lends his presence, but next to no information is publicly available about where he gives his money.) In any case, it seems churlish to mock any investor's 'failure' over a turbulent period of history when, for example, bank shares became the most dangerous investment imaginable: Elevation's assets, as of mid 2012, appeared to be ahead of where they had started roughly seven years earlier – that is, in the region of $2 billion, largely thanks to Facebook, and that scarcely sounds like failure.

Failure or success is not our reason for looking at Elevation. It's simply that it's part of Bono's public record. Over the years he has invested a great deal of his valuable time in many enterprises and causes, from U2 to Greenpeace, from Jubilee 2000 to (RED), but nothing else has ever appeared to have so much of his valuable money. 'Appeared' because, again, the fund's internal arrangements are opaque: Bono has, for most of its history, been one of six partners – at the last count it was five main men – and most commentators assume his stake is one-fifth of its $2 billion capital, but he himself has said: 'In Elevation, we invest other people's money, endowments, pension funds.'[29]

Like U2, another collective entity, all of Elevation's activities cannot be ascribed to Bono's desires, but it does help to complete the picture. Given his profile and the company's Bono-derived name, he can scarcely complain at any association between him and its investments.

Before Facebook, the one that raised most eyebrows was Elevation's 2006 investment in Forbes Media Inc., the company behind the magazine of the same name. That magazine's long-time advertising slogan was 'Capitalist Tool', and it remains an apt description of the contents of the publication and its website, which project themselves as useful instruments for the information and opinion-forming needs of the rich. *Forbes* also looks after their need for flattery, with its lists and profiles of the super-wealthy. Known historically as a family affair – the editor-in-chief was Steve Forbes, a right-wing flat-tax enthusiast and Fox News pundit who had chased the Republican presidential nomination in the 1990s – Forbes Media was in some financial difficulty by 2006, and happy for Elevation to buy what was reported to be a forty-something per cent stake for something over $250 million, an investment that was said to focus on the online side.[30]

According to his Elevation partner Roger McNamee, Bono was drawn to Forbes precisely because it had a 'point of view'; Bono, he said, 'drove this part of the discussion and likes the fact that there has been a consistent philosophy throughout its history'.[31]

To praise Forbes publicly for being consistently reactionary seemed, at least, somewhat superfluous. McNamee and Bono could have just said they thought it would eventually make money. By 2006 it was abundantly clear, especially in the US, that print media were in a parlous state, and beginning to become clear that some of the best prospects for profitable online survival were available to any company that could take a trusted brand on to the web and bring along an audience that was willing, and could afford, to pay for its contents. Business people with significant assets and expense accounts looked like the best candidates to constitute such an audience. Forbes might not be the most promising business brand – that lofty title was shared by the Wall Street Journal and Financial Times – but it was not far behind, and it was affordable. There was a straightforward business case for Elevation, which had media among its investment priorities, getting into Forbes (though the company continued to perform poorly), but no sensible reason to endorse its politics, which did not perceptibly change after Bono took an interest. Of course some sort of flattery is de rigueur in these situations, especially when the investment might be regarded as somewhat publicly embarrassing for the company on its receiving end; but surely the matter of the Forbes 'philosophy' could have been left quietly unattended.

Unless of course Bono really did like it, its consistency and its politics – a possibility that at this stage it would be extremely foolish to rule out. The investment in Forbes came, after all, within weeks of U2's tax move from Ireland to the Netherlands becoming public knowledge. Not long after Elevation got in, Forbes reportedly drastically curtailed its employee pension plan – right before the holiday season, as an anonymous employee noted in a message to the website Gawker: '[H]ey, Bono! Merry Christmas, you faux liberal asshole. Go buy some presents with our pension money.'[32] Three years later, Forbes began a programme of lay-offs of the sort that were becoming very familiar for journalists, including the closure of its London and Los Angeles bureaux.[33] The 'philosophy' looks all too consistent.

Elevation and Bono also chose to ignore protests from peace and global-solidarity campaigners about another of its investments – the $300 million it had sunk into a new partnership of California video-game makers, Pandemic and Bioware Studios. Again, electronic gaming was initially central to Elevation's self-image, and it didn't seem to matter when newspapers reported in 2006 on the development by Pandemic of

Mercenaries 2: World in Flames, in which part of the complicated and very violent game-play action involved players becoming mercenaries in the pay of an oil company attempting to overthrow a Venezuelan 'tyrant'. Any resemblance to a coup attempt against Hugo Chavez's government was more than coincidental.[34]

Bono, it seemed, had come a long way from his Sandinista sympathies and 'Bullet the Blue Sky' – indeed, he had never shown any sympathy or solidarity with the twenty-first-century wave of left-led governments in Latin America. Meanwhile, the game's release was delayed until 2008 – after the Pandemic and Bioware partnership had been sold on to the gaming giant Electronic Arts – but Bono never publicly commented on the complaints from Venezuelan politicians and activists, along with American clerics, who pointed out how fearful many people in Venezuela were of just such a US-backed coup against their country's government. Pandemic, it seems, had deep roots when it comes to war-games, having developed the *Full Spectrum Warrior* series, which grew out of training software for the US army, developed in conjunction with the CIA-funded Institute for Creative Technologies.[35] The US military makes no apologies about the usefulness of video-games when it comes to training young soldiers and soldiers-to-be, and this sort of 'overlap' is scarcely remarked upon in the fake-violent world of gaming. It was hardly likely that Bono, who had helped to whitewash the politicians responsible for the real war in Iraq, would have any serious misgivings about a virtual one in Venezuela, and there is no suggestion that Elevation's sale of its creators Pandemic and Bioware was motivated by anything other than money.

Bono was a personal investor at Facebook even before Elevation bought into it in 2009, and Elevation's myriad personal and financial connections with the company led a journalist in 2010 to call them 'one chummy bunch'.[36] Even with the rapid drop in the value of Facebook shares that occurred after its public launch in the summer of 2012, Bono and Elevation were still hugely in profit compared to their initial investments. More modest but still enormous profits – estimated at about $200 million in mid 2012 – were made by Elevation on Yelp!, a website and tool for word-of-mouth on restaurants and other service businesses. In 2012 Bono and The Edge invested an unknown sum of money in the online file-storage and sharing service, Dropbox.[37] On one of the many, many occasions when he has flattered politicians and business people by dressing them up in rock-star garb, Bono said of that company's founders: 'Meeting Drew and Arash is like meeting guys in a band.'[38]

This was scarcely visionary investment: the likes of Dropbox, Yelp! and Facebook each had tens of millions of users before Bono got involved;

Forbes was among the most established brands in American media. Suggestions in the fund's early days that Elevation would be involved in supporting music enterprises have thus far proved unfounded, perhaps because in recent years no one but Apple has found a reliable way to make money from tunes. And these investments made Bono a 'paper billionaire' only in the sense that a lot of ill-informed newspapers started calling him a billionaire. He still had quite some way to go before his net worth reached that glorious ten-figure sum, whether in dollars, sterling or euros.

However, the fact of this very public investment profile, complete with alleged windfall, conjoined with the widespread reporting of U2's tax, *ahem*, efficiencies, did contribute to a change in the public image of Bono between 2009 and 2012. Is this reputational damage justified? In reality he may simply be a highly visible illustration of the maxim that the rich get richer; his particular investment portfolio may just be suggestive, no more, about aspects of his character, connections and priorities. It would be absurd, surely, even to begin to judge Bono definitively on the basis of Steve Forbes's politics or Mark Zuckerberg's attempt to commercialise people's private information. Or even U2's tax arrangements. We should look, instead, at what Bono has said, and what he has continued to do, and on whose behalf, in the public sphere, as an alleged force for good in the world.

ZOOROPHILIA: FROM SALVADOR TO SARAJEVO

Whatever the limitations of his early politics – and we have already considered those at some length in relation to both Ireland and Africa – the relatively naive, earnest Bono of the 1980s did help to organise the Amnesty International 'Conspiracy of Hope' tour, volunteered in an Ethiopian orphanage, and even travelled in Central America. And while you couldn't call him a Catholic, exactly, he had been influenced by the Catholic liberation theology he encountered in the Western hemisphere: the director of Amnesty in the US, Jack Healey, had been both a monk and a priest, and had a big impact on U2's political commitments.

Bono went for a week to Central America in the mid 1980s in support of the US-based Sanctuary movement, which was largely based in churches, though not just Catholic ones.[39]

He recalled, in a twenty-first-century reminiscence published in *U2 by U2*, that the ideas of the Nicaraguan Sandinista revolution were 'a coming together of many of my interests: Christianity, social justice, artists in power'. That recollection, for the most part, badly garbled the politics of the 1980s situation. For example, he said Sanctuary was 'supporting peasant farmers who were caught in the crossfire of what was essentially a civil war in El Salvador'.⁴⁰ Most US members of Sanctuary would almost certainly not, in fact, have engaged in such mealy-mouthed neutrality about the revolution in El Salvador and its violent suppression by the US-backed government, and their support was not only for innocent victims of 'crossfire' – Bono's reflexively banal language by the time of his remembering – but, as the name suggests, for Salvadorans, of whatever profession or occupation, seeking refuge from that government in the US, against the hostility of the American immigration authorities.

Perhaps the book's U2-appointed editor is to blame for the further mess that arises as Bono tells of getting shot at while visiting 'our peasant farmers' in what appears at first reading to be Nicaragua. Summarising that country's situation, he appears to have inhaled a Ronald Reagan speech that he is spitting out randomly, mixing its metaphors: 'The powers that be [by which he appears to mean US leaders] felt the Sandinista revolution had to be squashed because it had the potential to catch fire, and had that happened in Mexico, the United States would have felt very unsafe.' His under-fire location turns out, however, to be El Salvador, where he appears to have witnessed the fire-bombing and mortaring of a rebel-sympathising village. 'I remember watching this horror happen on another hillside, in another world, next door to where we were but not so far away that we couldn't feel it.'⁴¹ One can only speculate as to how frustrated the young Bono might be at his middle-aged self losing the political point of his experience but managing to rhapsodise about it anyway; but Bono does pull his thoughts together long enough to rattle off a few more vaguely pointed clichés:

> I had this love affair with American literature happening at the same time as I became aware of how dangerous American foreign policy could be in the countries around it, with the brutal crushing of the Sandinistas. I started to see two Americas, the mythic America and the real America. It was an age of greed, Wall Street, button down, win, win, win, no time for losers. New York was bankrupt [sic – that was a decade earlier]. There was a harsh reality to America as well as the dream ... I wanted to describe this era of prosperity and Savings and Loan scandals as a spiritual drought. I started thinking about the desert ...⁴²

And thus was born the *Joshua Tree* album – though, contrary to what this memoir implies, the Sandinistas were by no means crushed yet by the time of its release in 1987. He put his Central American experience in a song: Bono's violent El Salvador experience was distilled in the chainsaw sound – mainly generated by The Edge – of the album's fourth track, 'Bullet the

Blue Sky'. In the version of the song performed in *Rattle and Hum*, Bono, speaking through the musical bridge in an exaggerated American accent, establishes that even in the 1980s geography was not his strong suit, as he locates the rural attack he witnessed – on 'women and children' naturally, because why else would he sympathise – in 'the hills of San Salvador', which was and is in reality the capital city.[43] This song and performance are, nonetheless, both very good, and as good as it gets when it comes to Bono and U2 manifestly – if not quite directly – attacking US policy. Especially when, as in that performance, the song follows a clip of Jimi Hendrix playing 'The Star-Spangled Banner'. It is impossible to imagine Bono, at that time, cosying up to President Reagan. Sadly, on subsequent tours the song was framed visually so that it referred to religious conflict, handguns, Nazis – almost anything other than US foreign policy.

But then, U2's general interest in America seemed to wane for several years anyway. That loss of interest has been read largely in aesthetic terms, in relation to their rebirth as postmodern poseurs, but it had a political dimension.

U2 were lucky, in a sense, that the crisis of 'authenticity' that saw their B. B. King partnership wearing so thin by the late 1980s (see Chapter 2) was immediately followed by the fall of communism in Europe, the reunification of Germany, and the rise of pop-cultural postmodernism to boot. Lucky, that is, because it gave them somewhere reasonably interesting to turn, as well as lots of old East German cars to hang from the rafters around their stage. Even the names of their first two albums of the 1990s alert us to their new setting: *Achtung Baby* and *Zooropa*, the latter with the twelve-star European flag on its cover. This is not the place to consider this turn as an aesthetic move for U2, though clearly their creative juices were initially revived by the change and by the thumping European dance scene they found themselves feeding off, developing musical and staging ideas that were, in Bono's words, 'more Eurocentric ... more decadent, more old world'.[44] Onstage, according to Bono, the band even 'played upon' the resemblance of a rock concert to a fascist 'night rally'.[45]

It is futile to try to determine with certainty if this turn also marked the start of a sea-change in Bono's politics, or if what changed in his outlook simply reflected global changes in what was deemed worth looking out upon. He would scarcely be the only person who lost interest in the Third World, and its relations with the US, in the 1990s; since developing countries were no longer a Cold War battleground, both policy elites and solidarity activists found their attention drifting.

His band's post-1990 turn to Europe was also an attempt to prove that U2 had a sense of humour, with funny costumes, pranks, all those televisions and cars and golden arches onstage. U2, we were assured, and contrary to their previous reputation, were not taking themselves too seriously – there was even a whole song full of commercial advertising slogans. It did not depoliticise Bono and U2 per se, but American imperialist violence soon disappeared permanently from their political target list. As they moved on from Salvador and South Africa, their world-view of the 1990s might be summarised with three more S's: Sellafield, Sarajevo and, briefly, Salman Rushdie.

These issues were being contested on home European turf, but that was not the only difference. Whereas the commitments of the 1980s were relatively low-key – how many U2 fans at that time would have known that Bono considered himself a Sandinista sympathiser? – the band's political actions of the 1990s were stunts, enacted for public impact.

Sellafield is a nuclear-waste reprocessing plant on England's northwest coast. In 1957, when it operated under the name Windscale, part of a reactor core had caught fire, releasing radioactive material into the environment. The change of name didn't dispel the controversy surrounding the plant; but by the early 1990s a second plant, known as THORP (thermal oxide reprocessing plant) nonetheless had approval, and was about to be built. Greenpeace – which U2 had been supporting for years – vigorously opposed the new plant, as did the Irish government, concerned at reports of illness clusters already occurring in regions just across the Irish Sea from Sellafield, at high levels of radioactivity in the sea, and at the increased transportation of dangerous material from as far away as Japan to the plant through the waters between the two countries. The Edge pointed out the links to the nuclear-arms industry: 'Just as the rest of the world was ending the arms race … Sellafield had the brainwave of building a multi-billion pound reprocessing plant to create more weapons-grade plutonium.'[46]

U2, with Public Enemy, Kraftwerk and Big Audio Dynamite II, put on a 'Stop Sellafield' concert for Greenpeace, but they did more besides. In 1992, along with Greenpeace activists, they carried out a highly publicised not-quite-civil-disobedience action in which they landed on the beach outside the plant – carefully staying on the public-domain side of the high-tide line. Bono recalled: 'It was high comedy. We stormed the beach and recreated the cover for the Beatles' *Help*, using semaphore, except we were dressed in protective clothing.'[47] In Bill Flanagan's long and amusing eyewitness account of the escapade – complete with a Greenpeace campaigner who joked with Bono about his ability to walk on water – Bono acknowledged that they were 'rock stars on a day trip', and the band discussed their agreement that this would be their only do-gooding of the year. But though they literally sipped champagne en route to the action, they come across in Flanagan's version of the story as knowledgeable and committed, and their action helped to raise the profile of the campaign, which earned increased media coverage and popular support for years to come, especially in Ireland but also in Britain.[48]

The second Sellafield plant went ahead, however. In an interview roughly twelve years later, Edge wondered whether 'our protest made any difference', but Bono, beside him, wasn't having any of that defeatism: 'After years and years of protest, including a campaign led by my own dear wife, Ali, who … organized a million and a half postcards from Irish people protesting to Tony Blair, the British government have finally concluded Sellafield has to be closed down. That's what I always tell people. These things take time.'[49] Bono's faith in gradual change through postcards is touching, but when the THORP plant eventually closed in 2010, several years after this interview, the evidence suggests that it was because it was losing so much money, not because of polite protest.[50] And other facilities at the scandal-ridden Sellafield site remain very much active.

If Sellafield was a group endeavour – Larry Mullen Jr appears to have been the most informed and active, but all of U2 were articulate on the subject – then Sarajevo, and Salman Rushdie, were largely Bono's passions. Sarajevo's siege by violent Bosnian Serb forces was scarcely the only horror of the bloody war being waged in Bosnia – tens of thousands of Bosnian Serb peasants had been killed or ethnically cleansed, for example; but since it was taking place in a modern, Westernised city, it aroused sympathy among the world's metropolitan journalists like no other story in the Balkans, and it was pretty easy to tell.

An American film-maker, Bill Carter, interviewed U2 for Bosnian TV in 1993. As Bono recalled: 'So I agreed in an emotional moment to do a gig there. And after I've agreed on Sarajevo Television, I then have to explain to the band why putting our lives at risk is going to help the people of Sarajevo.'[51] The explaining didn't go so well: Bono was voted down. So instead of doing a one-off publicity stunt *in* Sarajevo, U2 instead did a publicity stunt *for* Sarajevo at every one of their concerts for about a month on the European stadium leg of their 1993 Zoo TV tour: a live satellite-video link to the city for five or ten minutes, up on the big screens. Even the band's official autobiography doesn't gloss over the problems and tensions this created in the context of a rock concert, with band members arguing over whether it was exploitative. And, you know, a buzz-kill. Mullen recalled:

> We were playing a rock 'n' roll show and it was lots of fun, and although the political stuff was serious it was done with a smile. Then suddenly seeing

video footage of people being bombed and a satellite link-up with people in Sarajevo saying, 'We're being killed, please come and help us.' That was really hard to watch and hard to listen to … I remember saying to Bono, 'I don't know if I can handle this any more, it's really hard up there.' He just pushed through. He said, 'I want to do this and I'm going to do it.'[52]

Paul McGuinness took up the recollection:

The worst night was Wembley Stadium, when three women came up on the screen [from the Sarajevo studio] and said, 'We don't know what we're doing here. This guy dragged us in. You're all having a good time. We're not having a good time. What are you going to do for us?' Bono started to reply but they just cut him off. They said, 'We know you're not going to do anything for us. You're going to go back to a rock show. You're going to forget that we even exist. And we're all going to die.' Right in the middle of a show at Wembley. And the show never really recovered.[53]

McGuinness is one hard-hearted impresario – years later he boasted to a music magazine that he never paid the European Broadcasting Union bill for the Sarajevo satellite link.[54] There is some unintended black humour in the fact that he thought the correct way to finish this dreadful story of pain, anger and exploitation was to reflect, his head shaking regretfully no doubt, that 'the show never really recovered'. Bono, again, wasn't admitting defeat: 'It was very upsetting. But the next day Brian Eno was inspired to get involved with the War Child project and a lot of great things came out of that. So some people were inspired to take action and some people were just horrified.'[55] Bono couldn't help it if his chief measuring gauge for whether something was worthwhile had become whether it convinced a celebrity to support a charity. It must be said, though, that U2's efforts were at least a part of increased attention and sympathy among the media and public to Sarajevo's plight. Four years later, with the fighting over, U2 played in Sarajevo, but the summer of the satellite link had proved controversial, for obvious reasons, and it exposed divisions in the band. Ultimately, though, the question of whether U2's Sarajevo special was annoying and/or repulsive is less important than that of whether U2 contributed to a partial and one-sided anti-Serb version of the Balkan conflict, a version that was to have deadly consequences. Years later, NATO planes were bombing the Serbian capital, Belgrade – a series of attacks ostensibly intended to drive Serb troops out of Kosovo, but that got widespread popular support partly because Western audiences had been so conditioned to view the Serbs as aggressors. Bono and U2 showed no interest in protesting against these attacks, or in linking up with the Serbs who were now under fire.

Salman Rushdie, meanwhile, was seen in public for the first time in five years when he walked out onto the Wembley stage in front of 70,000 people on that same strange 'worst' night in 1993. (Someone should tell McGuinness that the fans really got their money's worth.) The writer had been living in hiding because of an Iranian fatwa prompted by his novel *The Satanic Verses*. He and Bono were friends – indeed, there was controversy and anger at the risk to the safety of Bono and his family when it was publicly revealed that Rushdie had visited Bono at his Dublin home – but it was extraordinary, strange, and even a bit brave nonetheless when Bono turned one of his regular onstage prank-phone call schticks into an introduction for Rushdie in person, not just on the phone. 'I have enormous respect for Islamic culture,' Bono said later, 'but I would encourage extremists to consider the murder of a novelist as sacrilegious to *my* faith.'[56]

THE SPIRITUAL AMERICAN: BEFRIENDING PRESIDENTS

During the early part of the Zoo TV tour, the White House was a target for those onstage prank phone calls, not a regular destination on Bono's social calendar. But that was in the days of Bush the Elder. Bono was making friends with Bill Clinton even before he was elected president in November 1992.

The relationship had got off to a ribbing, roaring start in late August of that year on a US radio programme called *Rockline*. Fans were phoning in to talk to the band, and on the line came caller 'Bill from Little Rock'. Clinton and Bono joshed a bit – 'You can call me Bill', 'And you can call me Betty' – then settled into an amiable discussion that earned nice PR for both parties.[57]

Two weeks later, the story goes, the band arrived at their Chicago hotel at 3 am, drunk and disorderly, to be told that Bill Clinton was staying there too. 'Well, go bring him here! We want him,' Bono joked. U2's flunkies took him at his word, but the Secret Service refused to wake the sleeping candidate. When Clinton rose at 7 am he was annoyed to hear that he had missed this invitation from Bono, and went looking for him. Bono had crashed in Edge's suite, but he was roused to meet the presidential favourite. Still in his stage clothes from a gig in Madison, Wisconsin the night before, Bono put on his sunglasses, lit a cigar and made an entrance down a spiral staircase. Clinton's laughter, it is said, sealed the friendship.[58]

Clinton's casual charm, legendary even by Ireland's elevated standards, was easily a match for Bono's. He impressed each and all of U2 over the course of an hour's chat. Larry challenged him, saying the system was corrupt, and Clinton looked him in the eye and said: 'This is going to sound corny. But I do love my country and I do want to help people. I know the system is corrupt, and I don't know if the president can change it. But I know this: no one else can.'[59]

The gory details of this encounter, including Clinton's gut-wrenchingly 'corny' response to Mullen, only emerged later, but the fact that it took place got wide publicity, and fitted right into the media narrative that suggested Clinton was a new, and ineffably cool, sort of candidate. Clinton's opponent, President George H. W. Bush, soon desperately attempted to mock Clinton's down-with-the-kids parlay. American journalist Bill Flanagan was with Bono to see Bush's speech on TV:

> 'Governor Clinton doesn't think foreign policy's important, but he's trying to catch up,' Bush tells the crowd. 'You may have seen this in the news – he was in Hollywood [*sic*] seeking foreign policy advice from the rock group U2!'
>
> Bono looks up. 'Rock group?'
>
> Bush continues: 'I have nothing against U2. You may not know this, but they try to call me every night during the concert! But the next time we face a foreign policy crisis, I will work with John Major and Boris Yeltsin, and Bill Clinton can consult Boy George!' Bush goes on to declare that if Clinton is elected *you, too,* will have higher inflation, *you, too,* will have higher taxes. *You, too! You, too!*
>
> Bono doesn't get it. 'Does he think I'm Boy George?' he asks.
>
> 'Nah,' I say. 'He's damning Clinton by association. He probably had a team of consultants sitting up all night trying to think of a rock star they could insult without offending any potential Bush voters. Madonna's too big, Springsteen – need those electoral votes in New Jersey. Boy George is foreign, gay, and no longer sells any records. He's perfect.'[60]

Between the president's Boy George jibes and Clinton's charming attentiveness, it's not surprising that Bono and his bandmates were jubilant at the latter's November victory, and the joy never really wore off. Half the band, though not the unavailable Bono, played at an inauguration party. Bono later called Clinton 'a new kind of politician, the first of our kind', with 'real brainpower, real charm, a real sense of humour'.[61] In 2003, speaking at a celebrity-heavy Grammy function in his own honour, Bono called Clinton 'more of a rock star than anyone else in this room'.[62] (Thankfully, Tony Blair and Gordon Brown weren't in the room to provide Beatle-like competition.)

Bono in 1992 was, like many people, swept up in what has appeared since 1960 to be a sixteen-year cycle of unwarranted hope that a seemingly idealistic Democrat is going to change the world by moving into the White House. It was not a hope that was limited to liberal elites, as Bono found when he attended an inner-city church full of society's outcasts in San Francisco the Sunday after the election. Much of the congregation was ecstatic, he said.

> That's the moment when I knew how important this small victory was. I was looking around and I was thinking, 'Wow, if you're HIV, if you're a homosexual, if you're a member of the underclass or if you're a woman or if you're an artist – and that covers just about everybody in this church – this is no small thing.' … This was from 'We don't exist' to 'We do exist', you know?[63]

Just as liberals had done in 1960 and 1976, and would do again in 2008, Bono even went so far as to speculate about the new president's inauguration and administration as an opportunity for America to expiate its past sins, from the carnage in Central America all the way back to the extermination of North America's native people.[64] It is not really clear why Bono or anyone else should have believed this to be likely, but the emotion appears to have been genuine, and based on some then-still-enduring progressive sympathies of someone who regarded the Reagan–Bush era as a nightmare from which he feared he would never wake up. Like many of Clinton's supporters, he shows no sign that he ever did wake up from such delusions – though any members of that San Francisco congregation who were, for example, reliant on Aid to Families with Dependent Children would have got a ringing signal of Clinton's true qualities when he abolished that welfare programme in 1996, most notably driving many single mothers off welfare and into menial, low-paid jobs, if they were lucky.

At any rate, these private thoughts about Clinton's election, recorded in 1992 by American journalist Bill Flanagan, amount to the last time Bono is on the record elucidating a politics that, however naively expressed, sounds connected to the anti-imperialist Left with which he had been associating in the 1980s. By the time he became involved publicly in the debate on global development more than six years later, he was speaking a language that was much more reconciled to the reality of US power. As discussed in Chapter 2, Bono would eventually work closely with the Clinton White House in 1999–2000 on African debt-cancellation, before moving seamlessly into that of Bush the Younger. Once you're in there close to power, it seems, the logic of remaining there is almost always impeccable. Bono, once its earnest critic, would become its servant.

By the turn of the millennium, Bono's Virgil, guiding him through the Washington underworld, was the ultra-smooth Bobby Shriver, who could introduce the singer not merely to the partisan players in the White House and on Capitol Hill, but to the permanent class of experts, technocrats and assorted influence-peddlers who lurk around them. Bono became one of them, effectively a Washington lobbyist.

Thus Bono recalled meeting such helpful figures as Pete Peterson, chair of the highly influential Council on Foreign Relations, and himself a former commerce secretary, Lehman Brothers CEO and co-founder of the powerful private-equity firm the Blackstone Group; Shriver's old venture-capital boss and friend Jim Wolfensohn, head of the World Bank; and even David Rockefeller himself, the living embodiment of the government–business–philanthropy nexus.[65] These people, as much as the politicians he also encountered, helped him to drive the debt and AIDS policy initiatives described in Chapter 2. It was no joke when Bono's name was floated by some as Wolfensohn's potential successor as president of the World Bank when the latter's term was due to run out in 2005: the Los Angeles Times editorialised in favour of Bono's appointment, and Treasury Secretary John Snow wouldn't rule it out when pressed on a TV talk show. Bono was widely rumoured to be on Bush's short-list. Such an appointment was unlikely, and would of course have been fundamentally a public-relations stroke by the Bush government, but it would also have reflected Bono's status as a trusted insider in the corridors of political and economic power where such men resided. None of the many stories that raised questions about whether Bono should guide the World Bank suggested that the problem had anything to do with some perceived radicalism – merely that he lacked sufficient financial background.[66]

When Bush instead nominated the notorious neocon hawk Paul Wolfowitz to the World Bank presidency, there was some disquiet among the denizens of those corridors of power. Although there was inevitably some spin to the effect that Wolfowitz had a soft, slightly social-democratic Brooklyn heart beating under his hard, Pentagon exterior, it was considered unduly offensive to global opinion about the tainted Iraq invasion, of which Wolfowitz had been a leading advocate and planner, and to the beloved bipartisanship in Washington, to pick such a partisan, 'ideological' figure. Part of Wolfowitz's response to the criticism was, inevitably, to reach out to Bono: within a few days of his being picked for the job, his team ensured that Reuters could report he had already had two long phone conversations with the Irishman. According to a Wolfowitz spokesman, uncontradicted by Bono, the men 'clicked': 'They were very enthusiastic, detailed and lengthy conversations … incredibly substantive about reducing poverty, about development, about the opportunity to help people that the World Bank presidency provides and about charitable giving and social progress around the globe.'[67]

Bono, for his part, was scarcely going to reject the overtures of the World Bank president in the run-up to the Gleneagles summit, which (as noted in Chapter 2) had become something of his own project. Thus Wolfowitz mingled backstage with Bono and other celebrities at the Live 8 concert, associated himself with Bono's priorities at every opportunity, and sang the singer's praises when he got the chance. In a worshipful profile of Bono in *Time* magazine late in 2005, Wolfowitz – no doubt to his own delight – featured in the first paragraph, and offered the perfect soundbite endorsement of the great man's common touch: 'Pomposity and arrogance are the enemies of getting things done. And Bono knows how to get things done.'[68]

If Bono cooperated with Wolfowitz by granting him humanitarian cover by association, it would be an exaggeration to say that he reciprocated all that affection. Wolfowitz resigned from his World Bank post in 2007, damaged by a minor scandal, mainly to do with pay increases to a World Bank employee with whom he was in a personal relationship. By that time, Bono was not in the running for the nomination to replace him – having moved on from concentrating on global lobbying efforts to shopping sprees with Oprah; but it is probably fair to assume that his guru, economist Jeffrey Sachs, spoke for them both when he said that Wolfowitz had been 'absolutely the wrong guy for the job'. More revealing than the criticism of Wolfowitz, however, was Sachs's cautious endorsement of Bush's new nominee, Robert Zoellick, formerly Bush's deputy secretary of state and a senior executive at Goldman Sachs; Sachs hoped Zoellick, yet another man who had spent his life spinning through the Washington–Wall Street revolving door, would offer 'less ideology'. The likes of Wolfowitz had contributed, Sachs said, to lost leadership for the US in the world, because they were 'obsessed with the Persian Gulf … a huge, huge distraction'.[69]

The problem for Sachs, in other words, was not that the US, with less than 5 per cent of the world's population, insistently claimed global leadership; it was that it had been failing in that leadership mission because it was caught up in this particular war, aka 'ideology' – an error embodied by Wolfowitz. 'Ideology', in such technocratic discourse, is always what the other guy is suffering from. Sachs also differed publicly with Wolfowitz's heavy emphasis on anti-corruption initiatives in countries receiving aid, with Sachs suggesting corruption should not be such a priority and was sometimes used as an excuse for inaction; it's an often-confusing argument that rages well beyond those two men.

Sachs is a complex character with an apparent penchant for the spotlight – he arrived, for example, at Occupy Wall Street in 2011 to associate himself with its goals. He was the director of the Millennium Development Project, a UN body set up to pursue anti-poverty measures, and before that Sachs advised governments in Latin America and eastern Europe. He is associated with the fast and shocking switch to market economics that radically increased poverty, reduced life expectancy and gave rise to a new oligarchy in Russia, and he has never repudiated his work there, though he has implied his ideas were imperfectly applied by Russians and inadequately assisted by the West.

Bono's foreword to Sachs's 2005 opus *The End of Poverty*, helped ensure it got noticed well beyond the development-economics journals. 'To Jeff', Bono wrote, global poverty is 'a difficult but solvable equation that crosses human with financial capital, the strategic goals of the rich world with a new kind of planning in the poor world.'[70]

To be sure, in the wake of the most recent global financial crisis, Sachs has often mouthed radical-sounding critiques of free-market economics and the way corporations distort politics. But in 2004, when he wrote that foreword, Bono had characterised Sachs exactly right, and had signed on to his agenda – a strategic agenda that would suit 'financial capital' and US hegemony, erasing poverty, eventually, it was hoped, through the working of markets and technocratic planning in Washington and on Wall Street, not through any democratic mobilisation of poor people on their own behalf. The problem of global deprivation would be solved through a congruence of interests, not conflict. The 'equation' had nothing to do with 'equality'.

In that foreword Bono underlined his own embrace of a US-centred strategic view – 'not just heart, it's smart' – warning that 9/11 made it 'too clear' that the 'destinies of the "haves" are intrinsically linked to the fates of the "have-nothing-at-alls"'. The 'wealthy Saudis' who perpetrated 9/11 'found succor and sanctuary', Bono wrote, in the 'collapsed, poverty-stricken state of Afghanistan ... Africa is not the front line in the war against terror, but it soon could be.'[71]

In linking anti-poverty goals to 'the war against terror' – and in accepting and repeating that absurd label – Bono was thinking strategically about how to find space in Washington, or, to put it more crudely, looking for a piece of the action. His efforts saw him forge some striking partnerships during those Bush years: for example, he attended, and was used to promote, the high-tone 'Business Summit' organised by the influential Corporate Council on Africa, a US-based trade body loaded with oil and infrastructure interests such as Halliburton, even as Halliburton's own man in the White House, Vice President Dick Cheney, helped lead the US into a bloody invasion of Iraq.[72]

MORE WAR: STANDING BESIDE BUSH

The build-up to the Iraq War in 2002 and early 2003 must have posed a considerable dilemma for Bono. Western elite opinion was genuinely divided over the prospect of a US-led invasion of Iraq, so it was possible to oppose the potential war without cutting oneself off from respectable society. Moreover, he and his band had come to prominence two decades earlier with an album called *War* and an anthem, 'Sunday, Bloody Sunday', that, as far as most listeners were concerned, expressed an abhorrence of violence as a means to political ends; they had drawn attention to the bloody siege of Sarajevo; they had earnestly attacked and playfully satirised all manner of militarism. And now there was a worldwide movement against this war even before it started – a gathering of benign forces with which, on the face of it, a campaigner for justice such as Bono would want to associate himself.

And yet, there were also his most powerful friends and patrons – Bush, Powell, Rice and, perhaps most importantly, Blair – all of whom had staked their reputations on this invasion. Blair, with his mad-eyed facsimile of idealism, had been a crucial instrument in rallying politically 'moderate' opinion to the war.

Bono's solution for quite some time was to be one of the few people in the world without a known view on the subject. On 15 February 2003 – five weeks before the invasion – a small, simple placard at the big anti-war protest in Dublin read: 'Where's Bono?' Perhaps the large, peaceful and media-friendly nature of those February demonstrations all around the world was enough to shake him into a statement of sorts. On Sunday, 23 February, an exclusive interview with him appeared in the mid-market tabloid newspaper *Ireland on Sunday*. The paper presented it as his coming-out against the war, but it was more like, 'Be careful now, pals', addressed to his friends Tony and George. In keeping with his revisionist post-peace process version of the conflict in Northern Ireland, Bono was now, in 2003, an advocate of inclusive dialogue rather than state violence. 'Over the top' responses to terrorism, he said, deploying all the local knowledge he could muster, only exacerbated the problem:

> I think the way terrorism in Ireland was encouraged by a very over the top British response is a good example. You had 300 active service members of the Provisional IRA in the '70s and '80s and they sent in 30,000 troops. They also interned everybody who was suspicious

without fair access to trial lawyers. Internment was the thing that actually grew the IRA.[73]

Leaving aside the familiar difference between such twenty-first-century pronouncements and Bono's unwaveringly one-sided pronouncements against IRA 'terrorism' when the Irish Troubles had raged, his formulation appeared to accept that the prospective invasion of Iraq was simply a response to terrorism. In comments directed toward his friends in Washington, he added: 'It would be wise at this moment in time to think about the mistakes that have been made. Irish people have a little bit of experience with terrorism, and America has none.'[74]

That statesman-like fence-sitting was clad by the media as an anti-war statement, and seemed to go down reasonably well. Bono clearly felt encouraged to say some more, and the perfect occasion presented itself in Paris the following week, when Bono was made a Knight of the Legion of Honour. An anti-war statement here, where his host Jacques Chirac was leading the 'old Europe' pressure for no war without UN Security Council agreement, could never be construed as radical. Why, it was practically just good manners: 'How can you not be for peace? I think America has no experience with terrorism or even with war. In Europe, we know a little bit more about these things. We must not make a martyr out of Saddam Hussein. He's good at propaganda. Let's not make it easier for him.'[75]

This pulling of historical rank on behalf of 'old Europe' was perhaps just a tad rude to the Americans, who had after all experienced some brutal terrorism and, further back in history, a bloody civil war; and it still left him with Tony Blair to address. Bono did so with his customary aplomb: 'Tony Blair is not going to war for oil,' he said. 'Tony Blair is to me a great politician. He is sincere in his convictions about Iraq but, in my opinion, he is sincerely wrong.'[76]

This, it must be said, was smooth positioning. Bono, he made clear, was not some crazy radical accusing the 'Coalition of the Willing' of representing corporate interests in Iraq; he wasn't screaming 'No blood for oil!'; he was not even worrying about the consequences for Iraqi civilians of an attack, nor of the sanctions that had been starving and sickening them for twelve years. No, he was merely on one side of a respectful difference of honest opinion among right-minded men about the best way to deal with terrorism, so as not to make it worse. The enemy, let there be no doubt, was not merely 'terrorism', it was also that master of propaganda, Saddam Hussein.

In a story that appeared on the MTV website just as the war was launched, he expressed clearly to a US audience the limits of his support for, and opposition to, the war:

> With the unimaginable levels of economic, cultural and military weight that the United States has, there must come humility and restraint … I'm all for President Bush trying to scare the sh— [sic] out of Saddam Hussein, but you have to bring along the rest of the world … People need to understand what this is about, and I support them all the way to the point where they go to war without the United Nations behind them. That is a mistake, because that looks like the US doesn't need to explain itself, and I think it does.[77]

Bono construed the threat to shower bombs and missiles on a sovereign country, then invade it, as an effort to scare the shit out of its dictator, and fully approved it. The execution of that threat, he cautioned, required further explanation, that was all – or else it might be construed as, horror of horrors, a mistake.

Then, having supported them 'all the way to the point' where they went to war, as they did, without a UN resolution, Bono showed no further sign of opposing the war. On the contrary, as the carnage of violent occupation piled up in Iraq over the following years, he cooperated with the British and US governments in what was, in effect, the most extraordinary effort to rehabilitate them in the eyes of the public as leaders of the global anti-poverty crusade, the saviours of Africa (see Chapter 2).

The grotesque irony of this effort was not lost on everyone. After Bono did a photo-op with Blair and Clinton to promote African debt relief early in 2005, Jim Kerr, singer from the band Simple Minds, accused him of 'sucking up' to 'creeps':

> How can Bono, having graced concert stages for over two decades, draped in the white flag of peace and screaming 'No More War' [sic] at the top of his lungs contemplate praising and back slapping Tony Blair? … I can't believe that anyone could fail to identify that no matter what gesture Blair may make towards African debt relief, his slippery hands are currently dripping in the fresh warm blood of Iraqi men, women and children.[78]

Bono paid Kerr no attention. When the leaders of the war-making world, Bush and Blair foremost among them, gathered in Gleneagles, Scotland, for the G8 summit in the summer of 2005, they were greeted not by the massive peace protests that would have been the very least they deserved, but by a pop concert, a backstage pass for Paul Wolfowitz, and a vast demonstration of welcome.

Bono did not bear the full responsibility for this, not by a long shot. We have no reason to believe he approached and created that event as cynically as, say, Blair clearly did, by the evidence of his own memoirs (see Chapter 2). Gordon Brown himself evidently played a close role in moulding activists into the image of the British government. Still, Bono must have had an inkling of the purpose he served. Bono's role in using Africa to whitewash Blair and Bush is reminiscent of the host who presents an attractive cake to guests, and, asked if he made it himself, replies, 'I made it … possible.' Bono was necessary, if not sufficient, for the task of presenting the dainty dish that was set before a deceived public that summer. He has not suffered nearly the opprobrium he deserves for helping to reshape a global peace-and-justice movement into a cheering section for those who led the slaughter in Iraq.

History has already proved a harsher judge of Bush's bona fides, and Bono's reputation will be haunted by the images that trailed through 2002 and 2003 of his stroll in the Rose Garden – perhaps flashing a juvenile peace sign for the cameras, or is it a V for victory? – then having a quiet word in the president's ear. Those images may prove to be the most enduring of his career on the fringes of American politics. As Richard Dienst writes of one such image,

> To a well-trained, cynical viewer, this photo does not need to be decoded at all, because the cynicism is built right into it. The image does not simply advertise that some kind of deal is being struck: the image is the substance of the deal itself. The only question is whether or not it is a good deal, and for whom.
>
> It is easy to imagine what people will say: Bono and Bush are simply using each other. Bono uses his celebrity to pressure Bush on debt relief and AIDS funding for Africa. Bush uses Bono to show that he is somehow in touch with popular tastes, and somehow sympathetic to the causes Bono espouses. Nobody will be surprised to see the pomp of state power mingling so freely with the glitz of pop stardom. Nobody needs to believe that these two men are actually having a serious conversation about the issues of global poverty. Instead everybody will assume that each of them has a good, if vague, reason to be seen in public with the other.

As Dienst also notes, 'During the same period that the [Bush] administration had such a hard time scraping together just over $4 billion for the Millennium Challenge [another name for the Sachs multilateral anti-poverty project], it spent more than sixty times that much on Iraq.'[79]

When Bush stood beside Bono on a White House platform in January

2002 and said, 'Bono, I appreciate your heart', you could nearly imagine that Bono had torn that organ from his chest and given it, tied up in a ribbon, to the president. Bush was clearly enjoying the largely make-believe contrast between president and rock star: 'Here's what I know about [Bono]. First, he's a good musician. Secondly, he is willing to use his position in a responsible way.'[80] That word 'responsible', as every child knows, generally translates as 'obedient'.

James Traub of the *New York Times*, an admirer of Bono though not of Bush, summarised what Bush meant by 'responsible': 'Bono says, in effect, I am willing to shed some of my liberal credibility on you.'[81]

Bono, cornered by the press afterwards, did exactly that: 'We just had a meeting with the President of the United States about the emergency of AIDS. It is the crumbs off our table that we offer these countries. And it is not good enough.' Bono threw his thumb over his shoulder in the direction of the Oval Office for emphasis. 'The President of the United States doesn't think it's good enough.'[82] As noted previously, Bush eventually thought AIDS funding for Africa was good enough to feature it in his 2003 State of the Union speech, just before the section that signalled his unwavering intention to attack Iraq.

A decade later, in a BBC interview, Bono was unrepentant: 'Even though people said "George Bush is using you", I beg to differ. I think we used him. And I think he wanted to be used, it turned out, in that way. We found that piece of him that wanted to show the world what he was *for* as well as what he was against.'[83] But what if the things that Bush was *for*, including endless war, runaway military spending, abstinence education against AIDS instead of condoms, deals with Big Pharma instead of generic drugs for the developing world – what if all those things killed more people, and made poverty and inequality more intractable, than more radical alternatives? Just what was Bono using Bush for?

DREAMING WITH OBAMA: WASHINGTON TO PALESTINE

Bono has rarely missed an opportunity to praise George W. Bush for his efforts on behalf of AIDS and Africa. As he insisted as recently as 2011, 'He's a controversial figure … but I can verify that at the very least there are a few million fathers, mothers, sisters and brothers that would not still be with us were it not for him.'[84] He never mentioned those who owed their deaths, rather than their lives, to Bush.

All the same, even Bono, the consummate salesman, would have to admit Barack Obama was an easier sell than Bush. In 2006 Oprah Winfrey had called Bono 'the reigning king of hope', but the singer seemed happy enough to relinquish his crown to the man who had made 'hope' his unique selling point when elected to the White House in 2008. As we saw in Chapter 2, Bono had featured Obama prominently when he edited *Vanity Fair* in 2007, and, given the new president's African origins and global popularity, it would have been astonishing if Bono had done anything other than seek to make an ally of him. The Obama campaign, in turn, used U2's 'City of Blinding Lights' as entrance music for the candidate in the run-up to the election.

Extravagant flattery followed for years to come. Obama, he said shortly before the president visited Ireland in 2011, 'represents the best of the political class':

> Whereas Bill Clinton is a very physical person in a room, he puts his hand on your shoulder, he's a great emotional arm-wrestler, Barack Obama has the demeanour of one you would play chess with. And then, of course, his secret weapon is his flash of a smile and a wicked sense of humour. He's very funny. You don't expect that from the chess player and that's his charm, and it is literally a winning smile because it's hard to stand up to – because it isn't insincere. A lot of politicians need to control their smile, it's like you can see the wires [laughs], but there's absolutely nothing fake about this man.[85]

In the same 2011 interview, however, Bono hinted that 'absolutely nothing fake' Obama was not always happy with the portrait of Africa that emerges from Geldof/Bono-style advocacy (note Bono's reflex to add heft to 'Africa' with additional verbiage, though at least this time it is not 'terrible beauty'):

> Obama was, and is, very keen to avoid the cliché of this majestic continent of Africa being portrayed as supplicant. I think that offends his African side and that's very understandable. Sometimes, with people like myself or Bob [Geldof], because our job is to raise the alarm, the drama that's necessary to get people to take unnecessary loss of life seriously means that you can project an image of the continent that's not dimensional or accurate. I have always found in my dealings with Obama that he's very keen to stress a relationship with Africa that is horizontal, not vertical – i.e. partnership not patronage.[86]

All this admiration for the way Obama talked about Africa is perhaps a substitute for being able to cite things that the first black president had actually done for Africa. In the financially straitened Obama years, there were no major and visible new initiatives to match Clinton's debt-cancellation or Bush's AIDS programme, whatever the limits and contradictions of those achievements. Could Obama's legacy on Africa be simply that he told Bono not to be so condescending about the continent?

Nothing, however, could staunch the flattery. Having willingly swept Bush's militarism under the carpet for so many years, Bono was positively admiring of Obama's version, especially the killing of Osama bin Laden in Pakistan:

> I guess he could have flattened the compound, but as with so much to do with this President, he shows his brains over brawn; the lives of the women and children were, under Obama's leadership, a critical part of the calculation. I don't believe it was an execution, as some have suggested. The safety of the Navy SEALs was and should be pre-eminent.[87]

Again with the women and children – though it appears that this time they take second and third place in Bono's mind, behind the Navy SEALs. The idea that the 'safety' of US troops attacking a compound full of civilians in a country in which the US was not at war should be 'pre-eminent' is some indication of how far Bono had come from 'Bullet the Blue Sky'. However, while mere photo-ops with Bush had earned Bono the anger of many US (and Irish) liberals, his lavish praise for Obama put him firmly in their company. Obama's policy of targeted drone strikes in Pakistan, Yemen and elsewhere – effectively killing some of the people Bush would have merely tortured, and taking hundreds of women and children with them – was still, in 2011, largely uncontroversial, evidence of the president's 'brains over brawn', and had bipartisan support in the US.

Indeed, Bono's admiration for Obama would be quite unremarkable, a mere marker of his familiar, and commonplace, political temperament, if it were not conjoined with an adoration of the US ruling class more broadly. Two decades on from Clinton's election, Bono was no longer exercised by America's need to expiate its original sins. It was clear from this Irish interview that it was the president's office, with its Irish-oak desk, rather than the man that really made him breathless:

> [T]his kind of very, very heightened feeling that you have from being around the White House, whether you try to talk yourself down from it or not, you tend to walk out of there with a slightly different walk from when you went in.
>
> ... I really believe in America – the idea, that is. America is an idea, not just a country, and I think it's an extraordinary idea and meant to be contagious ... I mean, here's this dude Jefferson who is a complicated guy for

sure, but he's 27 or maybe even younger when he's writing [the Declaration of Independence].[88]

Jefferson was thirty-three, as it happens. But what really impressed Bono was not the Founders' youth but the fact that they were 'not just farmers or urban workers; they are the most powerful people in the Americas. If you think of George Washington as the greatest landowner, that's like Bill Gates, in terms of his wealth.'[89] Lest we forget, George Washington's great wealth (unlikely to have been in the Gates bracket) was measured in the hundreds of human beings he owned as well as the land. What is intriguing about Bono's rhapsody is the part of the history lesson that really excited him: not democracy, but the ability of a group of rich men to bring about dramatic change, and to do so in the name of a ringingly good idea. The association of this peculiar form of greatness with Bill Gates, who had become something of a partner and patron to Bono, is surely no accident. (For more on the Gates connection, see below.)

Bono's version of America's 'idea', in short, is fully in keeping with his own campaigning practice: rich and powerful men making decisions and creating change that they say is in the interests of everyone else – who may or may not get a say in the matter.

Just as Bono had believed America's great principles were now ready to be fulfilled at Bill Clinton's election in 1992, part of his role at the Obama inaugural concert was to declare the new president to be the embodiment of the fulfilment. Joining the liberal chorus, Bono proclaimed that the inauguration of one black man as US president meant that Martin Luther King's vision of a multiracial republic of equality, freedom and justice had become reality or – as he put it rather awkwardly from the stage – 'On Tuesday, that dream comes to pass.'

One could have tried pointing out to Bono that white households in the US had on average twelve times the wealth of black households (a gap that stretched to 22:1 in the first four Obama years), or that black Americans live an average of five years shorter than whites, but there would have been no point. Not only has Bono generally shown little interest in the reality of poverty anywhere but in Africa, but his basic elite orientation probably meant that, for him, a more multicoloured ruling class really did look like living the dream.

Anyway, in the middle of 'Pride (In the Name of Love)', Bono made another little speech to annotate that 'dream' line: 'Not just an American dream. Also an Irish dream, a European dream, African dream, an Israeli dream …' Such an odd choice of dreams: two continents, two specific nationalities – what on earth could he be building to now with this dramatic pause as he stalked the platform? 'And also [further dramatic pause] … a Palestinian dream!' He turned to face the audience, looking ready to burst with, well, pride, then launched into the song's final sing-along chorus.[90]

Bono's mini-speech was actually a little confusing. Did he mean that Obama's inauguration caused the dream to 'come to pass' for all those other people too? Hardly. But it really did appear that he believed he had committed an act of great and redeeming courage by uttering the word 'Palestinian' in this context in Washington, where in actual fact politicians had for decades been paying lip-service to a Palestinian dream – if by the dream we mean some sort of Palestinian statehood – while at the same time buttressing Israeli intransigence. Indeed, in the quasi-official circumstances it would have been somewhat controversial if Bono had failed to pay the normal lip-service: once he said 'Israeli', he would have to balance it with, at the very least, 'Arab', if not 'Palestinian'. Yet in an interview more than two years later he was still extraordinarily impressed with himself for his (first and only) brave intervention on behalf of this oppressed people:

When [King] said 'I have a dream', people think he was talking about the American dream, and it's really not true. It was a dream big enough to fit the whole world. And then I mentioned that it was also an Irish dream, it was a Mexican dream, it was an Israeli dream, it was a Palestinian dream. And I got into terrible trouble for the 'Palestinian dream' piece. That's when they got fed up. That's when they said, 'go home!' And I'm thinking, how could you not regard the figure of Dr King as standing for universal human rights, whatever the geography? There was no problem in the new administration – but in the media there was some real push-back.[91]

It's interesting that Bono misremembered himself as saying 'Mexican dream', which would probably have been slightly controversial and even a little bit brave, had he actually done so, in the context of US immigration policy. But the notion that his Palestinian 'piece' led to his being scorned, abused, told to go home – that's an exaggeration, at the very least. A small number of mainstream reports of the concert suggest that Bono 'courted controversy', or words to that effect, but the controversy itself, the 'real push-back', is conspicuous by its absence from the online record.

This appears to be another example of Bono's version of himself as an activist, making dangerous noise and banging on doors, speaking truth to power. The reality is that he has not said anything that even begins to discommode Washington's powerful elite in at least two decades. Why would he, when he is part of that elite?

It is an elite that has been instrumental in suppressing the 'Palestinian dream', even while periodically alluding to its sort-of legitimacy. The phony neutrality of some American rhetoric about the Israel–Palestine conflict is crucial to the maintenance of the oppressive status quo, and Bono has been a part of that phenomenon. A year after the inauguration, Bono was again paying lip-service to Palestine, this time without mentioning Israel. In that decade-preview column for the *New York Times*, in a section headed 'Viva la (Nonviolent) Revolución', Bono lovingly quoted Obama, wished ill on the regimes of various official enemies – Iran, North Korea, Myanmar – and then said he was 'placing his hopes on the possibility … that people in places filled with rage and despair, places like the Palestinian territories, will in the days ahead find among them their Gandhi, their King, their Aung San Suu Kyi'.[92] The patronising ascription of raw, thoughtless emotions such as rage and despair to subordinate peoples was straight out of the imperial playbook; the same can be said for the hint that he blamed the Palestinians themselves – thousands of whom languished in Israeli jails without any proven connection to violent resistance – for failing to produce a nonviolent leader, and therefore blocking their own release from rage and despair.

Bono was not finished dreaming sweet dreams for Israel and Palestine. In April 2012 he paid what was described in the press as a 'private visit' to Tel Aviv and Jerusalem. One Palestinian report said he visited Bethlehem's Church of the Nativity and other sites on the West Bank.[93] In his suite at Jerusalem's King David Hotel – site of an infamous 1946 Zionist bombing that killed ninety-one people – he left behind a note, with a sketch of a rather vicious-looking 'dog called Hope'. Signed by him – and, it appears, Ali on her own behalf and that of their two young sons – it looked like a piece of poetic prose.

> In Jerusalem hope springs eternal. Hope is like a faithful dog sometimes she runs ahead of me to check the future, to sniff it out and then I call to her: Hope, Hope, come here, and she comes to me. I pet her, she eats out of my hand and sometimes she stays behind, near some other hope maybe to sniff out whatever was. Then I call her my Despair I call out to her. Heh, my little Despair, come here and she comes and snuggles up, and again I call her Hope.

Beside his signature, Bono added: 'with great thanks for great room in great hotel in great city'. The note was widely reported, especially in Israel, and seemed to be something along the lines of 'Bono's hope for the Middle East'. It took a U2 fan blog to spot on the note, in tiny writing, the words 'reading Amichai', and then to discover that Bono was merely quoting, from an English translation, the late Israeli poet Yehuda Amichai.[94]

The Israeli website Ynet reported that Bono had hired a top Israeli security firm for his trip – as used by Bill Gates and Warren Buffett – and turned down a meeting with President Shimon Peres, citing his promise to his children that it would be a low-key visit, but promising to have a pint with Peres at some future time. Ynet quoted a note from Bono to the president praising Peres's 'special mind' and the tourist attractions of Tel Aviv, noting that 'history is written in the Holy Land every day', and signing himself 'your admirer'.[95]

The Israeli authorities were happy to make use of Bono's apparent friendship. In late 2012, when controversy flared up about the many Irish artists who had chosen to boycott Israel, that country's eccentric deputy ambassador in Ireland, Nurit Tinari-Modai, told a newspaper not only that *Riverdance* had played in Jerusalem, Tel Aviv and Haifa, but that 'Bono is a regular visitor to Israel with his family'[96] – 'regular' being most likely a diplomatic exaggeration. (Unlike artists including Brian Eno, Roger Waters and Ken Loach, Bono has never backed a cultural boycott of Israel; but nor have he or U2 played there.)

This diplomatic implication of a Bono endorsement of Israel appeared even while Israel was again bombing Gaza – but Bono didn't see fit to make any public pronouncement distancing himself from it. And so, at the time of writing, the world still awaits – or it doesn't – a Bono pronouncement on Israel, the occupation, and the resistance to it, in words that go beyond carefully balanced dreams.

CUI BONO? PHILANTHROPY

No one can be in any doubt that, whatever the character of his interventions, Bono has been generous with his words and with his time for the causes he supports. But it would appear that Bono does not set out to do good in the world with much (relatively speaking) of his own money. Trevor Neilson, a man who enjoys the peculiar job description of 'celebrity philanthropy adviser', recalled in a *New Yorker* article how, as they were seeking to get their DATA lobbying organisation funded in 2001, Bono and Bobby Shriver came to him looking for help raising $3 million, a sum that even then Bono would easily have had at his fingertips.[97] (It is hard to imagine Shriver was not equally blessed.) *Time* magazine, ever-ready with a compliment and/or a rationalisation for its favoured public figures, said that Bono 'refused to bankroll it' to 'ensure that DATA was divorced from the stigma of vanity'.[98] Neilson, who was then working for the Bill and Melinda Gates Foundation, 'helped to get DATA off the ground' in

2002, said Bono, with Gates money, and other benefactors chipped in too. Presumably the Gates and Soros grants that funded DATA had never been married to 'the stigma of vanity'.

According to Neilson, who in the *New Yorker* article expressed his admiration and appreciation of the 'sweat equity' that Bono brings to causes, the singer 'doesn't spend millions of dollars of his own money. He rallies public opinion and lobbies governments.'[99] One suspects that Neilson's formulation is somewhat misleading, and that Bono has surely spent 'millions' of his own money on philanthropic causes – just perhaps not the same ones with which he is most publicly associated, nor on the same scale as some other rich celebrities. Nonetheless, Neilson's line is the nearest we can get, in the opaque world of Bono and his finances, to a flat statement from someone reasonably knowledgeable on the subject about the volume of Bono's charitable giving, and Nielson says it is not very large compared to some of his peers. Bono himself has said that U2 prefers to keep its philanthropy below the radar; the only amount that has been publicised recently in Ireland is €5 million, given by U2 as a whole, for an admirable music-education scheme for young people. At any rate, only the most crass and superficial observer would seek to judge someone's commitment to 'good causes' with a dollar amount; the question 'How much does he give?' has trailed Bono more than most in recent years because of publicity around his investments and tax arrangements, but he is perfectly entitled not to be drawn into answering it.

DATA, the Bono-founded organisation funded by Gates and Soros, stands not merely for Debt AIDS Trade Africa, but also for Bono's Sachs-bred devotion to hard, measurable facts when it came to poverty-reduction and AIDS treatment. With DATA as his lobbying arm, in 2004 Bono co-founded another US non-profit, ONE: The Campaign to Make Poverty History, to do the 'rallying [of] public opinion'; the short form, ONE, comes from the title of one of U2's best songs, and has stuck. ONE was initially a coalition of mainly US-based organisations, including Oxfam America, Save the Children, World Vision and (confusingly) DATA itself, and it also invited members of the public to join. Like DATA before it, it got a significant lump of its first money from the Gates Foundation.

By the end of 2007, it seemed the two organisations belonged together, and so they merged into ONE. The new body's first chief executive officer, David Lane, came straight from the Gates Foundation, where he had held various senior policy positions.[100] But Lane was no mere charity case: a Washington insider, he had also served in the Clinton administration and as a member of the Council on Foreign Relations, and when he left ONE in 2011 he slid back into government under Obama as an 'ambassador' to the UN's Food and Agriculture Organisation in Rome.[101] When he did so, ONE replaced him with an Englishman, Michael Elliot, who had been editor of *Time International*, the global version of *Time*, when Bono had all those nice things written about him, and was named the magazine's Person of the Year (along with his benefactors Bill and Melinda Gates) in 2005. Elliot had also worked as a journalist and columnist at such hotbeds of radical thought as *Fortune* and *Newsweek*. As of late 2012, ONE's board of directors is largely a parade of middle-aged white men, mostly Americans from the mingling worlds of business, government and philanthropy. Exceptions to the dominant race and gender include Condoleezza Rice and – the only one of the nineteen who actually lives and works in the developing world – Ngozi Okonjo-Iweala, Nigerian finance minister and a long-time Bono favourite.[102] She was, you may recall, the sole living, thinking African whose 'voice' was readable in Bono's 2006 edition of the London *Independent* (see Chapter 2). Her Harvard degree and spell at the World Bank no doubt render her suitable to sit beside, say, former US treasury secretary and Harvard president Laurence Summers at a ONE board meeting. A charitable view of the board is that its members were chosen for their powerful connections.

It is easy to mock the level of activism ONE encourages among its 3 million or so 'members' – 'joining' is as easy as entering a name and email address. Indeed U2 concert-goers have been given a chance to sign up on the spot, as an Irish journalist observed at a 2009 gig, when after the song 'One',

> Bono urged the crowd to take out mobile phones and sign up to the advocacy organization of the same name, which he co-founded, the number of which appeared on the giant screen. When only a sprinkling of phones lit up, he suggested that we take out our phones anyway, to show the power of one. It was an odd moment, one of a few in the show that gave it the sense of a sanitized branded experience rather than a rock show, something tweaked and streamlined to generate the optimal consumer reaction…[103]

However, despite such bland provenance and promotion, it is surprising that some of ONE's public work is actually reasonably spirited and engaging. The one.org website encourages 'ONE Act a Week'. In late August 2012 the act for the week was to send a tweet – the text was provided – to three US senators to thank them for helping to improve transparency about the lobbying efforts of US-based oil and gas companies in the developing world. (A perfectly decent campaign, by the way.) '*Time: 5 minutes. Level of difficulty: Easy.*' Five minutes was a generous allotment for this act, presumably allowing for the member to 'Read more' and thus begin to understand why they were being asked to do this. Beside this injunction to action is a nice little cartoony video featuring Bill and Melinda Gates explaining in numbingly simple, studiously uncontroversial terms why the right sort of aid works a treat for making things better in the developing world, from building schools to improving soil fertility.

Nonetheless, anyone regularly reading the blog on ONE's website – judging by the number of comments, there are very few who do so – would actually learn a thing or two about global poverty, including even some things that don't entirely fit with the Bono world-view: a link, for example, to a story (albeit on the official Voice of America website) about an academic study showing that the vast majority of the world's poorest people live *not* in very poor countries – in other words, the ones consistently targeted by Bono's campaigning over the years – but in middle-income countries, where the problem is not desperate national poverty but enormous internal inequality.[104] It is hard to imagine ONE will take this information on board, but at least it helped to disseminate it.

ONE clearly employs (in both paid and volunteer capacities) a lot of energetic young people skimming merrily along the surface of the serious issues that confront the world. Its publicity is full of images of shiny-faced workers in black ONE T-shirts gathered for a tiny 'demonstration', or stretched along the steps of the US Capitol with their fact-filled clipboards, or at the Republican convention with their iPads. Those young people and their activities on three continents are, to a huge extent, what ONE 'does', how it spends its money, what it is, largely within the limits set by its narrow and neoliberal leadership. What ONE *isn't* is a charitable foundation.

Some of the negative coverage of ONE has not quite caught the distinction that Bono's ONE is not a charitable organization, but rather one devoted to lobbying and public information campaigns. Thus, Britain's *Daily Mail* screamed in 2010: 'Bono's ONE foundation under fire for giving little over 1% of funds to charity'. (This was one of those 'under fire' headlines in which the newspaper itself appears to be the only one firing.) In fact, US tax records showed 98.8 per cent of ONE's $15 million intake for the year 2008 went on salary and expenses, with a negligible $180,000 slipping out to three charities.[105]

However, since ONE is not in fact a foundation but an advocacy non-profit, and since it does not, exactly, solicit money from the public, but gets most of its dough from the bottomless pit that is the Gates Foundation, this was something of a non-story, at least in standard media terms. (As it happens, the ONE annual report for 2010 acknowledges that improvement was needed in communicating the 'we don't want your money' message to the public. That report indicates that 'contributions', as opposed to 'grants', fell from more than $2.6 million in 2009 to less than $700,000 in 2010.[106])

Even the ONE salaries, apparently averaging out somewhere around $80,000 each in 2008, were not scandalous. What got the media's attention in 2010, however, was an example of the sort of 'expenses' often incurred by a lobbying organisation. The UN was meeting in New York to discuss progress, or otherwise, on the Millennium Development Goals, and the *New York Post* reported that a string of couriers had dropped by the Murdoch newspaper's office, bearing gifts from ONE:

Nothing says, 'Wipe out AIDS and poverty' like Band-Aids and a black-and-white cookie …

The items were part of a pricey pile of puzzling loot, which also included a $15 bag of Starbucks coffee, a $15 Moleskine leather notebook, a $20 water bottle and a plastic ruler.

The stash came in four, oversized shoe boxes, delivered one at a time via expensive messenger …

Kimberly Hunter, spokeswoman for DC-based ONE, declined to say how much money the organization shelled out for the publicity blitz.

'Sometimes it's pretty hard to get through to reporters with the information about the lives of the world's poorest people,' Hunter said. 'We think it's important enough to try and break through the clutter … That's why we sent the boxes.'

Poverty-stricken African kids live on less than $1.25 a day – 'about the cost of the cookie in this box', ONE contended [in a note in the box] …

The Starbucks brew – made with Ethiopian beans – came with a suggestion to drum up support for investing in African agriculture.[107]

Bono's name featured, inevitably and unflatteringly, in the headline.

It was a story custom-made for media righteousness: why spend a buck and a quarter on a cookie for a journalist when you could have doubled the money available to some kid in Africa? Journalists didn't, and don't, tend to reveal all the other times they got a goody bag from a PR agency working for some business client.

However, hidden behind the unsurprising story about ONE's devotion to corporate-style public relations, and the non-story about its non-charitable purpose, was an unexplored story about ONE's growing devotion to a particular form of 'sustainable agriculture' in the developing world, supposedly embodied in that Ethiopian coffee. Yet again, Bono's agenda was working in the service not simply of 'the world's poorest people' but of corporations seeking to depict what's good for them as what's good for the poor.

GRASSROOTS: AN AGRICULTURAL AGENDA

Bono's ONE has got a tremendous amount of funding from the Gates Foundation: a total of $83 million between 2006 and 2009 to last until the end of 2012, with a little $1 million top-up in March 2012, according to the Gates Foundation's own online records. (The campaign's annual report is not required to be fully and transparently detailed about its sources of money.) Given that fact, and given that the first CEO of the united ONE organisation came in directly from that foundation, ONE can legitimately be seen not only as Bono's main humanitarian vehicle of recent years, but also as part of the information and campaigning operation of the vast $30-plus billion Gates charitable fortune. That foundation is prepared to spend money in order to associate itself with allegedly credible voices on global issues: for example, in 2010 it began to part-fund (through a grant in 2011 of about $2.5 million, or less than 0.01 per cent of the Gates total endowment) an area of the British *Guardian* newspaper's website devoted to global development. The foundation's subtle logo can now be seen pasted onto legitimate journalistic stories in that section of one of the world's most popular journalistic websites.[108]

As it happens, one such legitimate 2010 *Guardian* story – a blog post framed politely in relation to Gates, wondering if the foundation might be a tad, er, 'hopelessly naive' – discussed how Gates had clearly and deliberately got into bed with two of the world's nastiest multinational agribusiness giants: Monsanto, which sells agrichemicals and is a leader in the development of genetically modified (GM) crops, and Cargill, a vast conglomerate involved in the production and distribution of food and fertiliser. The foundation was apparently working with Cargill on 'developing the soya value chain' in Mozambique, a phrase that the journalist recognised from corporate rhetoric about introducing GM seed; and the foundation had bought $23 million-worth of Monsanto shares, adding to its existing shareholding. *Guardian* environment editor John Vidal couldn't help but ask:

> Does Gates know it is in danger of being caught up in their reputations, or does the foundation actually share their corporate vision of farming and intend to work with them more in future?
>
> The foundation has never been upfront about its vision for agriculture in the world's poorest countries, nor the role of controversial technologies like GM. But perhaps it could start the debate here?

In the meantime, it could tell us how many of its senior agricultural staff used to work for Monsanto or Cargill?[109]

Vidal's question about the possible direct personal connections between the foundation and agribusiness was not meant to be rhetorical, but it was never directly answered, nor was it taken up elsewhere.

Philanthropic foundations get an extraordinarily uncritical press – not surprising, perhaps, when they may splash some cash around a struggling newspaper; but given that a US foundation such as Gates keeps vast amounts of its namesake's fortune out of the public tax coffers, and is in a position to advance its pet policy agendas to an extent that would be the envy of most governments, you might imagine it would be more closely scrutinised. In general, media commentary may gripe about where Bill Gates got his money – through a ruthless monopoly on computer operating software – but it rarely does anything other than praise how he has spent it.

The Gates Foundation's agenda, its vision, on agriculture has emerged clearly enough for those who choose to look for it. In 2006 it joined forces with the Rockefeller Foundation to establish the Alliance for a Green Revolution in Africa (AGRA), promoting scientific and technological solutions to increasing agricultural production, very much in partnership with companies such as Monsanto. Gates has also funded GM and other agri-science research in Western universities and institutions.[110]

So-called 'green revolutions' have been hotly debated in terms of their impact in countries such as Mexico and India, where they may have boosted production but also driven poor farmers into debt and off the land – in India, notoriously, into suicide by their thousands – because of the expense of repeatedly having to purchase the new high-tech inputs to seed and nourish increasingly exhausted soil. The respected Indian journalist P. Sainath has documented an incredible 270,940 farm suicides between 1995 and 2011, even while India's farm population has been falling, and 'despite an orchestrated (and expensive) campaign in the media and other forums by governments and major seed corporations to show that their efforts had made things a lot better'.[111] A 2005 American PBS documentary looked at the incredible spate of 'suicides by pesticide', and linked the phenomenon to GM promotion by, yes, Cargill and Monsanto.[112]

This has not deterred the foundations from pursuing more of the same in Africa, encouraging farmers to invest to produce higher yields of cash-crops that will integrate them into local and global markets. Even the idea, and reality, of Western companies buying African agricultural land meets with the approval of Bill Gates himself: 'Many of these land deals are beneficial, and it would be too bad if some were held back because of Western groups' ways of looking at things.' (It is a familiar and clever rhetorical strategy to attribute resistance to western corporate interference to 'Western groups', suggesting that Africans themselves have no problem with such 'progress' – though this is untrue, as we shall see.) Gates continued: 'When capital is put into Africa, that's a good sign.'[113] Even, that is, when the capital is 'put in' to take land out of African hands, forcing local farmers into dependence on Western owners and Western-supplied technology.

Make no mistake, this development has not escaped Bono's attention. On the contrary, he and ONE have embraced the AGRA 'sustainable agriculture' agenda, and Bono himself was one of the initiative's frontmen at the G8's latest re-branding exercise, a 'Global Food Summit' hosted by the US at Camp David in May 2012. Employing the techno-positivism beloved of Gates and their like, Bono told an interviewer: 'You know, no one wants to see those extended [*sic*] bellies … Hunger is a ridiculous thing. And we know what to do in order to fix it. There's, you know, these whole new approaches to agriculture to increase productivity.'[114] Bono was not called upon to specify what 'these whole new approaches' might be; his task, in any case, is not to make the technical case for GM and chemical-laden farming, but to mutter the emollient words that will assure audiences that such developments must surely be for the good of Africa's poor.

And what's good for Africans, Bono added in the same interview, is good for America. Africans 'are future consumers for the United States. The president [Obama] is talking business. This is good.'[115] The idea of 'trade not aid' to help the 'entrepreneurial poor' is of course attractive on the face of it. As Bono said, echoing almost word for word his earlier recollection of Obama's rhetorical priorities: 'It's partnership, it's not the old paternalism. These are sort of horizontal relationships, not vertical ones.'[116]

Unsurprisingly, given the resources available, there are a great many Africans willing to be horizontal partners in this new 'revolution' with Gates, Bono and Western states and companies. But what is more surprising, and inspiring, is that so many people are willing to stand against it. When that same G8 meeting announced a 'New Alliance for Food Security and Nutrition' – an alliance that included the G8, African governments, and forty-five companies ranging from Unilever to the alcoholic drinks giant Diageo to Monsanto – a number of campaigners were quick to spot what was going on. Oxfam, which had been such a reliable ally of Bono in 2005, was no longer on board: its press release was headlined, sarcastically, 'G8 food security alliance answers question hungry people have not asked' – the new 'answer' being heightened involvement by multinational companies. Oxfam saw the 'new alliance' not only as a way of getting corporations in on the act, but as a diversion, as the G8 continued to ignore old promises it had made of providing aid: the 2009 G8 meeting at L'Aquila, Italy, had promised $22 billion in increased aid, much of which still hadn't appeared. Now, in a crisis-ridden global economy, aid pledges were being sidelined in favour of this new 'partnership'. Oxfam's Lamine Ndiaye was critical of the corporate agenda: 'Smallholder farmers need the freedom to pursue their own growing strategies, not take overly-prescriptive tips on farming from G8 leaders, or one size fits all technologies from far away CEOs.'[117] Other groups and alliances from African civil society had already joined in the condemnation, with an 'open letter' statement in advance of the summit:

> If the private sector is to play a productive role, there needs to be strong evidence that these kinds of partnerships can actually deliver for small-scale producers. For the initiative to truly be an alliance, women small-scale producers, youth, and pastoralists should have been consulted in the drafting of the plan. Instead, G8 leaders are merely asking African governments for a rubber stamp. Donors increasingly claim to target the small-scale producers who make up the majority of the world's poor, but they are rarely consulted, and these resources seldom actually reach them.[118]

As with other issues, there is room for legitimate disagreement about the role of GM and increased market integration in the development of African agriculture and the relief of hunger. It is striking, however, that yet again Bono finds himself on the side representing Western 'philanthro-capitalism' and the interests of multinational companies seeking to expand their businesses, and their profits, in the fertile soil of the global poor.

Even some of those who give Gates and Bono the benefit of the doubt believe they are getting it wrong when pursuing a new Green Revolution in the wake of the failure of previous ones. Kavita N. Ramdas is an Indian-born researcher in 'social entrepreneurship' at Stanford University who has worked with the Gates Foundation – her CV, indeed, is a resumé of good causes that even Bono would envy. Ramdas has said that the foundation's 'good intentions' are turned into bad policy in this area because of the obsession with 'measurable impacts', and certain ideological blinkers:

> At the root of the difference in approach is what we believe causes hunger or poverty. If you think that people are poor because there is not enough food, then you will concentrate on making measurable gains, in growing more food, and more nutritious food, more efficiently. But if you think that

people are poor because of problems with equality, with access, with education, then developing a concrete strategy is far more difficult; these things
are not readily measurable.[119]

The emphasis on production, efficiency, things you can measure, is in
some ways understandable. How else can you know what you are achiev-
ing? When Bono spoke at the World Bank in November 2012, he was
asked what was the most important thing 'we' could do to end extreme
poverty; he replied, 'We need open data … We need better data.'[120] But
the problem with 'measurable impacts' is the things that are left out – not
only the factors Ramdas mentions, but also all the alternative approaches
that are ignored.[121] As researchers such as those at the Institute of Food
and Development Policy have long argued, the problem in Africa is not
a shortage of food, but food systems that have been distorted by the push
to export crops, by the needs of local and foreign elites, and by promotion
of technological solutions that push farmers and their knowledge out of
decision-making.[122]

Why, in this context, and keeping Ramdas's words in mind, do Gates
and Bono 'believe' that the problem is too little food, and 'think' that
agriculture-on-steroids is the answer? To which one might answer, people
mostly 'believe' what they want to believe, and 'think' what it suits them to
think. For Bono to continue to ally himself with the sorts of government
and company with which he had stood side-by-side since the late 1990s,
and for him to continue to be a useful front to their interests, he had to
speak the language of equality, access and education, but also to 'think' that
the interests and desires of the rich and powerful happily coincide with
the making of a better world that would finally deliver upon those values.

WITH OR WITHOUT YOU: BONO TODAY

In truth, in recent years Bono may have begun to outlive his usefulness as a
fashionable accessory to power. If anything, he has probably been too loyal
to the forces and figures that were so widely discredited in the post-2007
global crisis – to the Rubins, Clintons and Browns who opened the door
to the financial catastrophe, to the Bushes and Blairs who unleashed hell
on Third World countries. A little more distance, even in retrospect, might
have preserved some of his credibility. But then he wouldn't be Bono. A
decade ago, one might arguably have suggested that he stood outside the
system, bringing some moral authority to bear on questions of global
poverty and disease and what to do about them. Today, as a high-profile
multimillionaire investor, as part of a band of notorious tax-avoiders who
assured us that financial innovation was the route to success, as the man

who dressed a bunch of multinational corporations in his favoured shade of (RED), as the Blairite who applauded when the world's war-mongers pretended to lavish some relief on a few poor countries while saddling them with more neoliberal conditions – today, he is hard to see as anything other than one of Them, the elite 1 per cent of 1 per cent.

This perception of him is increasingly widespread, which means that, from the point of view of those who would use him, Bono has perhaps become a too-easy target, the villain of a thousand online comment threads. For every Mike Huckabee – who cited Bono's great work, and his great love for the USA, from the platform at the 2012 Republican National Convention – there's a Sinead O'Connor mocking his tax status and calling him "Bozo".

It probably doesn't help that as of early 2013 he appears to have run out of steam artistically. Bono's pet musical-theatre project with The Edge, *Spider-Man: Turn Off the Dark*, was a logistical fiasco, pilloried especially for its music – and will need to run for several years on Broadway (its only home thus far) just to pay its debts.[123] It may eventually achieve such a run, thanks to its special effects and the touristic pull of the spidery franchise, but it is unlikely ever to be removed from its already-honoured place, earned via accidents, injuries, at least one major lawsuit and month after month of 'previews', as one of Broadway's greatest ever messes.

It would be unwise, a dangerous hostage to fortune, to rule out an artistic comeback for Bono. Sensible people may legitimately differ on how long it has been since a good U2 album – is the time best measured in years or decades? – and indeed on the question of Bono's contribution to the band's best material. (In his recent lyrics, a noted critic writes, 'every platitude yields to an obscurantist pretension and back again'.[124]) In mid 2012 he appeared on an Irish television talk-show and suggested that new U2 music was being delayed from reaching the public by Edge's unjustified doubts about his own genius; Bono added, with typical (if somewhat wearing) self-deprecating charm, that he himself suffered from the opposite flaw, excessive confidence in his genius. It is very difficult to spend any extended time wading through his interviews and writings and then to disagree with the latter assessment: for all his reflexive self-put-downs, Bono is, in his own mind, part of an exceedingly small rock pantheon of true greatness. There is every possibility that, in his early fifties, he still has work ahead of him, with or without U2, that will compel many others to agree.

A renewal of his artistic standing might also improve his political profile. But it's not like he hasn't been working on the latter: he remains, despite his setbacks, a favoured symbol of soft power for the global elite when it gathers. His campaign, ONE, is nothing like the mass movement that it pretends to be, but it is present and visible, getting signatures on petitions and lobbying not only in Washington or at the G8, but in various lower-level parliaments and councils in Europe and Africa, where it now boasts offices in Nigeria and South Africa. Politically, Bono is not a 'fraud', not in the sense that word is usually understood. The oft-heard assertion that his humanitarian work is a means of garnering free publicity for his profitable music is a half-truth, at best, that significantly underestimates the scale and below-the-radar detail of his advocacy. He is not lacking in genuine commitment, even if the demands of his half-billion-dollar rock band and two-billion-dollar private-equity fund may intrude on his campaigning. (His physical frailty, in the form of back problems, has also intruded on all these activities.) He has given a lot of his time and built up political and organisational nous: his work and his campaigns are linked to real achievements, from marginal debt relief to AIDS drugs to the high visibility of African poverty in Western celebrity circles. It is not the existence of those achievements that is questioned in these pages: it is their meaning, and the interests they represent.

Bono and his supporters have, for example, pointed proudly to the rather dramatic rates of economic growth taking place over the last decade in several poor African countries where his agenda has been active.[125] (You might imagine the fate of the Celtic Tiger would make them wary of very rapid growth rates, but apparently not.) However, the vision of Afro-optimism is punctured once you look closely at those numbers, as even the UN acknowledges: a 2012 report shows that 'the current pattern of growth is neither inclusive nor sustainable' – that it is growth that is unequally shared and largely fuelled by the extraction of quickly depleting natural resources.[126] That sort of 'development' is good news for someone, but that someone is not the vast majority of Africa's poor.

The phenomenon of Bono is profoundly linked to efforts over recent decades by Western leaders, both in and out of political office, to project themselves as humanitarian visionaries. (Two of Bono's best political pals, Bill Clinton and Tony Blair, both have global charitable foundations in their names; both have got money from the Bill and Melinda Gates Foundation.) Various endeavours, from violent interventions in Iraq and the former Yugoslavia to the neoliberal restructuring of whole economies in the developing world, have been portrayed as arising from a desire to better the lives of various poor and oppressed peoples, while in fact serving the strategic and economic goals of the West. This is not to be conspiratorial, nor to fail to recognise that there are internal divisions among Western elites, so that they don't always speak with one voice on such matters. Nonetheless, it has become an important part of the legitimation of the neoliberal project, often as destructive to the lives, circumstances and democratic voices of people in 'rich' developed countries as in the global South, to portray it as a drive for a more just globalised system that will value, include and reward the very people who were beggared by previous versions of imperialism. That's where Bono comes in.

A transnational class of elites, experts and technocrats in largely unaccountable state institutions and completely unaccountable corporations and foundations continues to lead the way in this project. Celebrity humanitarians have become instrumental to their work. Bono may not have realised it when he climbed aboard a largely admirable campaign against developing-world debt in the late 1990s, but his reputation for integrity and the love for his music felt by millions of people would become important weapons in the arsenal of those seeking to maintain and extend their influence, power and profit in a changing world. He fronted for the G8; he fronted for Tony Blair and Gordon Brown and George Bush; he fronted for Nike and Apple and Motorola; he fronted for Bill Clinton and Bill Gates and the Irish Financial Services Centre to boot.

Whether he believed in his heart that it was worthwhile to advance the plans and interests of such people and organisations in order to achieve larger benign goals is a moot question. He should be judged not on his motivations or intentions, which are invisible, but on the plain reality of his actions. Bono cannot be expected to support every righteous cause, but it is striking to note some he has not. For example, right on his doorstep in Ireland, there are the campaigners in County Mayo in the west of the country who are fighting to keep a dangerous Shell gas pipeline and refinery out of their community, and making powerful links with Ogoni people in Nigeria who have waged similar struggles against the petroleum giant. The Irish locals in this boggy, remote landscape sometimes call themselves 'the Bog-oni', and they have invited Nigerians and others from around the world to come share their experiences; they have fought in the courts and lain down in front of trucks; they have sailed their fishing boats in front of giant pipe-laying vessels; they have been beaten off the roads by police and security men and been locked up in jail for months at a time; they have drawn attention to the political cowardice and corruption that saw Ireland sell off the rights to its offshore gas and oil to foreign companies at a rate so low it would make a Third World dictator laugh all the way to his Swiss bank.[127] And they have done all this fighting without an ounce of support from the Irishman who claims to be a campaigner for justice and global solidarity.

Then there are those Africans who have been fortunate or unfortunate enough to have actually left Africa, and thus lost Bono's support. Tens of thousands of African migrants live in Ireland, many thousands as asylum-seekers forced into an inhumane system called 'direct provision'. Under this system, some 2,000 asylum-seeker children and 4,000 adults live packed into hostels, denied the right to work and given a pittance of €19 per week each (less for the kids) as an allowance.[128] For many years one such hostel, Kilmarnock House, housing 100 or more residents and owned by a controversial Protestant pastor, was located in Bono's home village of Killiney – perhaps he could even see it, a mile or so away, from his hillside mansion. It wasn't one of the better hostels: residents said conditions there were 'prison-like', and indeed at one point it was closed temporarily on health-and-safety grounds.[129] A grim 2004 'needs assessment' of its residents said that 'due to the extremely limited availability of funding, most of the recommendations are constrained to activities that could be implemented by the community and voluntary sectors'.[130] A number of people and organisations in Ireland campaign visibly for migrant rights, but Bono is not one of them. Chinedu Onyejelem, a Nigerian-born community activist who edits a 'multicultural' newspaper in Ireland and is usually adept at securing support from the great and good, was emphatic when asked if Bono had been of help to Ireland's Africans: 'The answer is NO. I tried several times to contact him and to get him to do something with us, but never got beyond his agent.'[131]

Perhaps contact with real grassroots activism of this sort would interfere with Bono's rhetorically crucial claims to 'represent' the world's poor. He periodically laughs at the cheekiness of his unelected representation, and recently even wished for the day when it would no longer be necessary, and he could 'fuck off'.[132] However, Bono has nonetheless not been shy of making the claim: 'I'm representing the poorest and most vulnerable people. On a spiritual level, I have that with me. I'm throwing a punch, and the fist belongs to people who can't be in the room, whose rage, whose anger, whose hurt I represent.'[133] Richard Dienst has dismantled this claim with brilliant and bitter precision:

> He does not claim to represent their interests, their perspectives, or even their hopes, but rather their 'rage, anger, and hurt': That is to say, he does not represent human beings, he represents affects, detached from real lives and filtered through his celebrity image ... It is not as if 'the poorest and most vulnerable people' do not express themselves, in countless ways, all the time. They are articulate, deliberate, and far too various to be summed up just by their pain or their poverty. They have many representatives, too, in and out of governments. All of them are aching to be heard. None of that

seems to matter when Bono goes to the White House. Indeed, we should make no mistake about it: he can stand there precisely because those people are so absent; he can speak for them exactly insofar as they are silenced; he can 'throw a punch' at Bush, Blair, Obama, or any of the others only because he disguises the immense material force of their lives with the soft 'moral force' of his rhetoric ... What is missing, invisible, off the agenda, is any belief that economic development can be a mode of collective self-determination, opening up a realm of freedom for the poor beyond that envisioned for them by billionaires.[134]

There can scarcely have been a more perfect expression of the way anything that might ever have been good or real about Bono has become corrupted, and of the relationship between the West and the global South he has come to 'represent', than what happened in the summer of 2012 on a popular African television programme. This was *Big Brother Africa: Stargame*, the seventh season of a pan-African version of the vicious and voyeuristic 'reality' show that puts a group of strangers into a fully televised house and pits them against each other around the clock, with a cash prize at stake; they must often appear to cooperate with each other in tasks in order for each to advance his or her strategy for success, achieved partly through public voting. The show is, as its title suggests, a depiction of a microcosm of the surveillance state portrayed in George Orwell's famous novel *Nineteen Eighty-Four*; but it is also, intentionally or not, a metaphor for, and embodiment of, the savage world of deceit, betrayal, false appearances, ruthless competition and commercial exploitation of even the most humane relationships that characterise neoliberal capitalism; the African version adds implied competition between nations to this happy script. Needless to say, it was popular over its three full months in the forty-seven African countries that screened it, sixteen of which were represented among the 'housemates'. Bono's ONE Campaign had got itself involved with a gardening task on the show, as part of its 'Thrive' campaign on African agriculture. Housemates also had to design T-shirts for 'Thrive'. Thrive-related tasks were ongoing when, on one July day, with most of the housemates bearing the ONE logo on their chests, there on the big screen from where Big Brother normally addressed the housemates appeared a Thrive logo, followed by a video of Bono. He was beamed in, on tape, straight from Dublin, speaking bland phrases of encouragement, Big Brother personified. The full Orwellian effect, whereby words mean the opposite of what they should really mean, was underlined by the giant 'RESPECT' flashing electronically beneath his visage. Obviously aware, albeit insufficiently, of the relationship implied by his appearance in this role, he blathered, to the accompanying fast-moving video graphics: 'This is your Irish rock star fan, Bono. You are my big brothers and little sisters.' He continued: 'I hear that you're growing and farming the future, and that the fruit is the hope and change that we're all hungry for.'[135]

Here was Bono, back where he had started so modestly in Ethiopia twenty-seven years before, entertainingly telling Africans how to grow their food, but now coming through in rapid jump-cuts, dressed in full celebrity regalia, for a European TV-show franchise specifically designed to bring out, and display, the worst in people, and speaking – vaguely, but in the context of the visuals and the show, unquestionably – on behalf of an agricultural partnership that included Monsanto, in soundbites borrowed from Obama.

'This is so surreal, I cannot believe it,' a housemate said, in apparent awe. But you'd better believe it: it's all too real.

ACKNOWLEDGEMENTS

The late, great Alexander Cockburn used to ask his interns and acolytes, 'Is your hate pure?' I wasn't either of those things, exactly, but he asked me anyway. I doubted his seriousness, as I also doubted the purity of any aspect of my being. (Or of his, for that matter.) I couldn't say Yes, and I hope it was just a long-running joke, because otherwise he might have been sorely disappointed with me and with this book, which is not animated by hatred, pure or otherwise, of its subject. Like all the work I've ever done as a journalist it was, however, animated by him, and it was my great good fortune that in the last decade he helped to bring that work to a wider audience.

Although I cannot repay Alexander, I hope I may find some way to thank his fine friend and co-editor at *CounterPunch*, Jeffrey St Clair, to whom this book owes its very existence, as well as its rocking short title. The magical *CounterPunch* chain of acquaintance also found me linked with another of my animating heroes, Dave Marsh, whose excellent writings on Bono have all-too-obviously been an inspiration for these pages, and whose conversations on- and offline always make me think deeper.

Beside Jeff and Dave, at the top of the list of people who might have done this book better is my extraordinary friend Andy Storey, who over the decades has freely shared with me his deep analytical expertise on Africa, economics, music, and even Bono. (His thoughts on football and films haven't made the cut this time.) In countless sessions he made the Swan bar in Aungier Street my classroom, and he is directly responsible for a significant chunk of the bibliography and several crucial improvements in this text. The errors are of course all my own, but I would never have been smart enough to make them without him.

Margaret Kelleher was responsible in another way, offering her empty home and the company of her beautiful cat Shelley when a deadline threatened and a writing retreat was needed. The book's back was broken under her print of a sixteenth-century map, 'Africae Tabula Nova', a welcome reminder of the long history of European efforts to inscribe meanings on that continent.

I am grateful to numerous librarians, in my home institution the Dublin Institute of Technology, in Trinity College Dublin and in the Dublin public library system, who made my research easier. Paddy Prendeville of *Phoenix* magazine was a guide to that fine and dangerous publication's daunting print and digital archives, and was also one of the many, many people around Ireland who, either at my request or simply on hearing of my topic, launched fascinating, insightful, provocative conversations. Many of them will recognise their insights, and I hope they do not mind the borrowing. Most of them would probably prefer to go unnamed, but particular thanks must go to scholar Sean Dunne, who offered formidable ideas and a great graffiti sighting. Also special thanks to the vegetable-seller who mentioned the *South Park* episode about Bono!

A book that is not in my notes but which was nonetheless useful is Nathan Jackson's *Bono's Politics: The Future of Celebrity Political Activism*, self-published in 2008 and with its text available free at bonospolitics.com. Jackson might not relish the mention, since his views and conclusions are so different from my own, but his book is a clear, thorough presentation of what might be called the case for the defence.

At Verso, I am indebted to Andy Hsaio for showing the confidence to commission this from me, and to Audrea Lim for her extraordinarily valuable editorial input, which was friendly but challenging, thorough and thought-provoking. Similar thanks and praise are due to a wise and sympathetic copy-editor, Charles Peyton.

My brilliant eldest daughter Louisa was the first I heard enunciate clearly the Irish reaction to Bono's tax controversy a few years back. 'No one can stand him anyway – this just gives us a reason for how we already felt.' Even allowing for exaggerated teenage certitude, the thoughts of her and her equally brilliant sister Cara have been enormously treasured, and their company too.

I think my youngest, Stella, has particularly enjoyed speaking the phrase, 'so you can work on your Bono-book'. I look forward with pleasure to her next phrase, and my next excuse. Her mother, my wife Catherine Ann Cullen, has for more than ten years been the best of all possible companions, interlocutors, editors, exemplars. She is inspiring and strengthening, and a helluva lotta fun. I can scarcely conceive of this work, or anything else, without her.

NOTES

INTRODUCTION

1 Michka Assayas, *Bono on Bono: Conversations with Michka Assayas* (London: Hodder & Stoughton, 2005), 17.
2 'Leadership at a Time of Transition and Turbulence – A Conversation with Peter Sutherland KCMG', *Gresham College*, 8 March 2011, at gresham.ac.uk.
3 'Give Us the Money', *Why Poverty?* (BBC Four, 25 November 2012).
4 Marina Hyde, 'Bono: The Celebrity Who Just Keeps Giving', *Guardian*, 23 September 2010; Jane Bussmann, 'Kony2012 Made up for the Flaws of Bono, Geldof and Co', *Guardian*, 3 April 2012.
5 Eamonn McCann, 'Make Bono Pay Tax', *CounterPunch*, 26 February 2009, at counterpunch.org.
6 'Give Us the Money'.
7 Daniel Schorn, 'Bono And The Christian Right', *CBS News*, 20 November 2005, at cbsnews.com.
8 Ibid.
9 George Monbiot, 'Africa's New Best Friends', *Guardian*, 5 July 2005.

1 IRELAND

1 Shane Hegarty, 'The Sad Ballad of Bruce and Bono', *Irish Times*, 24 January 2009.
2 Michka Assayas, *Bono on Bono: Conversations with Michka Assayas* (London: Hodder & Stoughton, 2005), 112.
3 Bill Flanagan, *U2: At the End of the World* (London: Random House, 1996), 78.
4 David Kootnikoff, *U2: A Musical Biography* (Oxford: Greenwood Press, 2010), 8.
5 Eamon Dunphy, *Unforgettable Fire: The Story of U2* (London: Penguin, 1987), 22–31.

6   Bono, 'Transcript: Bono Remarks at the National Prayer Breakfast', *USA Today*, 2 February 2006.

7   Kootnikoff, *U2: A Musical Biography*, 3–6.

8   Michael Gray, *The Bob Dylan Encyclopedia* (London: Continuum, 2008), 689.

9   Dunphy, *Unforgettable Fire*, 26–8.

10 Dan Wooding, 'Whatever Happened to U2?', n.d., at prayforsurf.net.

11 Bono, The Edge, Adam Clayton and Larry Mullen Jr, *U2 by U2* (London: HarperCollins, 2006), 135.

12 Bill Graham, *U2: The Early Days* (London: Mandarin Paperbacks, 1989), 24–5.

13 Ibid., 30–2.

14 Assayas, *Bono on Bono*, 94.

15 Bono et al., *U2 By U2*, 118.

16 Graham, *U2: The Early Days*, 30.

17 Ibid., 42.

18 Ibid., 37.

19 Sean Campbell and Gerry Smyth, *Beautiful Day: Forty Years of Irish Rock* (Cork: Atrium, 2005), 4.

20 Graham, *U2: The Early Days*, 33.

21 Ibid., 23.

22 Ibid., 10.

23 Dave Fanning, 'U2 – Just Beginning', *Magill*, June 1985.

24 Graham, *U2: The Early Days*, 36.

25 'U2 and the USA', *U2 Magazine*, November 1983. This story of principled withdrawal is somewhat confused by a photograph of the band walking under umbrellas in the 1982 parade, taken by the well-known photographer Lynn Goldsmith and available online at morrisonhotelgallery.com.

26 Bill Graham, 'Irish Ways ... Irish Laws: The Moving Hearts Interview', *Hot Press*, 24 October 1981.

27 Eamonn Sweeney, *Down, Down Deeper and Down: Ireland in the 70s and 80s* (Dublin: Gill & Macmillan, 2010), 231.

28 'Fitzgerald Launches Youth Committee', *Irish Times*, 16 September 1983.

29 Laura Jackson, *Bono: The Biography* (London: Piatkus, 2003), 43.

30 Initially the British claimed that they were returning fire in Derry, and a first official inquiry whitewashed the slaughter; a long peace-process-inspired British investigation confirmed in 2010 what everyone in Ireland had already known for decades: that the victims were completely innocent.

31 Bono et al., *U2 by U2*, 135.

32 Brian Trench, 'See the Conquering Heroes Come', *Magill*, June 1987; Bill Rolston, '"This is Not a Rebel Song": The Irish Conflict and Popular Music',

Race and Class 42(3) (2001): 49–67; Barbara Bradby and Brian Torode, 'To Whom Do U2 Appeal?', *The Crane Bag* 8: 2 (1984): 73–8.

33 Kootnikoff, *U2: A Musical Biography*, 22. The extent to which the specifics of Bloody Sunday in Derry had become a forgotten embarrassment to the southern Irish establishment by the 1980s can be measured by the fact that respected journalist Eamon Dunphy's U2 'biography', published in 1987, got the year of the atrocity wrong, and mentioned sniffily that 'many' of the day's victims had been innocent. The errors were not corrected in the 1993 edition.

34 'A Social History of U2: 1976-2005', *The Dubliner*, April 2007.

35 'Band FAQ', *U2FAQS.COM: Frequently Asked Questions About U2*, n.d., at u2faqs.com.

36 Bono et al., *U2 by U2*, 130.

37 Phil Joanou, *U2: Rattle and Hum*, DVD (Paramount, 1999).

38 Bono et al., *U2 by U2*, 130.

39 Bono, 'In Ireland, Tuesday's Grace', *New York Times*, 19 June 2010.

40 Isaac Guzman, 'No Bombast, But U2 Bands Together With N.Y.', *New York Daily News*, 26 October 2001.

41 Sweeney, *Down, Down Deeper and Down*, 353.

42 Jim Carroll, 'Self Aid, 22 Years On', *Irish Times*, 19 May 2008.

43 Dunphy, *Unforgettable Fire*, 327.

44 *U2: Bad (Live Dublin '86 – Self Aid) HQ Stereo*, n.d., at youtube.com.

45 Dunphy, *Unforgettable Fire*, 327–30.

46 'Pillar of Society: Paul McGuinness', *Phoenix*, 27 August 1993.

47 'Bono's Bum Deal', *Phoenix*, 11 February 2000; 'Bono, the Law and His Ass', *Phoenix*, 25 February 2000; 'L'ETAT C'EST MOI! KING BONO INVOKES OFFENCES AGAINST THE STATE ACT', *Phoenix*, 25 February 2000.

48 'Ali Hewson's Celestial Offer', *Phoenix*, 29 March 2002.

49 James Henke, 'U2: Here Comes the Next Big Thing', *Rolling Stone*, 19 February 1981.

50 Trench, 'See the Conquering Heroes Come', *Magill*, June 1987.

51 Ross, Michael, "All That They Can't Leave Behind," *Sunday Times*, July 12, 2009, Ireland edition.

52 Assayas, *Bono on Bono*, 289.

53 Bono et al., *U2 by U2*, 172.

54 Andrew Cockburn, 'Bono Betrays Ireland', *Counterpunch*, 10 August 2002, at counterpunch.org.

55 'How Bono Staged the Hume and Trimble Handshake', *U2log*, 9 June 2004, at u2log.com.

56 Gary Grattan and Maeve Quigley, 'U2 Say Yes to New Two', *Belfast Telegraph*, 20 May 1998.

57 Bono et al., *U2 by U2*, 285–6.

58   Assayas, *Bono on Bono*, 172–3.

59   'Give Us the Money', *Why Poverty?* (BBC Four, 25 November 2012).

60   Trench, 'See the Conquering Heroes Come.'

61   Matt Cooper, *Who Really Runs Ireland? The Story of the Elite Who Led Ireland from Bust to Boom … and Back Again* (Dublin: Penguin Ireland, 2009), 124.

62   Ibid.

63   Mary Carolan, 'Call for Retention of Artists' Tax Exemption', *Irish Times*, 15 September 2005.

64   Ibid.

65   Marie O'Halloran, 'Call for Analysis of Benefits of Arts Tax Scheme', *Irish Times*, 14 October 2005.

66   Hugh Linehan, 'When the Band Has No Shame', *Irish Times*, 12 August 2006.

67   Eamonn McCann, 'Make Bono Pay Tax', *CounterPunch*, 26 February 2009, at counterpunch.org.

68   Richard Tomlinson and Fergal O'Brien, 'Bono, Who Preaches Charity, Profits From Buyouts, Tax Breaks', *Bloomberg*, 25 January 2007.

69   ' "Double Irish With a Dutch Sandwich" ', n.d., at nytimes.com.

70   Cooper, *Who Really Runs Ireland?*, 124.

71   Ibid., 126.

72   McCann, 'Make Bono Pay Tax'.

73   'Pillar of Society: Diarmuid Martin', *Phoenix*, 15 August 2003.

74   'Give Us the Money'.

75   Brian Boyd, 'Bono "Hurt" by Criticism of U2 Move to Netherlands to Cut Tax', *Irish Times*, 27 February 2009.

76   Cooper, *Who Really Runs Ireland?*, 125–127.

77   See, for example, Jim Stewart, 'Financial Innovation and the Financial Crisis' (presented at the International Schumpeter Society Conference 2010 on Innovation, Organisation, Sustainability and Crises, Aalborg, 2010), at schumpeter2010.dk.

78   Boyd, 'Bono "Hurt" by Criticism'.

79   Eamonn McCann, 'The Emperors of Bombast', *CounterPunch*, 14 July 2009, at counterpunch.org.

80   Boyd, 'Bono "Hurt" by Criticism'.

81   Olaf Tyaransen, 'There Is Absolutely Nothing Fake About This Man', *Hot Press*, 2 June 2011, at hotpress.com.

82   'Ireland's Greatest', RTE, n.d., at rte.ie.

83   Photographs of both sets of graffiti are in the author's possession.

84   'U2 and Tax Avoidance', *Irish Times*, 6 March 2009.

85   Lara Gould, ' "Heavy Handed" Glastonbury Guards Break up U2 Protest', *Mail Online*, 26 June 2011, at dailymail.co.uk.

86   Ibid.

87   James O'Shea, 'Sinead O'Connor Slams Bono, Bob Geldof as "Bozo" and "Lily Livered Cowards"', *IrishCentral.com*, 19 June 2012, at irishcentral.com.

88   Visnja Cogan, *U2: An Irish Phenomenon* (Cork: Collins Press, 2006), 162.

89   'U2 Put Their House in Order', *Phoenix*, 20 October 2006.

90   'Pillar of Society: Ossie Kilkenny', *Phoenix*, 14 January, 2000.

91   Tomlinson and O'Brien, 'Bono, Who Preaches Charity, Profits From Buyouts, Tax Breaks'.

92   Cogan, *U2: An Irish Phenomenon*, 164.

93   Paul Colgan, 'U2's Tangled Financial Web', *Sunday Business Post*, 19 June 2005.

94   'U2 Put Their House in Order'.

95   Ibid.

96   Ibid.

97   Donal O'Donovan, 'U2 Firm Pays Tax Bill of Just €16,500 as Profits Plummet', *Irish Independent*, 2 December 2011.

98   Colgan, 'U2's Tangled Financial Web'.

99   Gordon Deegan, 'Bono and the Edge Help Clarence Hotel Back to Profit', *Irish Examiner*, 15 October 2011.

100   Frank McDonald, 'Clarence Group Gets Permission to Redevelop', *Irish Times*, 18 July 2008.

101   Ibid.

102   Boyd, 'Bono "Hurt" by Criticism'.

103   Frank McDonald, 'Bono Sees a Dublin "Defaced" by Developers', *Irish Times*, 13 November 2002.

104   'U2 Tower Land to Help Settle NAMA Debts', *RTE News*, 25 November 2011.

105   Accumulated losses in the Gerenger consortium that was to build the tower, only partly owned by U2, were €2.8 million according to accounts filed early in 2010. See 'Bono's Birthday Blues', *Phoenix*, 21 May 2010.

106   Tyaransen, 'There Is Absolutely Nothing Fake About This Man'.

107   Bono Addresses the American Ireland Fund 35th Anniversary New York Gala, 2010, at youtube.com. The quotes that follow are all transcribed from that video.

108   Bono, despite occasional efforts, lacks a common touch when it comes to sport, and sports personalities are in general notable by their absence from his celebrity-filled campaigns.

109   'When Bono Meets the Queen', *Mysterious Distance*, 24 May 2012, at mysteriousways-mysteriousdistance.blogspot.ie.

110   'Bow Before His "Demigodness": Bono Knighted', *TODAY.com*, 29 March 2007, at today.msnbc.msn.com.

111   Eamonn McCann, 'Simon, Sir Bono and Tinkerbelle', *CounterPunch*, 16 April 2007, at counterpunch.org.

2 AFRICA

1 Bono, The Edge, Adam Clayton and Larry Mullen Jr, *U2 by U2* (London: HarperCollins, 2006), 179.

2 Olaf Tyaransen, 'There Is Absolutely Nothing Fake About This Man', *Hot Press*, 2 June 2011, at hotpress.com.

3 Tom Lodge, 'An "Boks Amach": The Irish Anti-Apartheid Movement', *History Ireland* 14: 4 (August 2006).

4 'STRIKE!', *Diatribes of a Dilettante*, n.d., at cake1983.wordpress.com.

5 Bono et al., *U2 by U2*, 351.

6 Ibid., 158.

7 'Give Us the Money', *Why Poverty?* (BBC Four, 25 November 2012).

8 Bono et al., *U2 by U2*, 158.

9 Ibid.

10 Ibid.

11 Ibid.

12 *U2 – Sunday Bloody Sunday – Live Aid 1985*, 2011, at youtube.com.

13 *U2 BAD Live Aid 1985*, 2006, at youtube.com.

14 Bono et al., *U2 by U2*, 164.

15 Ibid.

16 *U2 At Live Aid*, 2009, at youtube.com.

17 *Frank Zappa On Howard Stern Show 1985 (pt. 1)*.

18 *U2 At Live Aid*.

19 Bono et al., *U2 by U2*, 162.

20 Pete Paphides, 'U2 Become Stars After Live Aid', *Observer*, 12 June 2011.

21 Bono et al., *U2 by U2*, 167.

22 Bono, *A String of Pearls: Photographs of Ethiopia*, 1988.

23 Bono et al., *U2 by U2*, 167.

24 Ibid.

25 Ibid., 167–9.

26 Ibid., 169.

27 Ibid.

28 Phil Joanou, *U2: Rattle and Hum*, DVD (Paramount, 1999). Bono concludes his speaking interlude with the injunction, 'Play the blues, Edge', to which Edge replies with a not very bluesy solo, underlining both Bono's desire to connect this song to the blues and U2's incapacity to make that connection.

29 Noel McLaughlin and Martin McLoone, *Rock and Popular Music in Ireland Before and After U2* (Dublin: Irish Academic Press, 2012), 188.

30 At the risk of excessive literalism, it should be noted that the limousine trip in which Bono allegedly heard Holiday on WBLS, on the band's first night in New York in 1980, occurred on a Thursday, when an oldies show would have been highly unlikely. See Matt McGee, *U2: A Diary* (London: Omnibus Press, 2008).

31   Bono et al., *U2 by U2*, 207.

32   Ibid., 211.

33   Ibid., 213.

34   McLaughlin and McLoone, *Rock and Popular Music in Ireland Before and After U2*, 190.

35   *Save the Children*, 1995, at youtube.com.

36   Bono, 'World Debt Angers Me', *Guardian*, 17 February 1999.

37   'Give Us the Money'.

38   Nick Buxton, 'Debt Cancellation and Civil Society: A Case Study of Jubilee 2000', in Paul Gready, ed., *Fighting for Human Rights* (London: Routledge, 2004).

39   Charlotte Denny, 'Brown's $50bn Demand', *Guardian*, 20 February 1999.

40   Bono et al., *U2 by U2*, 293.

41   Michka Assayas, *Bono on Bono: Conversations with Michka Assayas* (London: Hodder & Stoughton, 2005), 89.

42   Ibid.

43   Bono et al., *U2 by U2*, 290.

44   James Traub, 'The Statesman', *New York Times*, 18 September 2005.

45   'Give Us the Money'.

46   Traub, 'The Statesman'.

47   'Washington Wire', *Wall Street Journal*, 22 September 2000.

48   Bono et al., *U2 by U2*, 290.

49   Quoted in Sean O'Hagan, 'Pro Bono', *Observer*, 26 September 2004.

50   Mark Memmott, 'Rocker Leads Drive to Lift Third World Debt', *USA Today*, 14 June 2001, at usatoday.com.

51   Traub, 'The Statesman'.

52   Ibid.

53   Ibid.

54   'Bono, Mar. 4, 2002', at time.com.

55   Traub, 'The Statesman'.

56   Assayas, *Bono on Bono*, 263.

57   Quoted in Traub, 'The Statesman'.

58   Robert Pollin, *Contours of Descent: US Economic Fractures and the Landscape of Global Austerity* (London: Verso, 2003), 165–7.

59   Traub, 'The Statesman'.

60   'Give Us the Money'.

61   Daniel Schorn, 'Bono And The Christian Right', *CBS News*, 20 November 2005, at cbsnews.com.

62   Alex de Waal, 'The Humanitarian Carnival: A Celebrity Vogue', *World Affairs* 171: 2 (Fall 2008), 47.

63   Traub, 'The Statesman'.

64 'AIDS: Too Much Morality, Too Little Sense', *Economist*, 28 July 2005, at economist.com.

65 Kapya John Kaoma, *Colonizing African Values: How the US Christian Right Is Transforming Sexual Politics in Africa* (Somerville, MA: Political Research Associates, 2012).

66 Riina Yrjölä, 'From Street into the World: Towards a Politicised Reading of Celebrity Humanitarianism', *British Journal of Politics and International Relations* 14: 3 (August 2012), 361–2.

67 Quoted in ibid., 359.

68 Audrey Bryan, 'Band-Aid Pedagogy, Celebrity Humanitarianism, and Cosmopolitan Provincialism: A Critical Analysis of Global Citizenship Education', in Charles Wankel and Shaun Malleck, eds, *Ethical Models and Applications of Globalization: Cultural, Socio-Political and Economic Perspectives* (Hershey, PA: Business Science Reference, 2012), 276.

69 Riina Yrjölä, 'The Invisible Violence of Celebrity Humanitarianism: Soft Images and Hard Words in the Making and Unmaking of Africa', *World Political Science Review* 5: 1 (2009), 1.

70 Yrjölä, 'From Street into the World', 367.

71 Bono, 'Transcript: Bono Remarks at the National Prayer Breakfast', *USA Today*, 2 February 2006.

72 Assayas, *Bono on Bono*, 264.

73 Yrjölä, 'From Street into the World', 369.

74 Ibid., 358.

75 Yrjölä, 'Invisible Violence', 4.

76 Yrjölä, 'From Street into the World', 361–2.

77 Summarised in John Street, 'Do Celebrity Politics and Celebrity Politicians Matter?', *British Journal of Politics and International Relations* 14: 3 (August 2012), 351.

78 Yrjölä, 'From Street into the World', 359.

79 Quoted in Nathan Farrell, 'Celebrity Politics: Bono, Product (RED) and the Legitimising of Philanthrocapitalism', *British Journal of Politics and International Relations* 14: 3 (August 2012), 397.

80 Traub, 'The Statesman'.

81 de Waal, 'Humanitarian Carnival', 49.

82 Tony Blair, *A Journey* (London: Random House, 2010), 555.

83 Quoted in Stuart Hodkinson, 'G8 – Africa Nil', *Red Pepper*, November 2005.

84 ' "Get Real" on Africa, Urges Bono', BBC.co.uk, 29 September 2004.

85 Quoted in Julie Hollar, 'Bono, I Presume: Covering Africa Through Celebrities', *Extra!*, June 2007, at fair.org.

86 Josh Tyrangiel, 'The Constant Charmer', *Time*, 19 December 2005.

87 Traub, 'The Statesman'.

88   Blair, *A Journey*, 555. Blair's book is awash with idiotic facsimiles of natural speech such as this one.

89   Ibid.

90   Street, 'Do Celebrity Politics and Celebrity Politicians Matter?', 350.

91   Blair, *A Journey*, 570.

92   Hodkinson, 'G8 – Africa Nil'.

93   Kate Nash, 'Global Citizenship as Show Business: The Cultural Politics of Make Poverty History', *Media, Culture and Society* 30: 2 (1 March 2008), 175.

94   Ibid., 179.

95   Ibid., 176.

96   Ibid., 177.

97   'Albarn Criticises Live 8 Concerts', *BBC*, 10 June 2005.

98   Maxine Frith, 'Celebrities "Hijacked" Poverty Campaign, Say Furious Charities', *Independent*, 27 December 2005.

99   Ibid.

100 Hodkinson, 'G8 – Africa Nil'.

101 Ibid.

102 Ibid.

103 George Monbiot, 'Bards of the Powerful', *Guardian*, 21 June 2005.

104 'Bob, Bono and Africa', *Guardian*, 27 June 2005.

105 Hodkinson, 'G8 – Africa Nil'.

106 The colour and the capital letters denote emergency, apparently, and the parentheses are like embracing arms. Confusingly, when attached to products the brand often appears as (PRODUCT)[RED], supposedly with the product name occupying the embrace in place of the word 'product', though in practice this doesn't always happen. Some of the passages quoted in this section did not employ the parentheses at all, and I have retained the original presentation in each case.

107 Ray Waddell, 'U2 Set to Wrap Biggest Concert Tour Ever', *Billboard*, 29 July 2011.

108 Bono, 'Message 2U', *Vanity Fair*, 1 July 2007.

109 Alex Shoumatoff, 'The Lazarus Effect', *Vanity Fair*, 1 July 2007. Nike would eventually board the bandwagon in 2009 with some (RED), and red, shoelaces.

110 Eric Dash and Louise Story, 'Rubin Leaving Citigroup; Smith Barney for Sale', *New York Times*, 10 January 2009.

111 Sarah Dadush, 'Profiting in (RED): The Need for Enhanced Transparency in Cause-Related Marketing', *New York University Journal of International Law and Politics* 42: 4 (Summer 2010), 1269–336.

112 'One Great Color. One Great Cause', *Apple.com*, n.d., at apple.com.

113 Dadush, 'Profiting in (RED)', 1336 n. 21.

114 Ibid., 1336 n. 19.

115 Farrell, 'Celebrity Politics', 399.

116 Dadush, 'Profiting in (RED)', 1284–5.

117 'Costly Red Campaign Reaps Meager $18 Million', n.d., at adage.com.

118 Farrell, 'Celebrity Politics', 399.

119 Jane Martinson, 'The Amex Chief Providing Backing for Bono', Guardian, 17 March 2006.

120 Ibid.

121 Farrell, 'Celebrity Politics', 402.

122 Ibid., 404.

123 See Norma Anderson, 'Shoppers of the World Unite: (RED)'s Messaging and Morality in the Fight Against African AIDS', Journal of Pan African Studies 2: 6 (September 2008), 32–54.

124 Lisa Ann Richey and Stefano Ponte, 'Better (Red)™ Than Dead? Celebrities, Consumption and International Aid', Third World Quarterly 29: 4 (June 2008), 719–21.

125 Colleen O'Manique and Ronald Labonte, 'Rethinking (Product) RED', Lancet 371: 9624 (May 2008), 1561–3.

126 Colleen O'Manique and Ronald Labonté, 'Seeing (RED) – Authors' Reply', Lancet 371: 9627 (May 2008), 1836.

127 Bono, ' "We Need Europe to Be a Melting-Pot. We Need to Melt" ', Independent, 16 May 2006.

128 Bono, 'Bono, Guest Editor: I Am a Witness. What Can I Do?', Independent, 16 May 2006.

129 Bono, 'The Africa Issue: Still Optimistic, but No Sleep Until G8 Promises Fulfilled', Independent, 16 May 2006.

130 Paul Vallely, 'Can Rock Stars Change the World? The Big Question', Independent, 16 May 2006.

131 Ciar Byrne, ' "We Just Look for the Stuff That Feels Most Visceral" ', Independent, 16 May 2006.

132 Bob Geldof, 'Aid Isn't the Only Answer. Africa Must Be Allowed to Trade Its Way Out of Poverty', Independent, 16 May 2006.

133 Lisa Robinson, 'It's Bono, on Line 1', Vanity Fair, July 2007.

134 Bono, 'Meanwhile, in the Next White House …', Vanity Fair, 1 July 2007.

135 David Carr, 'Citizen Bono Brings Africa to Idle Rich', New York Times, 5 March 2007.

136 Bongani Madondo, quoted in Natasha Himmelman and Danai Mupotsa, '(Product)Red: (re)Branding Africa?', Journal of Pan African Studies 2: 6 (September 2008), 1.

137 Ibid., 2.

138 Zine Magubane, 'The (Product) Red Man's Burden: Charity, Celebrity,

and the Contradictions of Coevalness', *Journal of Pan African Studies* 2: 6 (2008).

139 Karon Liu, 'Bono and Bob Geldof Bring Their Bleeding Hearts (and Headline-Writing Skills) to the Globe', *Toronto Life*, 5 May 2010.

140 Jason Pontin, 'TED Day 1: Bono Heckles the Stage – Technology Review', *Technology Review*, 5 June 2007.

141 Felix Salmon, 'Mwenda vs Bono in Tanzania', 5 June 2007, at upstart.bizjournals.com.

142 Pontin, 'TED Day 1'.

143 *U2Miracle.com = Bono & Ali Hewson by Annie Leibovitz for Louis Vuitton's Core Values Ad Campaign*, 2010, at youtube.com.

144 'EU Court Rules Against Louis Vuitton in Nadia Plesner Copyright Case', *Eyeteeth*, 4 May 2011, at eyeteeth.blogspot.com.

145 'De Beers Jewellery – About De Beers', *De Beers Jewellery*, n.d., at debeers.com.

146 Tamara Abraham, 'Stuck in a Louis Vuitton Moment: Bono and Ali Hewson Pose for French Megabrand … in Clothes from Their Own Ethical Label', *Mail Online*, 2 September 2010, at dailymail.co.uk.

147 Ibid.

148 'Ad Nauseum: How Many Messages Can Bono, Designer Wife Ali Hewson and Louis Vuitton Fit in One Ad?', *New York Daily News*, 3 September 2010.

149 Chrissie Russell, 'Ali Hewson: It's a Wonderful Life Being Mrs Bono', *Independent.ie*, 27 August 2011, at independent.ie.

150 Bono, 'Message 2U'.

151 David Lipke, 'Q&A: Ali Hewson and Bono', *WWD*, 13 September 2011, at wwd.com.

152 See Carr, 'Citizen Bono Brings Africa to Idle Rich'.

153 Nathalie Atkinson, 'Ali Hewson and Bono's Return to Edun', *National Post*, 5 March 2011.

154 'Bono's Hotel Bills', *Phoenix*, 3 November 2006.

155 'Ali Hewson's Perfume', *Phoenix*, 28 August 2009.

156 Marina Hyde, 'Stella McCartney v Ali Hewson: Who Has the Right to Be "Nude"?', *Guardian*, 14 August 2009.

157 'Ali Hewson's Ethical Losses', *Phoenix*, November 2009.

158 The Hon. Mr Justice Floyd, *Nude Brands Ltd v Stella McCartney Ltd & Ors [2009] EWHC 2154 (Ch)* (EWHC (Ch) 2009).

159 Atkinson, 'Ali Hewson and Bono's Return to Edun'.

160 'Ali Hewson's Headaches', *Phoenix*, 24 September 2010.

161 'Ali Hewson's Perfume.'

162 'Bono and Ali Drop $10m', *Phoenix*, 7 October 2011.

163   Jennifer Bray, 'Ali Calls on Alicia Keys as Sometimes You Can't Make It on Your Own', *Irish Daily Mail*, 11 September 2012.

164   Atkinson, 'Ali Hewson and Bono's Return to Edun'.

165   Ibid.

166   Quoted in ibid.

167   'About Edun', *Edun*, n.d., at edun.com.

168   Bruce Wilson, 'KONY 2012 Effort a Ministry in Antigay Evangelical Barnabas Group, Reports LGBT Rights Nonprofit', *Huffington Post*, 10 April 2012, huffingtonpost.com.

169   Elizabeth Flock, 'Invisible Children Responds to Criticism About "Stop Kony" Campaign', *Washington Post Blogs*, 8 March 2012, at washingtonpost. com.

170   Most hilariously by Charlie Brooker in *Kony 2012 NWO Sinister Logos and Invisible Children – 10 O'Clock Live*, 14 March 2012, at youtube.com.

171   'Bono Comments on Invisible Children's Kony 2012 Campaign', 12 March 2012, at one.org.

3 THE WORLD

1   'Media Monkey Goes to Pebble Beach', *Guardian*, 2 August 2006.

2   'Bono's Secret: Frontman for Genocide', *Infowars*, n.d., at infowars.com.

3   I am indebted to Eric C. Lott, whose stimulating paper at the UCD Clinton Institute conference on 'Ireland and African America' in March 2012 dealt with Springsteen's induction speech for U2. The usual disclaimer applies about Lott's views being distinct from mine.

4   One of Dublin's favourite 'Bruce Springsteen is a lovely fella' stories, told again and again when his name is mentioned, recounts his very kind behaviour, when he was out in a restaurant with Bono, to fans who were seeking photos and autographs from Bono without recognising Springsteen.

5   Bruce Springsteen, 'Transcript: Bruce Springsteen Inducts U2 into the Rock and Roll Hall of Fame', *U2 Station*, 17 March 2005, at u2station.com.

6   Ibid.

7   Ibid.

8   Ibid.

9   'History FAQ', *U2faqs.com*, n.d., at www.u2faqs.com.

10   'Songs/Lyrics FAQ', *U2faqs.com*, n.d., at u2faqs.com.

11   All quoted in 'Apple Introduces the U2 iPod', *Apple.com*, 26 October 2004, apple.com.

12   'iTunes Music Store. Facelift for a Corrupt Industry', *Downhill Battle*, n.d., at downhillbattle.org.

13   Bryan Chaffin, 'Bono: Steve Jobs Is The Dalai Lama of Integration', *Mac Observer*, 15 October 2003, at macobserver.com.

14 'Pillar of Society: Paul McGuinness', *Phoenix*, 27 August 1993.

15 Ibid.

16 Ibid.

17 Bill Flanagan, *U2: At the End of the World* (London: Random House, 1996), 282–3.

18 *U2's Lost Song NEGATIVLAND*, 2007, at youtube.com.

19 'Negativland Interviews U2's The Edge', *Negativworldwidewebland!*, n.d., at negativland.com.

20 'U2 V. Negativland', *What Is Fair Use?*, 24 February 2008, at whatisfairuse.blogspot.ie.

21 'Negativland Interviews U2's The Edge'.

22 Ibid.

23 Edna Gundersen, 'U2's "Horizon" Premieres with Sky-High Sales Numbers', *USA Today*, 12 March 2009.

24 Bono, 'Ten for the Next Ten', *New York Times*, 2 January 2010.

25 Ibid.

26 Ibid. The American metaphor 'bully pulpit' was coined by Teddy Roosevelt, who used 'bully' to mean 'excellent'. It refers to an office, role or platform that confers authority, credibility and a guaranteed audience on those who speak from it. It can refer to the US presidency; to being a top humanitarian rock-star and *New York Times* op-ed writer; perhaps to making an induction speech at the Rock and Roll Hall of Fame. But it's a wishful, or ignorant, stretch of the phrase's meaning, even in the corporate media environment, to assume that the 'next Cole Porter', selected by Bono to front an industry campaign against music piracy, would have a bully pulpit.

27 'U2's Pension Plans', *Phoenix*, 2 November 2007.

28 'Bono Becomes The Worst Investor In America', *247wallst.com*, 24 March 2010, at 247wallst.com.

29 Crystal Bell, 'Bono, Facebook IPO: U2 Singer to Become the World's Richest Musician (UPDATED)', *Huffington Post*, 18 May 2012, at huffingtonpost.com.

30 'Bono Becomes The Worst Investor In America'.

31 David Carr, 'Investors, Including Bono, Buy a Piece of Forbes', *New York Times*, 7 August 2006.

32 'Irresponsible Rumormongering: "Forbes", The Pensions Stripped Bare, What Does Bono Care?', *Gawker*, 18 December 2006, at gawker.com. The same anonymous Forbes staffer ruefully added: 'Nobody is complaining because a) this is the kind of unbridled asshole capitalism we're always praising in our pages; and b) we're all pussies.'

33 Ryan Tate, 'Forbes Layoffs are Here, and They're Brutal', *Gawker*, 28 October 2009, at gawker.com. A commenter on this Gawker story wrote: 'Next issue: Forbes' Top 50 Most Unemployed People in America'.

34   'New Wargames for Sir Bono's Profit', *Phoenix*, 6 April 2007.

35   Ibid.

36   Ibid.

37   Lisa O'Carroll, 'U2's Bono and the Edge Invest in Dropbox', *Guardian*, 3 April 2012.

38   'Dropbox to Locate International HQ in Dublin', *Silicon Republic*, 3 December 2012, at siliconrepublic.com.

39   Bono, The Edge, Adam Clayton and Larry Mullen Jr, *U2 by U2* (London: HarperCollins, 2006), 172–7.

40   Ibid., 175.

41   Ibid., 177.

42   Ibid.

43   Phil Joanou, *U2: Rattle and Hum*, DVD (Paramount, 1999).

44   Bono et al., *U2 by U2*, 247.

45   Michka Assayas, *Bono on Bono: Conversations with Michka Assayas* (London: Hodder & Stoughton, 2005), 121.

46   Bono et al., *U2 by U2*, 238.

47   Ibid.

48   Flanagan, *U2*, 68–78.

49   Bono et al., *U2 by U2*, 238.

50   'BNFL Denies Sellafield THORP Closure Report', *RTE News*, 26 August 2003.

51   Bono et al., *U2 by U2*, 252.

52   Ibid., 253.

53   Ibid.

54   Tom Doyle, '10 Years of Turmoil Inside U2', *Q*, 10 October 2002.

55   Bono et al., *U2 by U2*, 253.

56   Ibid.

57   Flanagan, *U2*, 95.

58   Ibid., 96–7.

59   Ibid., 97–8.

60   Ibid., 99.

61   Bono et al., *U2 by U2*, 242.

62   'Bill Clinton, Stars, Turn Out for Bono', *Foxnews.com*, 23 February 2003.

63   Flanagan, *U2*, 100.

64   Ibid., 101.

65   Bono et al., *U2 by U2*, 290.

66   See 'Could Bono Handle the Bank?', *CNN Money*, 9 March 2005.

67   Tim Grieve, 'Wolfowitz Reaches Out to Bono', *Salon.com*, 18 March 2005, at salon.com.

68   Josh Tyrangiel, 'The Constant Charmer', *Time*, 19 December 2005.

69 Matthew Benjamin, 'Zoellick Better Fit at World Bank Than Wolfowitz, Sachs Says', *Bloomberg*, 31 August 2007, at bloomberg.com.

70 Jeffrey D. Sachs, *The End of Poverty: Economic Possibilities for Our Time* (New York: Penguin, 2005), xv.

71 Ibid., xv–xvi.

72 'Photo Gallery of Summits Past', *Corporate Council on Africa*, at africacncl. org; George Monbiot, 'Africa's New Best Friends', *Guardian*, 5 July 2005.

73 Newspaper interview quoted contemporaneously in Harry Browne, 'The Curse of Bono!', *CounterPunch*, 4 March 2003, at counterpunch.org.

74 Ibid.

75 'Bono's Peace Medal Blast', *Daily Mirror*, 1 March 2003.

76 Ibid.

77 Shaheem Reid, 'Pride, Shame, Confusion Abound as War Reactions Surface', *MTV*, 20 March 2003.

78 'Simple Minds' Kerr Rips Bono', *UPI*, 2 February 2005, at upi.com.

79 Richard Dienst, *The Bonds of Debt: Borrowing Against the Common Good* (New York: Verso, 2011), 99, 104.

80 'Give Us the Money', *Why Poverty?* (BBC Four, 25 November 2012).

81 Ibid.

82 Ibid.

83 Ibid.

84 Olaf Tyaransen, 'There Is Absolutely Nothing Fake About This Man', *Hot Press*, 2 June 2011, at hotpress.com.

85 Ibid.

86 Ibid. Bono used much the same self-critical language about his past errors in depicting Africa, albeit without citing Obama as its source, during a public meeting with World Bank staff late in 2012.

87 Ibid.

88 Ibid.

89 Ibid.

90 *U2 Live from Lincoln Memorial Obama Inaugural Celebration (Pride & City of Blinding Lights)*, 2009, at youtube.com.

91 Tyaransen, 'There Is Absolutely Nothing Fake About This Man'.

92 Bono, 'Ten for the Next Ten'.

93 'U2's Bono Visits West Bank', *Ma'an News Agency*, 11 April 2012, at maannews. net.

94 Tim Neufeld, 'Bono Leaves Jerusalem, and Offers a Poem for the Hotel Staff (Update #2)', *@U2blog*, 19 April 2012, at atu2blog.com.

95 Based on Google Translate from Hebrew of *Ynet*, 16 April 2012, at ynet.co.il.

96 Harry Leech, 'Discord over Irish–Israeli Song Contest', *Sunday Times*, 18 November 2012, Ireland edition.

97   John Colapinto, 'Letter from Hollywood – Looking Good: The New Boom in Celebrity Philanthropy', *New Yorker*, 26 March 2012, 59.

98   Tyrangiel, 'Constant Charmer'.

99   Colapinto, 'Letter from Hollywood', 63.

100 'Bono's US-Based Anti-Poverty Groups to Merge', *Reuters*, 29 October 2007, at reuters.com.

101 'US Ambassador to the United Nations Agencies in Rome, Italy: David J. Lane', *United States Mission to the UN Agencies in Rome*, 23 July 2012, at usun-rome.usmission.gov.

102 'Board of Directors', *ONE*, n.d., at one.org.

103 Ross, Michael, "All That They Can't Leave Behind," *Sunday Times*, July 12, 2009, Ireland edition.

104 Joe DeCapua, 'Where Do the World's Poor Live?', *VOA*, 28 August 2012, at voanews.com.

105 'Bono's ONE Foundation Under Fire for Giving Tiny Percentage of Funds to Charity', *Mail Online*, 23 September 2010, at dailymail.co.uk.

106 See one.org. My query to ONE through its website seeking an explanation of this number and other aspects of the campaign's financing went unanswered.

107 Jeane MacIntosh, 'Poor Idea, Bono', *New York Post*, 20 September 2010, at nypost.com.

108 'About This Site', *Guardian*, 14 September 2010.

109 John Vidal, 'Why Is the Gates Foundation Investing in GM Giant Monsanto?', *Guardian*, 29 September 2010.

110 Behrooz Morvaridi, 'Capitalist Philanthropy and Hegemonic Partnerships', *Third World Quarterly* 33: 7 (August 2012), 1191–210.

111 P. Sainath, 'Farm Suicides Rise in Maharashtra, State Still Leads the List', *Hindu*, 3 July 2012, at thehindu.com.

112 Chad Heeter, 'Seeds of Suicide: India's Desperate Farmers', *Frontline/World*, PBS, 26 July 2005.

113 Quoted in ibid.

114 'U2's Bono Talks Curbing Hunger with NBC's Andrea Mitchell', *First Read*, 18 May 2012.

115 Ibid.

116 Ibid.

117 Oxfam, 'G8 Food Security Alliance Answers Question Hungry People Have Not Asked', *Oxfam International*, 18 May 2012, at oxfam.org.

118 "Open Letter to the G8 from African Civil Society," *Stick to Africa's Plans:*, 4 May 2012, at africasplansforg8.org.

119 Quoted in Maria Bustillos, 'Our Billionaire Philanthropists', *Awl*, 13 June 2012, at theawl.com.

120 Grant Cameron, 'Bono and Data Beyond 2015: How Can the Bank Measure

Up?', *Open Data: The World Bank Data Blog*, 16 November 2012, at blogs. worldbank.org.

121   See for example the passage in Chapter 2 that describes Robert Pollin's measurement of the failure of the Bono–Paul O'Neill approach to development when gauged beside an earlier developmental-state model, which had become 'unthinkable' since the 1980s because of an ideological assault from neoliberalism.

122   Melissa Moore, 'The Myth – Scarcity: The Reality – There IS Enough Food', *Food First: Institute for Food and Development Policy*, 8 February 2005, at foodfirst.org.

123   Patrick Healy, ' "Spider-Man", a Year After First Preview, Is on Solid Ground', *New York Times*, 27 November 2011.

124   Dave Marsh, 'Sir Bono: The Knight Who Fled From His Own Debate', *CounterPunch*, 19 March 2009, at counterpunch.org.

125   See for example the end of "Give Us the Money," *Why Poverty?* (BBC Four, 25 November 2012).

126   United Nations Conference on Trade and Development, *Economic Development in Africa Report 2012*, 2.

127   See Lorna Siggins, *Once Upon a Time in the West: The Corrib Gas Controversy* (Dublin: Transworld Ireland, 2010).

128   See Gavan Titley, 'Asylum Seekers in Ireland Languish in the Magdalene Laundries of Our Time', *Guardian*, 3 October 2012.

129   'PASTOR PARCEL BY JIM GALLAGHER Sunday World December 4, 2011', *Dialogue Ireland*, at dialogueireland.wordpress.com; 'Pastor Hade's "Prison-Like" Conditions', *Phoenix*, 17 December 2004.

130   Dervla King, *A Needs Analysis of Asylum Seekers Resident in Kilmarnock House, Killiney* (Southside Partnership, May 2004).

131   SMS message to author, 4 December 2012.

132   'Give Us the Money'.

133   Jann Wenner, 'Bono: The Rolling Stone Interview', *Rolling Stone*, 20 October 2005.

134   Dienst, *Bonds of Debt*, 117–18.

135   ' "Attention Housemates, This Is Bono": U2 Front Man Makes Guest Appearance on Big Brother Africa', *Independent.ie*, 26 July 2012, at independent.ie.